I0118606

TC 3-55.1

Reconnaissance and Surveillance Brigade Collective Task Publication

June 2011

Headquarters, Department of the Army

Published by Books Express Publishing
Books Express Publishing, 2011
ISBN 978-1-78039-953-9

Books Express publications are available from all good retail and online booksellers. For
publishing proposals and direct ordering please contact us at: info@books-express.com

Training Circular
No. 3-55.1

Headquarters
Department of the Army
Washington, DC, 8 June 2011

Reconnaissance and Surveillance Brigade

Contents

Distribution Restriction: Approved for public release; distribution is unlimited.

Contents

Figures

Tables

Preface

Purpose

This training circular is a tool that commanders can use during training strategy development. The products in this training circular are developed to support the brigade's full spectrum operations mission-essential task list training strategy.

Scope

This training circular provides guidance for commanders, staff, leaders, and Soldiers who plan, prepare, execute, and assess training of the reconnaissance and surveillance brigade.

Intended Audience

The primary target audience for this training circular is reconnaissance and surveillance brigade commander, staff, and other leaders. The secondary audience is training developers who develop training support materials for professional military education.

Applicability

This publication applies to Active Army, the Army National Guard (ARNG)/Army National Guard of the United States (ARNGUS), and the United States Army Reserve (USAR) unless otherwise stated.

Feedback

The proponent for this publication is the United States Army Training and Doctrine Command. The preparing agency is the United States Army Maneuver Center of Excellence. Send comments and recommendations by any means, United States mail, e-mail, fax, or telephone, following the Department of the Army Form 2028, *Recommended Changes to Publications and Blank Forms*. More information is available by phone. Point of contact information is as follows:

E-mail:	BENN.MCoE.DOCTRINE@CONUS.ARMY.MIL
Phone:	COM 706-545-7114 or DSN 835-7114
Fax:	COM 706-545-8511 or DSN 835-8511
U.S. Mail:	Commanding General, MCoE
	Directorate of Training and Doctrine (DOTD)
	Doctrine and Collective Training Division
	ATTN: ATZB-TDD
	Fort Benning, GA 31905-5410

Unless otherwise stated in this publication, masculine nouns and pronouns refer to both men and women.

Chapter 1

Introduction

The reconnaissance and surveillance (R&S) brigade conducts reconnaissance and surveillance operations—including the military intelligence (MI) discipline collection—to answer division, corps, or joint force priority intelligence requirement (PIR) and other intelligence requirements. These actions enable the commander to focus joint six warfighting functions. The R&S brigade also provides assets to enhance the reconnaissance and surveillance capability of other brigades, including brigade combat teams (BCTs) and, when directed, produces intelligence for its supported higher headquarters (HQ) (FM 3-55.1). To accomplish these goals and more, R&S brigade commanders must train units to standard. This training circular (TC) provides information on the Army approach to training and highlights several training considerations and enablers, when implemented and used, can make training successful.

SECTION I - TEXT REFERENCES

1-1.   Table 1-1 contains the references used in this chapter.

Table 1-1. Chapter 1 text references

Reference	Subject
FM 3-55.1	Battlefield Surveillance Brigade
FM 3-0	Operations
TRADOC Pamphlet 525-3-0	Army Capstone Concept
FM 7-0	Training Units and Developing Leaders for Full Spectrum Operations
FM 1-01	Generating Force Support for Operations
FM 6-22	Leadership
Army Posture Statement	Army Posture Statement
ATN	Army Training Network link: https://atn.army.mil/index.aspx
FM 1-02	Operational Terms and Graphics
FM 3-90.6	Brigade Combat Team
JP 3-13	Joint Doctrine for Information Operations
JP 1-02	Department of Defense Dictionary of Military and Associated Terms
FM 6-0	Mission Command: Command and Control of Army Forces
JP 3-0	Joint Operations
AR 350-1	Army Training
TRADOC Pam 350-70-1	Guide for Unit Training Products and Processes: Analysis, Design, and Development
AR 220-1	Army Unit Status Reporting and Force Registration–Consolidated Policies
AR 350-28	Army Exercises

SECTION II - ARMY APPROACH TO TRAINING

1-2. Before commanders and staff begin planning, preparing, executing, and assessing unit training, they must have a clear understanding of the Army's training and leader development strategies, training systems, and training management.

ARMY TRAINING STRATEGY

1-3. The Army goal is to routinely generate trained and ready units for both current missions and future contingencies at an operational tempo that is sustainable (Army Training and Leader Development Guidance, FY 10-11). To accomplish this goal, the Army G-3/5/7 developed a comprehensive training strategy called the Army Training Strategy (ATS).

1-4. The ATS describes the ends, ways, and means required to adapt Army training programs to an era of persistent conflict, to prepare units and leaders to conduct full spectrum operations (FSO), and to rebuild strategic depth. The ATS generates cohesive, trained, and ready forces that can dominate at any point on the spectrum of conflict, in any environment, and under all conditions.

1-5. The ATS has identified 10 goals. Each goal has supporting objectives that detail the ATS. Obtaining each goal ensures the Army generates trained and ready units. For further information on the ATS, refer to Deputy Chief of Staff, G-3/5/7 memorandum, *Army Training Strategy*. The goals are—

- Train units for full spectrum operations.
- Enable adaption of training.
- Train and sustain Soldier skills.
- Train and sustain Army civilian skills.
- Sustain and improve effectiveness of combat training centers (CTCs).
- Provide training at home Station and while deployed.
- Provide training support system live, virtual, constructive, and gaming (LVCG) enablers.
- Increase culture and foreign language competencies.
- Provide supporting and integrating capabilities.
- Resource the Army Training Strategy.

ARMY LEADERSHIP DEVELOPMENT STRATEGY

1-6. While the ATS was being developed, the commanding general of the Training and Doctrine Command (TRADOC) concurrently developed a leader development strategy (LDS). *The Army Leader Development Strategy for a 21st Century Army* discusses how the Army will adapt the way in which it develops leaders. This strategy presents the challenges of the operational environment (OE), the implications of the OE on leader development, and the mission, framework, characteristics, and imperatives of and how to implement the strategy. The LDS describes eight specific imperatives designed to guide the policy and actions necessary to produce the future leaders the Army will need.

1-7. The LDS is part of a campaign of learning. It seeks to be as adaptive and innovative as the leaders it must develop. The LDS is grounded in Army leadership doctrine (FM 6-22) and seeks to deliver leader qualities described in both Army doctrine and capstone concepts. For further information on the LDS refer to the *Army Leadership Development Strategy for a 21st Century Army*.

1-8. The following documents describe leadership qualities:

- FM 3-0. This manual describes an operational concept where commanders employ offensive, defensive, and stability or civil support operations simultaneously as part of an interdependent joint force to seize, retain, and exploit the initiative, accepting prudent risk to create opportunities to achieve decisive results.

- <u>TRADOC Pamphlet 525-3-0.</u> This pamphlet describes the broad capabilities the Army will require in 2016-2028. It serves as a guide as to how the Army will apply available resources to overcome adaptive enemies and accomplish challenging missions.

ARMY TRAINING SYSTEM

1-9. The Army Training System prepares Soldiers, Army civilians, organizations, and their leaders to conduct FSO. The training system is built upon a foundation of disciplined, educated, and professional Soldiers, civilians, and leaders, adhering to principles that provide guidance.

FOUNDATIONS OF ARMY TRAINING

Training Principles

1-10. The Army provides combatant commanders with adaptive individuals, units, and leaders. Army expeditionary forces are trained and ready to conduct FSO in support of unified action anywhere along the spectrum of conflict. The Army accomplishes this by conducting tough, realistic, standards-based, performance-oriented training. (FM 7-0). The principles provide a broad but basic foundation to guide how commanders and other leaders plan, prepare, execute, and assess effective training. The 11 principles of training in accordance with (IAW) FM 7-0 are—

- **Commanders and other leaders are responsible for training.** Commanders are responsible for training their units. The unit commander is the unit's primary training manager and trainer. Commanders hold their subordinate leaders responsible for training their respective organizations. This responsibility applies to all units in both the operational Army and the generating force.
- **Noncommissioned officers (NCOs) train individuals, crews, and small teams.** Noncommissioned officers are the primary trainers of enlisted Soldiers, crews, and small teams. Their experience and knowledge are critical to determining the right collective tasks for the unit to train. Noncommissioned officers also determine the individual tasks necessary for collective tasks and, ultimately, FSO METL proficiency. Noncommissioned officers ensure that the objectives of individual Soldier training and development are met.
- **Train to standard.** A task is a measurable action performed by individuals or organizations. A standard is the accepted proficiency level required to accomplish a task. The standard for training is mastery, not just minimum proficiency. Mastery of a task is being able to perform the task intuitively, regardless of the conditions. Units master tasks by limiting the number of tasks to train to a few essential tasks that support accomplishing the mission. Leaders train their organizations until they achieve the standard, which may mean training longer than planned.
- **Train as you will fight.** "Train as you will fight" means training for the mission under the conditions of expected, anticipated, or plausible operational environments. It also means varying the training conditions to improve operational adaptability, training combined arms operations, and ensuring units can operate with all types of military and nonmilitary partners."Fight," in the context of training, includes lethal and nonlethal skills in FSO.
- **Train while operating.** Training continues when a unit is engaged in operations. Combat builds experience, but not necessarily effectiveness. To adapt to constantly changing situations, units continue to train even in the midst of campaigns. Unit leaders use available time to rehearse mission execution and prepare for likely contingencies. They conduct after action reviews (AARs) after completing operations—and after completing intermediate tasks—to capture lessons learned for future operations.
- **Train fundamentals first.** Fundamentals include warrior tasks and battle drills as well as FSO METL tasks. Company-level units establish the foundation. They focus training on individual and small-unit skills. These tasks typically cover basic soldiering, drills, marksmanship, fitness,

and military occupational specialty proficiency. Typically, units that are proficient in the fundamentals can more easily integrate and master the more complex collective tasks.

- **Train to develop operational adaptability.** Although planning is critical to successful training, circumstances may cause plans to change. Leaders prepare for personnel turbulence and equipment shortages even though the ARFORGEN system tries to ensure personnel and equipment objectives are met before training begins. Leaders develop training, manning, and equipping contingency plans. They train their personnel to assume other positions on short notice. They know that because the unit mission could change, the time to prepare for a deployment could be greatly compressed; consequently, they prioritize training tasks to ensure the most important tasks are trained first.

- **Understand the operational environment.** Commanders understand the OE and how it affects training. They replicate operational conditions, including anticipated variability, in training. For example, the conditions and collective and individual tasks required to accomplish a mission differ depending on where the operation falls on the spectrum of conflict. Tasks required to accomplish a mission in a combined arms maneuver role can be different from the tasks required in a wide area security role. Army forces need to be proficient in both and often execute them simultaneously.

- **Train to sustain.** Sustain, in the context of training, refers to resiliency and endurance. Training integrates short-term objectives with long-term goals. Soldiers must be capable of operating over long stretches of time while deployed. Commanders and leaders design training to sustain the proficiency of the unit and to build the capability of individuals to sustain themselves mentally and physically for the demands of combat. Training includes mental and physical training to develop individuals who are resilient enough for frequent deployments in an era of persistent conflict. Leaders incorporate comprehensive Soldier fitness programs into training plans.

- **Train to maintain.** Commanders allocate time for units to maintain themselves and their equipment to standard during training events. This time includes scheduled and routine equipment maintenance periods and assembly area operations. Leaders train their subordinates to appreciate the importance of maintaining their equipment. Organizations tend to perform maintenance during operations to the standards they practice in training.

- **Conduct multiechelon and concurrent training.** Commanders structure training events to allow subordinates maximum latitude to train their units. Through multiechelon training, they ensure subordinate units have the opportunity to train essential tasks during the higher unit's training event. Multiechelon training is a training technique that allows for the simultaneous training of more than one echelon on different or complementary tasks. It is the most efficient and effective way to train. It requires synchronized planning and coordination by commanders and other leaders at each affected echelon. Concurrent training occurs when a leader conducts training within the scope of another type of training. It complements the execution of primary training objectives by allowing leaders to make the most efficient use of available time.

TRAINING AND EDUCATION

1-11. The Army Training System comprises training and education. Training is not solely the domain of the generating force; similarly, education continues in the operational Army (FM 7-0). The operational Army consists of those Army organizations whose primary purpose is to participate in FSO as part of the joint force (FM 1-01). In contrast, the generating force consists of Army organizations whose primary mission is to generate and sustain the operational Army's capabilities for employment by joint force commanders (FM 1-01).

1-12. Training and education occur in all three training domains: institutional, operational, and self-development. Training prepares individuals for certainty and enables action. Education prepares individuals for uncertainty and enables agility, judgment, and creativity.

TRAINING DOMAINS

1-13. Reconnaissance and surveillance brigade commanders lead and assess training to ensure that training is high-quality and that individuals meet established standards. To meet the challenge of preparing for FSO, the Army takes advantage of the training capabilities found in the following three training domains:

- The **institutional** training domain is the Army's institutional training and education system, which primarily includes training base centers and schools that provide initial training and subsequent professional military education (PME) for Soldiers, military leaders, and Army civilians. Institutional training can take place within the Army at the many Centers of Excellence, such as Fires (Fort Sill, OK); Maneuver (Fort Benning, GA); and Maneuver Support (Fort Leonard Wood, MO).
- The **operational** training domain consists of the training activities organizations undertake while at home station, at maneuver CTCs, during joint exercises, at mobilization centers, and while operationally deployed.
- The **self-development** training domain includes planned, goal-oriented learning that reinforces and expands the depth and breadth of an individual's knowledge base, self-awareness, and situational awareness; complements institutional and operational learning; enhances professional competence; and meets personal objectives. The self-development domain consists of three components (2009 Army Posture Statement):
  - **Structured self-development** is required learning, progressively sequenced across a career. It is closely linked to and synchronized with operational and institutional domains.
  - **Guided self-development** is a set of recommended, but optional, learning that enhances professional growth and fosters continuous learning.
  - **Personal self-development** is self-initiated learning where the individual defines the objective, pace, and process.

1-14. Commanders play a critical role in each of these domains by—

- Providing their Soldiers and unit leaders the best opportunity to attend military education schools.
- Being responsible for unit training.
- Setting the example in self-development training.

1-15. This TC concentrates on the operational domain of training that R&S brigade commanders perform. For further information on the Army Training System refer to FM 7-0.

ARMY TRAINING MANAGEMENT

1-16. Army training management is the process used by Army leaders to identify training requirements and subsequently plan, prepare, execute, and assess training. Army training management provides a systematic way of managing time and resources and of meeting training objectives through purposeful training activities.

1-17. Training management is the practical application of the training doctrine and is found in FM 7-0. The training management information contained in FM 7-0 supersedes FM 7-1, *Battle Focused Training*.

1-18. FM 7-0 and training management are posted within the Army Training Network (ATN). The ATN is an Internet Web site provided by the Army to provide on-line training management processes, products, and resources.

1-19. These resources are linked together and are designed to be used in concert as a digital resource. FM 7-0 provides the intellectual framework of what Army training is, while training management provides the practical and detailed how-to of planning, preparing, executing, and assessing training. The ATN, as the digital portal to both documents, provides a wealth of other training resources, including the latest training news, information, products and links to other Army training resources such as combined arms training strategy (CATS), warfighter training support packages (WTSPs), and unit task lists (UTLs). For further information on Army training management refer to FM 7-0 and the ATN.

SECTION III - OTHER TRAINING CONSIDERATIONS

1-20. In addition to understanding the ATS and the training management model, commanders and staffs should also consider—
- Operational environment.
- Full spectrum operations.
- Full spectrum operations mission-essential task lists.
- Army force generation (ARFORGEN).
- Training enablers.

OPERATIONAL ENVIRONMENT

1-21. An OE is a composite of the conditions, circumstances, and influences which affect the employment of military forces and bear on the decisions of the unit commander (FM 1-02). The complex nature of the OE requires commanders to simultaneously combine offensive, defensive, and stability or civil support tasks to accomplish missions domestically and abroad (FM 3-0).

OPERATIONAL VARIABLES

1-22. Military planners describe the OE in terms of variables or of broad aspects of the military and nonmilitary environment that may differ from one operational area to another. These variables can affect major operations and form the basis for planning at any level. Although they are too broad for tactical planning, the R&S brigade commander must understand their influence and how the brigade's collection efforts provide the supported commander with better operational understanding (FM 3-55.1).

1-23. Army divisions and corps normally conduct assessments during the reset and ready phases of the ARFORGEN cycle prior to receipt of the mission based on priorities established by the supported commander. The R&S brigade does not conduct independent analysis; instead, it relies on the supported unit's staff for that analysis. However, because these variables are constantly changing over time and have a direct impact on the R&S brigade, it collects and provides input on each operational variable to the supported unit. (FM 3-55.1)

1-24. This analysis is based on the operational variables easily remembered using political, military, economic, social, information, infrastructure, physical environment, and time (PMESII-PT). For further information on operational variables refer to FM 3-0. The variables are defined as follows:
- The **political** variable describes the distribution of responsibility and power at all levels of governance.
- The **military** variable includes the military capabilities of all armed forces in a given operational environment.
- The **economic** variable encompasses individual and group behaviors related to producing, distributing, and consuming resources.
- The **social** variable describes societies within an operational environment. A society is a population whose members are subject to the same political authority, occupy a common territory, have a common culture, and share a sense of identity.
- The **information** environment is the aggregate of individuals, organizations, and systems that collect, process, disseminate, or act on information (JP 3-13).

- **Infrastructure** comprises the basic facilities, services, and installations needed for a society's functioning.
- The **physical environment** includes the geography and man-made structures in the operational area.
- **Time** is a significant consideration in military operations. Analyzing it as an operational variable focuses on how an operation's duration might help or hinder each side.

MISSION VARIABLES

1-25. Operational variables are directly relevant to campaign planning; however, they may be too broad for tactical planning. Upon receipt of a warning order or mission, Army tactical leaders narrow their focus to six mission variables. Mission variables are those aspects of the OE that directly affect a mission. They outline the situation as it applies a specific Army unit. Mission variables are comprised of mission, enemy, terrain and weather, troops and support available, time available, and civil considerations (METT-TC). For further information on mission variables refer to FM 3-0. The variables are defined as follows:

- The **mission** is the task, together with the purpose, that clearly indicates the action to be taken and the reason therefore (JP 1-02). Commanders analyze a mission in terms of specified tasks, implied tasks, and the commander's intent two echelons up.
- The **enemy** is not only the known enemy but also other threats to mission success. These include threats posed by multiple adversaries with a wide array of political, economic, religious, and personal motivations.
- **Terrain and weather** are natural conditions that profoundly influence operations. Terrain and weather are neutral; they favor neither side unless one is more familiar with—or better prepared to operate in—the physical environment. For tactical operations, terrain is analyzed using the five military aspects of terrain: observation and fields of fire, avenues of approach, key and decisive terrain, obstacles, and cover and concealment (OAKOC).
- **Troops and support available** are the number, type, capabilities, and condition of available friendly troops and support. These include resources from joint, interagency, multinational, host-nation, commercial (via contracting), and private organizations. They also include support provided by civilians.
- **Time available** is critical to all operations. Controlling and exploiting it is central to initiative, tempo, and momentum. By exploiting time, commanders can exert constant pressure, control the relative speed of decisions and actions, and exhaust enemy forces.
- **Civil considerations** reflect how man-made infrastructure, civilian institutions, attitudes, and activities of the civilian leaders, populations, and organizations within an area of operations influence the conduct of military operations (FM 3-0). Civil considerations are comprised of areas, structures, capabilities, organizations, people and events (ASCOPE).

THREATS

1-26. Threats facing U.S. forces vary today. They are not always enemy forces dressed in uniforms who are easily identified as foes, aligned on a battlefield, and opposite U.S. forces. Threats can be nation-states, organizations, people, groups, conditions, or natural phenomena able to damage or destroy life, vital resources, and institutions.

1-27. Threats are described in four major categories or challenges: traditional, irregular, catastrophic, and disruptive. While helpful in describing the threats the Army is likely to face, these categories do not define the nature of the adversary. Adversaries may use any and all challenges in combination to achieve the desired effect against the U.S. (FM 3-0). The four threats are defined as follows:

- **Traditional**. States employing recognized military capabilities and forces in understood forms of military competition and conflict.

- **Irregular**. Opponent employing unconventional methods and means to counter traditional U.S. advantages.
- **Catastrophic**. Enemy that involves the acquisition, possession, and use of weapons of mass destruction and effects.
- **Disruptive**. Enemy using new technologies that reduce U.S. advantages in key operational domains.

Hybrid Threats

1-28. The term hybrid threat has recently been used to capture the seemingly increased complexity of operations and the multiplicity of actors involved. While the existence of innovative enemies is not new, today's hybrid threats demand that U.S. forces prepare for a range of possible threats simultaneously.

1-29. Hybrid threats are characterized by the combination of regular forces governed by international law, military tradition, and custom with irregular forces that are unregulated and as a result act with no restrictions on violence or targets for violence. This includes militias, terrorists, guerillas, and criminals. Such forces combine their abilities to use and transition between regular and irregular tactics and weapons. These tactics and weapons enable hybrid threats to capitalize on perceived vulnerabilities making them particularly effective (FM 3-0). For further information on threats to the Army refer to FM 3-0.

FULL SPECTRUM OPERATIONS

1-30. An R&S brigade operates in a framework of FSO. FM 3-0 provides a discussion of FSO, which includes the elements of offensive, defensive, and stability or civil support conducted simultaneously. As a full-spectrum force, the R&S brigade conducts reconnaissance and surveillance missions and provides assets that enable the supported commander to gain a better understanding of the OE and to develop the situational understanding (SU) that enables informed decision-making. The R&S brigade may be augmented with additional forces for any or all of these operations to enhance its capabilities. To successfully accomplish its assigned mission, the R&S brigade may require additional reconnaissance assets for offensive and defensive operations or civil affairs and engineer assets for stability and civil support missions (FM 3-55.1). These operations are defined as follows:

- **Offensive operations** are combat operations conducted to defeat and destroy enemy forces and seize terrain, resources, and population centers. The R&S brigade was not designed to conduct independent offensive operations. As a supporting brigade focused within the intelligence warfighting function, the R&S brigade provides capabilities to supported units that enhance and enable their capability to conduct offensive operations.
- **Defensive operations** are combat operations conducted to defeat an enemy attack, gain time, economize forces, and develop conditions favorable for offensive or stability operations. Defensive operations can secure and protect areas in which forces conduct stability operations. Defensive operations counter enemy offensive operations. They defeat attacks by destroying as much of the attacking enemy as possible. They also preserve control over land, resources, and populations. Defensive operations retain terrain, guard populations, and protect critical capabilities against enemy attacks. As with offensive operations, the R&S brigade does not have the capability to conduct defensive operations other than to provide its own unit protection. As a part of broader-range defensive operations, the R&S brigade conducts operations according to the supported unit's overall intelligence, surveillance, and reconnaissance (ISR) plan to provide information about the enemy that the commander uses to support battlefield visualization and make critical decisions. It has the ability to conduct some security operations.
- **Stability operations** encompass various military missions, tasks, and activities conducted outside the U.S. in coordination with other instruments of national power. The goals are to maintain or reestablish a safe and secure environment, and provide essential governmental services, emergency infrastructure reconstruction, and humanitarian relief (JP 3-0). Forces can

conduct stability operations in support of a host nation or interim government or as part of an occupation when no government exists. Stability operations involve both coercive and constructive military actions. They help to establish a safe and secure environment and facilitate reconciliation among local or regional adversaries. Stability operations also can help establish political, legal, social, and economic institutions and support the transition to legitimate local governance. The R&S brigade is one of the key enablers in making the successful execution of stability tasks possible.

- **Civil Support** is Department of Defense (DOD) support to U.S. civil authorities for domestic emergencies and for designated law enforcement and other activities (JP 1-02). Civil support includes operations that address the consequences of natural or manmade disasters, accidents, terrorist attacks, and incidents in the U.S. and its territories. Army forces conduct civil support operations when the size and scope of events exceed the capabilities or capacities of domestic civilian agencies. The National Guard is suited to conduct these missions; however, the scope and level of destruction may require states to request assistance from federal authorities.

1-31. The simultaneous conduct of FSO requires careful assessment, prior planning, and unit preparation as commanders shift their combinations of FSO. This begins with an assessment of the situation to determine which primary tasks are applicable, and the priority for each. For further information on FSO refer to FM 3-0.

FULL SPECTRUM OPERATIONS MISSION-ESSENTIAL TASK LIST

1-32. To meet the demands of FSO, the Headquarters, Department of the Army (HQDA) has standardized FSO METL for brigades and above. This standardization ensures that like units deliver the same capabilities and gives the Army the strategic flexibility to provide trained and ready forces to operational-level commanders (Figure 1-1).

- CONDUCT COMMAND AND CONTROL (ART 5.0)
    - 71-8-5100 TG: EXECUTE THE OPERATIONS PROCESS (BN-CORPS)

- PERFORM INTELLIGENCE, SURVEILLANCE, AND RECONNAISSANCE (ART 2.3)
    - 71-8-2321 TG: DEVELOP THE INTELLIGENCE, SURVEILLANCE, AND RECONNAISSANCE PLAN (BDE-CORPS)
    - 17-8-2300 TG: PERFORM INTELLIGENCE, SURVEILLANCE, AND RECONNAISSANCE (ISR) (BN-CORPS)
    - 34-6-2050 TG: CONDUCT LONG RANGE SURVEILLANCE (LRS) STAFF PLANNING (BDE)

- CONDUCT RECONNAISSANCE (ART 2.3.3)
    - 17-6-9314 TG: CONDUCT ZONE RECONNAISSANCE
    - 17-6-9315 TG: CONDUCT AREA RECONNAISSANCE
    - 17-6-9225 TG: CONDUCT A SCREEN
    - 07-6-1272 TG: CONDUCT AREA SECURITY (BN-BCT)

- DECIDE SURFACE TARGETS (ART 3.1)
    - 06-6-1118 TG: CONDUCT FIRE SUPPORT PLANNING USING MDMP

Figure 1-1. Reconnaissance and surveillance brigade FSO METLs

1-33. The FSO METL does not change between home station and theater of operations. The mission-essential tasks (METs) trained in preparation of deploying are the same tasks the unit expects to perform when deployed. What can change, however, are the collective tasks that support the FSO METL based on assigned missions or out-of-design requirements. The R&S brigade commander and staff manage their unit training towards proficiency in these collective tasks. Training management, like the operational process, uses the planning, preparation, execution, and assessment process steps.

1-34. An FSO METL crosswalk table showing the relationships between the FSO METs and task groups for the R&S brigade with the collective tasks that support those tasks is located within this TC in Chapter 2. For additional information regarding HQDA-approved METL, refer to the FSO-METL Department of the Army (DA) standardized (brigade and higher) list found within the ATN.

ARMY FORCE GENERATION

1-35. Army force generation is a process that progressively builds unit readiness over time during predictable periods of availability to provide trained, ready, and cohesive units prepared for operational deployments. For additional information on ARFORGEN refer to FM 7-0.

1-36. Army force generation drives training management within the Army. Training management is the process used by Army leaders to identify training requirements and subsequently plan, prepare, execute, and assess training. Army training management provides a systematic way of managing time and resources and of meeting training objectives through purposeful training activities.

1-37. The Army prepares and provides campaign-capable expeditionary forces through ARFORGEN, which applies to Active Army and Reserve Component (RC) (Army National Guard and U.S. Army Reserve) units.

1-38. Army force generation takes each unit through a three-phased readiness cycle (known as pools): reset, train/ready, and available. The reset, train/ready, and available force pools provide the framework for the structured progression of increased readiness in ARFORGEN (AR 350-1). The force pools are defined as follows:

- **Reset force pool.** Reconnaissance and surveillance brigades enter the reset force pool when they redeploy from long-term operations or complete their window for availability in the available force pool. The AC units remain in the reset force pool for at least 6 months; RC units remain in the reset force pool for at least 12 months. Reconnaissance and surveillance brigades in the reset force pool have no readiness expectations.

- **Train/ready force pool.** An R&S brigade enters the train/ready force pool following the reset force pool. The train/ready force pool is not of fixed duration. Reconnaissance and surveillance brigades in the train/ready force pool will increase training readiness and capabilities as quickly as possible, given the resource availability. Reconnaissance and surveillance brigades may receive a mission to deploy during the train/ready force pool.

- **Available force pool.** Reconnaissance and surveillance brigades in the available force pool are at the highest state of training and readiness capability and are ready to deploy when directed. The available force pool window for availability is 1 year.

1-39. Reconnaissance and surveillance brigades move from the available force pool to the reset force pool following a deployment or the end of their designated window of availability.

1-40. Keys components of the ARFORGEN process that R&S brigade commanders may consider regarding training include—

- **Contingency expeditionary force (CEF)/deployment expeditionary force (DEF).** When beginning the AFRFORGEN process, R&S brigades are designated either as a CEF or a DEF. Training objectives and events are planned IAW the unit designation. Other considerations for these forces are the following:

  - Contingency expeditionary force units remain (not in a DEF) available force pool units, and are task organized to meet operational plans and contingency requirements. These forces are capable of rapid deployment but are not yet alerted to deploy (AC) or alerted for mobilization (RC). Contingency expeditionary forces will transition into DEF(s) if alerted.

- Deployment expeditionary force units are task organized units designed to execute planned operational requirements and those currently executing deployed missions to include homeland defense and homeland security.
- **Use of aim points**. ARFORGEN aim points are readiness benchmarks, established at specified points in time that enable leaders to meter and monitor effective collective training, thereby ensuring units are ready to execute contingencies and operational missions (FORSCOM Cir 350-1).
- **Progressive training**. The ARFORGEN process progressively builds unit readiness over time during predictable periods of availability to provide trained, ready, and cohesive units prepared for operational deployments.
- **Multiechelon training**. Sequential training programs successively train each echelon from lower to higher. However, limited resources (such as time) often prevent using sequential training programs. Therefore, commanders must structure each training event to take full advantage of multiechelon and concurrent training (FM 7-0).
- **Surge**. The "surge force" is defined as selected CEF units designated for emergency or contingency operations (FORSCOM Cir 350-1). Deploying units from the train-ready force pool constitute a surge. Reconnaissance and surveillance brigades deploy when directed, or if not directed to deploy, the R&S brigade will continue to train on FSO METL or as directed.

Note. Reserve Component units in a DEF are sourced against a future requirement, have been alerted for mobilization, or are currently mobilized.

ARFORGEN TEMPLATE

1-41. The R&S brigade commander and staff have at their disposal ARFORGEN doctrinal training templates. These templates are developed for units with standardized FSO METL. These templates can also be used to assist the commander and staff to maintain visibility on major events their unit conducts as well as their unit's progression through the ARFORGEN process.

1-42. Active Army (Figure 1-2) and RC (Figure 1-3) R&S brigades progress through the ARFORGEN pools in the same manner, with some variations, to the number of aim points and different timelines.

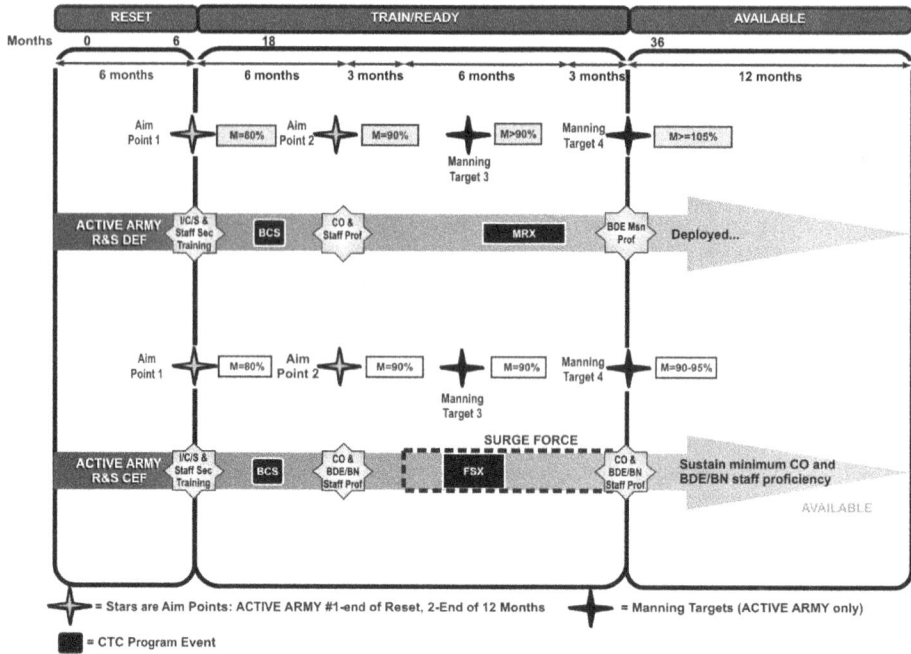

Figure 1-2. Example ARFORGEN doctrinal training template for an Active Army R&S brigade

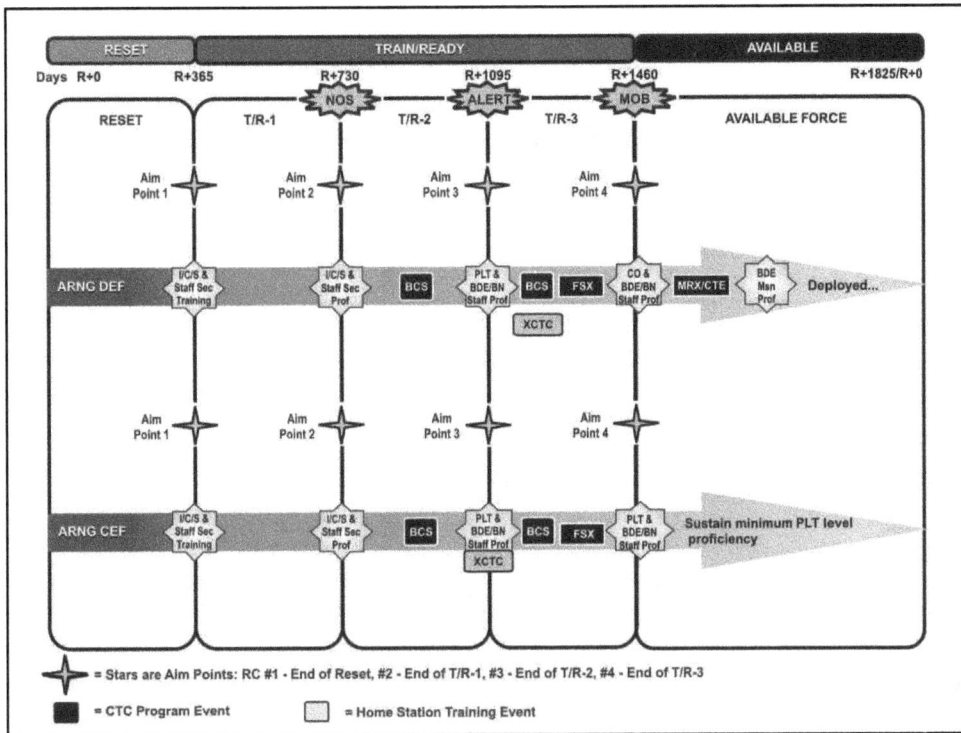

Figure 1-3. Example of an ARFORGEN doctrinal training template for an RC R&S brigade

EVENT MENU MATRIX

1-43. An event menu matrix (EMM) is a one-page synopsis/list of events used by HQDA to help determine requirements. Event menu matrixes are based on the ARFORGEN doctrinal training template. An EMM provides a multiechelon, events-based, progressive training strategy designed to achieve capability levels depicted on the ARFORGEN doctrinal template. Each EMM is extracted from and linked to an associated combined arms training strategy (CATS). Event menu matrixes are living documents, changing as needed as the events and resources change.

TRAINING ENABLERS

1-44. Reconnaissance and surveillance brigade commanders determine a training strategy for their unit and prepare training plans that enable the unit to be ready within the ARFORGEN process. Commanders develop training plans that enable them to attain proficiency in the METs needed to conduct FSO under conditions in the OE.

1-45. Several training products are available that the R&S brigade commander can use to train his unit to FSO METL proficiency based on readiness requirements. Each training enabler has been designed and developed within the TRADOC to fill specific training needs of the R&S brigade. Commanders should consider LVCG when considering training enablers. The following training enablers can be used throughout the training process of planning, preparation, execution, and assessment-of-unit training:

- Individual and collective tasks.
- Unit task lists.
- Combined arms training strategies.
- Warfighter training support packages.

INDIVIDUAL AND COLLECTIVE TASKS

1-46. Both individual and collective tasks are performed during unit training to assess the proficiency of individuals and groups on their ability to perform the tasks to standard.

Note. This TC focuses on collective tasks and how they are used to support unit training. It addresses individual tasks minimally.

Individual Tasks

1-47. An individual task is a clearly defined, observable, and measurable activity accomplished by an individual. It is the lowest behavioral level in a job or duty that is performed for its own sake. An individual task supports one or more collective tasks or drills and often supports another individual task. Individual tasks can consist of both leader and staff tasks (TRADOC Pam 350-70-1). For further information on individual tasks refer to TRADOC Regulation 350-70. The tasks are defined as follows:

- **Leader task.** An individual task (skill level 2 or higher) a leader performs that is integral to the performance of a collective task.
- **Staff task.** A clearly defined and measurable activity or action performed by a staff (collective) or a staff member (individual) of an organization that supports a commander in the exercise of unit mission command.

Collective Tasks

1-48. A collective task is a clearly defined, observable, and measurable activity or action that requires organized team or unit performance, leading to the accomplishment of a mission or function. Collective task accomplishment requires the performance to standard of supporting individual or collective tasks (TRADOC Pam 350-70-1).

1-49. There are two types of collective tasks, shared and unique:

- A **shared** collective task applies to or is performed by more than one unit (for example to units which have different proponents [different such as Infantry and Armor]), or to different echelon/table of organization and equipment (TOE) units within a single proponent's authority (a combined arms battalion [CAB] performing the same task as that performed at the R&S brigade level). Since the task, conditions, standards, task steps, and performance measures of shared collective tasks do not change, the collective task is trained and performed in the same way by all units that "share" the task. An example of a shared collective task would be Task # 71-8-2210, Perform Intelligence Preparation of the Battlefield (Battalion - Corps), which can be conducted by various organizations from battalion to corps levels (such as a CAB or an R&S brigade).
- A **unique** collective task is clearly defined and unit-specific. For a collective task to be classified unique, no other unit or proponent (such as Infantry or engineers) may have the capability or requirement to perform the task. The designated proponent is solely responsible for the development and maintenance of a unique collective task. An example would be Task # 07-6-1154, Conduct an Airborne Assault (which is a unique task performed to standard by an airborne-qualified battalion-brigade).

1-50. Collective tasks are primarily performed in the operational domain, so the emphasis is on unit performance. For further information on collective tasks refer to TRADOC Pamphlet 350-70-1. Each collective task contains the following components:

- **Assessment information.** Commanders and staffs review the measures of performance and measures of success, whether the R&S brigade had performed those previously, and what the assessment was when performed. If an assessment was conducted, it can provide information that states whether the unit has performed the tasks and is considered trained, partially trained, or untrained.
- **General information.** This includes task title and warfighting function.
- **Task data, conditions, and standards.**
- **Task attributes.** This includes whether the task is trained at night, under mission-oriented protective posture (MOPP) conditions, and task steps.
- **Supporting information.** This includes products/references, individual tasks, drills, collective tasks, and prerequisite collective tasks.

UNIT TASK LISTS

1-51. The UTL is a product of mission analysis which identifies all collective tasks (shared and unique) that a unit is organized, manned, and equipped to conduct. The UTL is produced for each unit with a TOE/modified TOE or table of distribution and allowance.

1-52. A mission analysis reviews unit missions from which the entire set of collective tasks (UTL) is derived. The UTL provides the baseline for a unit CATS. A training developer creates the UTL by linking collective tasks to those missions identified on the TOE. This process ensures that units train the appropriate tasks to required proficiency levels.

1-53. Reconnaissance and surveillance brigades report readiness on their FSO METL. Readiness is adapted to ARFORGEN training time and the chief of staff of the Army's training guidance. Training and Doctrine Command training products align these requirements through narrowing the UTL to tasks required for the R&S brigade to achieve proficiency in its FSO missions. For further information on unit status reporting refer to Army Regulation (AR) 220-1. For further information on UTLs refer to TRADOC Pamphlet 350-70-1.

UTL Locations

1-54. An assembled UTL is located in Appendix A of this TC. This list contains the tasks that support the HQDA-directed R&S brigade FSO METL and can be used by the R&S brigade commander for training management.

1-55. The R&S brigade UTL is also maintained and accessed within the Digital Training Management System (DTMS). The DTMS is a Web-based training management system that allows the R&S brigade to conduct mission and METL development; training planning, and management. It tracks unit training by implementing the doctrine, tactics, techniques, and procedures outlined in FM 7-0 and training management.

COMBINED ARMS TRAINING STRATEGY

1-56. The CATS is the Army's overarching strategy for the current and future training of the force. It describes how the Army trains the total force to standard in the institution and unit, and through self-development. It also identifies, quantifies, and justifies the training resources required to execute the training (TRADOC Pamphlet 350-70-1). Unit CATSs are built using unit missions and the UTL, are designed to reflect the FSO METL, and can be executed using the WTSPs.

1-57. Combined arms training strategies have replaced mission training plans (MTPs). Combined arms training strategies provide a crawl/walk/run training path with recommendations of what, who, and how to train. Combined arms training strategies support unit METL training and readiness reporting and are synchronized with ARFORGEN. The primary users of CATSs at the R&S brigade level are unit commanders and staffs.

Types of CATSs

1-58. Combined arms training strategies are based on the unit's TOE mission (that supports the FSO METL), employment, capabilities, and functions. For more information about CATSs refer to TRADOC Pamphlet 350-70-1. There are two types of CATSs, unit and functional.

Unit CATS

1-59. Unit CATSs are TOE-based and unique to a unit type. Unit CATS development considers organizational structure, METL, and doctrine to organize the unit's collective tasks to achieve task proficiency.

1-60. Every CATS consists of a menu of task selections that provide a base strategy for unit commanders to plan, prepare, and assess training for flexibility. A CATS is also designed to train a capability with supporting training events and resources. The events are designed to be trained in a logical sequence, starting with the lowest echelon or staff level and adding echelons or staff sections as the events get progressively more complex. The culminating, or run event, for a CATS is usually the highest level event designed to train and/or evaluate the entire unit.

1-61. Unit CATSs provide commanders a training strategy from which they develop their unit training plan to achieve collective task proficiency and support the reporting of training readiness. They integrate Army-required METL readiness reporting as well as support the ARFORGEN phases. These strategies are flexible and are not intended to constrain commanders; rather, they provide them with a menu of core mission/capabilities based training events. They also provide commanders with a method to train all tasks that a unit is designed to perform and estimate the required resources to support event-driven training. Unit CATS provide commanders with tools to plan, prepare for, and evaluate unit training.

Functional CATS

1-62. Functional CATSs address a functional capability common to multiple units and echelons. Functional CATS supplement unit CATS. They may be based on missions or functions performed by most units that are not unique to a specific unit type or they may be developed to train warfighting functions or operational themes that were not incorporated into unit CATS. Two examples of functional CATSs are mission command (formerly listed in CATS as command and control) and personnel protection. Functional CATSs contain most of the same data elements as unit CATSs (TRADOC Pamphlet 350-70-1).

Task Selections

1-63. Reconnaissance and surveillance brigade commanders and staffs can utilize task selections, which are grouped collective tasks together within a CATS. Combined arms training strategy developers determine what collective tasks would be logically trained together and place them in task selections. Task selections describe a specific capability/mission and include collective tasks that support developing that capability. A frequency of training and types of events that could be used to train the capability are also recommended.

1-64. Task selections are usually trained utilizing a series of crawl-walk-run events. Using crawl-walk-run events provide options to commanders to accommodate training at the appropriate level of difficulty based on their training readiness assessment. Each event provides recommendations for who and how to train and resources required that support that training (TRADOC Pamphlet 350-70-1).

1-65. The commander can consolidate necessary collective tasks needed to be trained to support FSO METs to help determine the time and resources needed to train these tasks to proficiency. A matrix showing CATS task selections used within the R&S brigade that support the task groups of the unit's FSO METL are located in Appendix C of this TC.

1-66. Commanders and staffs review applicable task selections in CATSs to develop select events that nest with externally directed events. Task selections also identify training gate events for key R&S brigade training events. Additionally, CATSs provide the recommended frequency and sequence for scheduling R&S brigade training events.

Training Events

1-67. Combined arms training strategies organize collective and individual tasks into standard Army training events that, when conducted, adhere to the principles of training mentioned earlier in this chapter.

1-68. Training events are the means to attaining FSO METL proficiency and CATSs provide the foundation to success in the plan, prepare, execute, and assessment phases of training. Reconnaissance and surveillance brigade training events can be directed by installation and higher HQ such as brigade full spectrum exercise, new equipment training, deployment exercises, exportable combat training center or Maneuver Combat Training Center rotations.

1-69. The R&S brigade commander and staff can also develop training events internally, such as classes, sergeants time training, maneuver readiness exercises, field training exercises (FTX), situation training exercises (STXs), combined arms live fire exercises, and command post exercises (CPX). When using the crawl-walk-run training path provided with CATSs, commanders can utilize the training gates developed for assessment of unit proficiency of each training event. For additional information on training exercises refer to Army Regulation 350-28.

1-70. The R&S brigade commander may create different versions of unit training plans using the CATS. A unit's progress through its training strategies is based on time available and the commander's assessment of task proficiency using the doctrinal process of assessing training, missions, and METs while preparing or updating unit training plans.

CATS Locations

1-71. Combined arms training strategies are available digitally from both the DTMS and the ATN. In digital format, CATSs provide numerous links to training materials which can assist the R&S brigade commander, staff, and unit training managers to develop the commander's plan and conduct training.

WARFIGHTER TRAINING SUPPORT PACKAGES

1-72. The WTSP is a complete, stand-alone, exportable training package that integrates training products and materials needed to train one or more critical collective tasks and supports critical individual tasks (including leader and staff). Warfighter training support packages are task-based information packages that provide structured situational training scenarios for LVCG unit and institutional training.

1-73. Heavy/Infantry/Stryker BCT WTSPs are used to assist commanders in training their unit's FSO METL. This is accomplished by basing the WTSP on a revised Caspian Sea scenario for differing echelons within the BCT. Each WTSP includes materials to support planning, preparing, executing, and assessing training exercises at respective echelons.

Using WTSPs in Training Management

1-74. Warfighter training support packages aid the R&S brigade commander and staff throughout the management of their unit during various training exercises. Warfighter training support packages have several benefits. They provide information needed in the development of long-range training plans. They also provide recording and reporting information for after-action reviews following completion of training on the R&S brigade FSO METL and supporting collective tasks.

1-75. The contents of a BCT WTSP are shown in Table 1-2. This example uses the Infantry brigade combat team (IBCT) WTSP, but each BCT WTSP is configured the same way. The BCT WTSP is one of a set of WTSPs comprising the overall BCT series. The WTSP provides the material to support exercise planning, preparation, execution, and assessment. Each WTSP includes five TSPs, a guide, and various tactical/support materials.

Table 1-2. Contents of the IBCT WTSP series

TSP #	Exercise Type	IBCT TSPs	HHQ OPORD
1	CPX JCATS	Brigade combat team	Division
2		Infantry battalion	Brigade combat team
3		Reconnaissance squadron	
4	STX VBS2	Infantry battalion-companies and platoon TSP	Infantry battalion
		Rifle company	
		Weapons company	
		Battalion reconnaissance platoon	
		Battalion mortar platoon	
		Infantry platoon	Infantry company
		Weapons platoon	Weapons company
5		Reconnaissance squadron-troop and platoon TSPs	Reconnaissance squadron
		Mounted reconnaissance troop	
		Dismounted reconnaissance troop	
		Mounted reconnaissance platoon	Mounted reconnaissance troop
		Dismounted reconnaissance platoon	Dismounted reconnaissance troop

1-76. The tactical materials for each WTSP provides higher HQ operation orders (OPORDs) and fragmentary orders (FRAGOs) and are intended to drive the R&S brigade's order development and planning process.

1-77. The BCT WTSPs are provided to assist commanders in the training of every reconnaissance and Infantry unit within the R&S brigade. The WTSPs are built from the FSO METL at the BCT level and can be used by the R&S brigade. When combined with CATSs, WTSPs can help to attain FSO METL proficiency through use of LVCG training.

WTSP Contents

1-78. All training products provided within the WTSP enable a structured training environment where certain events cause specific tasks, steps, or actions to occur. Structured training includes specific feedback on the performance of these actions as well. This structured training is supported in details by the products within the WTSP. These products provide a good starting point for a commander to use in the planning, preparation, execution, and assessment of any training event. Explanations and examples of the content of the BCT WTSP folder are—

- **Open first (guide).** Provides an overview of the specific WTSP and, in greater detail, exercise planning (organization and support requirements), preparation, execution, and assessment.
- **Tab A FSO METL.** Provides a matrix relating each of the WTSP tasks to the echelons trained within each FSO METL.
- **Tab B small group exercises.** Provides details on information engagement and other collective tasks detailed in mission training plan format.
- **Tab C enemy operations.** Provides guidance to the opposing forces for the exercises to include specific tasks.
- **Tab D observer/trainer (OT) guidance.** Provides guidance and briefing for the duties and responsibilities of the OTs. Gives specifics for what OTs do during each phase of the unit exercise; also gives an overview of how OTs collect data.
- **Tab E Maneuver Control System (MCS) files.** Provides information for MCS graphics. Grid reference sheets and MCS extensible markup language files are included. Graphics may be loaded into MCS by the R&S brigade training elements for the exercise.
- **Tab F command post exercise support requirements.** Provides information in matrix format of personnel, equipment, and petroleum, oil, and lubricant (POL) necessary to conduct the CPX.
- **Tab G mission briefing.** Details the mission used for the command post exercise.
- **Tab H master scenario events list (MSEL) options.** Provides MSEL event matrices detailing events occurring during training missions.
- **Tab I FSO METL task summaries.** Provides summaries of the FSO METL tasks (as shown in the Tab A matrix); also can be used for task performance criteria to support assessments of the IBCT staffs and subordinate elements.
- **Tab J training support package (TSP) glossary.** Provides a glossary of terms used in the WTSP.
- **Tab K brigade offense operations.** Provides offensive operations OPORD and annexes supporting the CPX.
- **Tab L brigade defense operations.** Provides defensive operations OPORD and annexes supporting the CPX.
- **Tab M brigade stability operations.** Provides stability operations OPORD and annexes supporting the command post exercise.

WTSP Locations

1-79. The WTSPs are exportable for use by the R&S brigade.

1-80. The WTSPs are located within the Maneuver Center of Excellence (MCoE) Collective Training Branch Web site on Army Knowledge Online (AKO). To access this Web site:

- Log into AKO.
- Copy and paste the following Web address (https://www.us.army.mil/suite/grouppage/130823) into the address bar.
- Select enter.
- When the MCoE Collective Training Branch home page opens, find the MCoE collective training documents, Heavy/Infantry/Stryker BCT WTSPs.
- Select desired WTSP.

LIVE, VIRTUAL, CONSTRUCTIVE, AND GAMING TRAINING

1-81. Reconnaissance and surveillance brigade commanders can use LVCG training to enhance training, replicate battlefield conditions, balance resources, and sustain readiness. Commanders consider each of the components to dictate the degree of simulation they plan for their unit during training events. Utilizing simulations within their unit training enables commanders to maximize many of the principles of training and to manage scarce resources.

LIVE

1-82. Live training is training executed in field conditions using tactical equipment. It involves real people operating real systems.

1-83. Live training may be enhanced by training aids, devices, simulators, and simulations and tactical engagement simulation to simulate combat conditions. An example of live training is the Multiple Integrated Laser Engagement System used during an STX as specified in both the CATS and WTSP.

VIRTUAL

1-84. Virtual training is executed using computer-generated battlefields in simulators with the approximate characteristics of tactical weapon systems and vehicles. Virtual training is used to exercise motor control, decision-making, and communication skills.

1-85. Sometimes called "human-in-the-loop training," it involves real people operating simulated systems. Individuals practice the skills needed to operate actual equipment, for example, flying an aircraft. An example of virtual training is using the Engagement Skills Trainer 2000 System to prepare the unit for a live fire exercise qualification and other training events.

CONSTRUCTIVE

1-86. Constructive training uses computer models and simulations to exercise command and staff functions. It involves simulated people operating simulated systems.

1-87. Constructive training can be conducted by units from platoon through echelons above corps. A CPX is an example of constructive training. Another example of constructive training is the Battle Command Training Center that utilizes the WTSP-supported Joint Conflict and Tactical Simulation (JCATS) System during a R&S brigade training exercise.

GAMING

1-88. Gaming is technology that employs commercial or government off-the-shelf, multi-genre games in a realistic, semi-immersive environment to support education and training. The military uses gaming technologies to train individuals and organizations.

1-89. Gaming enables individual, collective, and multiechelon training. Gaming operates in a stand-alone environment or is integrated with live, virtual, or constructive enablers. It can also be used for individual education. Employed in a realistic, semi-immersive environment, gaming can simulate operations and capabilities.

1-90. Gaming can also be used with live, virtual, and constructive training enablers. An example of gaming supported by the WTSP is the Virtual Battlespace 2 (VBS2) System, which is a mission rehearsal tool for Soldiers to practice tactics, techniques, and procedures prior to conducting an actual mission. The VBS2 system is tailored to train Soldiers at the company level and below but may be used at higher levels such as the battalion staff.

Chapter 2

Crosswalks and Outlines

This chapter provides the R&S brigade commander and staff an FSO METL crosswalk and the FSO METL supporting collective task training and evaluation outlines (T&EOs) found within that table. Each item assists the commander and subordinate leaders with training for the R&S brigade.

SECTION I - FSO METL CROSSWALK

2-1. The FSO METL crosswalk matrix (Table 2-1) identifies the DA-approved FSO METL for the R&S brigade by METs and task groups along with collective tasks that support each.

2-2. The tasks are listed in the matrix under the appropriate mission-essential task (MET). A specific mission is trained by identifying the supporting collective tasks in the vertical column for that mission marked with an "X" in the box below the MET that they support. Based on the proficiency of the unit, training can then be focused on operational weaknesses.

Table 2-1. FSO METL crosswalk

HHC, R&S Brigade		METs and Task Groups								
		C2	Perform ISR			Conduct Reconnaissance				Decide Surface Targets
Task Number	Task Title	Execute the Operations Process	Develop the ISR Plan	Perform ISR	Conduct LRS Staff Planning	Conduct Zone Reconnaissance	Conduct Area Reconnaissance	Conduct a Screen	Conduct Area Security	Conduct Fire Support Planning Using MDMP
71-8-2321	Develop the Intelligence, Surveillance, and Reconnaissance Plan (BDE - Corps)	X	X							
34-4-0823	Plan Multifunctional Team Missions		X							
34-5-0820	Manage Prophet Sensor Missions		X							

Table 2-1. FSO METL crosswalk (continued)

HHC, R&S Brigade		METs and Task Groups									
		C2	Perform ISR			Conduct Reconnaissance				Decide Surface Targets	
Task Number	Task Title	Execute the Operations Process	Develop the ISR Plan	Perform ISR	Conduct LRS Staff Planning	Conduct Zone Reconnaissance	Conduct Area Reconnaissance	Conduct a Screen	Conduct Area Security	Conduct Fire Support Planning Using MDMP	
71-8-2210	Perform Intelligence Preparation of the Battlefield (IPB) (BN-Corps)		X								
71-8-2311	Develop Information Requirements (Division - Corps)		X								
71-8-2300	Perform Intelligence, Surveillance, and Reconnaissance			X							
17-6-1007	Conduct Intelligence, Surveillance, And Reconnaissance (ISR) Synchronization and Integration (Battalion - Brigade)			X		X	X	X	X		
34-4-1723	Perform Intelligence Synchronization			X							
34-5-0221	Synchronize the HUMINT Collection Effort (S2X)			X							
34-5-0331	Coordinate HUMINT Operations (OMT) (R&S Brigade)			X							
34-5-0702	Process Incoming Signals Intelligence (SIGINT) Information			X							
34-6-2034	Perform Analysis (brigade/battalion)			X							

Table 2-1. FSO METL crosswalk (continued)

Task Number	Task Title	C2 — Execute the Operations Process	Perform ISR — Develop the ISR Plan	Perform ISR — Perform ISR	Perform ISR — Conduct LRS Staff Planning	Conduct Reconnaissance — Conduct Zone Reconnaissance	Conduct Reconnaissance — Conduct Area Reconnaissance	Conduct Reconnaissance — Conduct a Screen	Conduct Reconnaissance — Conduct Area Security	Decide Surface Targets — Conduct Fire Support Planning Using MDMP
34-6-2042	Process Specific Information Requirements (SIR)			X						
34-6-2044	Disseminate Combat Information and Intelligence			X						
34-6-2050	Conduct Long Range Surveillance (LRS) Staff Planning (BDE)				X					
1-4-7927	Conduct Unmanned Aircraft System (UAS) Surveillance Missions				X					
17-6-9314	Conduct Zone Reconnaissance (Battalion-Brigade)			X		X				
17-1-4025	Conduct a Reconnaissance Handover (Battalion-Brigade)			X		X	X			
17-6-9315	Conduct Area Reconnaissance (Battalion-Brigade)			X			X			
17-6-9225	Conduct a Screen (Battalion-Brigade)							X		
17-6-3809	Conduct Battle Handover (Battalion-Brigade)							X		
07-6-6082	Conduct Mobility, Countermobility, and or Survivability (Battalion-Brigade)			X		X	X	X	X	

HHC, R&S Brigade

Table 2-1. FSO METL crosswalk (continued)

HHC, R&S Brigade		METs and Task Groups								
		C2	Perform ISR			Conduct Reconnaissance				Decide Surface Targets
Task Number	Task Title	Execute the Operations Process	Develop the ISR Plan	Perform ISR	Conduct LRS Staff Planning	Conduct Zone Reconnaissance	Conduct Area Reconnaissance	Conduct a Screen	Conduct Area Security	Conduct Fire Support Planning Using MDMP
07-6-1272	Conduct Area Security (Battalion-Brigade)								X	
07-6-6073	Secure Civilians During Operations (Battalion-Brigade)								X	
17-6-9406	Conduct Lines of Communication Security (Battalion-Brigade)								X	
06-6-1118	Conduct Fire Support Planning using MDMP	X								X
01-6-0436	Coordinate Air-Ground Integration and the Close Combat Attack	X				X	X	X	X	X
06-6-5059	Coordinate Target Attack									X
06-6-5066	Employ Lethal Fires in Support of the BCT			X		X	X	X	X	X
17-6-0308	Synchronize Close Air Support (Battalion – Brigade)	X		X		X	X	X	X	X
71-8-5100	Execute the Operations Process (Battalion – Corps)	X								
71-8-5111	Conduct the Military Decision-Making Process (Battalion – Corps)	X								
71-8-5120	Prepare for Tactical Operations (Battalion – Corps)	X								
71-8-5130	Assess Tactical Situation and Operations (Battalion – Corps)	X								
71-8-5131	Execute Tactical Operations (Battalion – Corps)	X								

SECTION II - TRAINING AND EVALUATION OUTLINES

2-3.   This section contains the T&EOs of all supporting collective tasks found in the R&S brigade FSO METL crosswalk table. These T&EOs can be used to evaluate units during training events.

INTRODUCTION

2-4.   This section provides the R&S brigade FSO METL supporting collective tasks in the form of T&EOs. All T&EOs support R&S brigade missions, and individual T&EOs may support multiple missions within the FSO.

2-5.   The task outlines have multiple uses. Leaders and Soldiers within the R&S brigade can use them as a reference on how to perform a task. Commanders and staff members may use them to identify subordinate unit supporting tasks. Observers or evaluators can use them to record and document the unit's task performance.

STRUCTURE

2-6.   Each T&EO provides the task conditions and standards. Each T&EO also provides a series of task steps and performance measures that serve as a logical guide for performing the task. Task steps are generally sequential, but they may be performed concurrently, or even omitted, based on the mission variables of METT-TC. The unit's ability to accomplish the task steps and performance measures indicates whether or not it is executing the task to standard. Table 2-1 lists R&S brigade FSO METL tasks by R&S brigade METs and task groups. For additional T&EO information refer to TRADOC Pamphlet 350-70-1.

FORMAT

2-7.   Each T&EO displayed in this TC consists of the following:

- **Element**. This identifies the unit or unit elements that perform the task.
- **Task**. This is a description of the action to be performed by the unit, and provides the task number.
- **References**. The reference that contains the most information (primary reference) about the task is listed first and is underlined. These are in parenthesis following the task number.
- **Iteration**. This is used to identify how many times the task is performed and evaluated during training. The "M" identifies when the task is performed in MOPP 4.
- **Commander/leader assessment**. This is used by the unit leadership to assess the proficiency of the unit in performing the task to standard. Assessments are subjective in nature, use all available evaluation data, and submit leader input to develop the organization's overall capability to accomplish the task. Assessments use the following ratings:
  - **T-Trained**. The unit is trained and has demonstrated its proficiency in accomplishing the task to standards.
  - **P-Needs practice**. The unit needs to practice the task. Performance has demonstrated that the unit does not achieve standard without some difficulty or has failed to perform some task steps to standard.
  - **U-Untrained**. The unit cannot demonstrate an ability to achieve proficiency.
- **Condition**. The condition is a written statement of the situation or environment in which the unit performs the collective task.
- **Task standard**. There are two components:

- The task standard states the performance criteria that a unit must achieve to successfully execute the task. This overall standard should be the focus of training and understood by every Soldier.

- The trainer or evaluator determines the unit's training status using performance observation measurements (where applicable) and his judgment. The unit must be evaluated in the context of METT-TC conditions. These conditions should be as similar as possible for all evaluated elements, which establishes a common base line for unit performance.

● **Task steps and performance measures.** These are actions that are required to complete the task. These actions are observable performances for evaluating training proficiency. The task steps are arranged sequentially along with supporting individual tasks and their reference. Leader tasks within each T&EO are indicated by an asterisk (*). Performance measures are listed under each task step. Each measure must be accomplished to correctly perform the task step. If the unit fails to correctly perform a task step to standard, it has failed to achieve the overall task standard.

● **Go/no-go column.** This column annotates the unit's performance of task steps. When assessing training, each performance measure must be evaluated for a task step by placing an "X" in the appropriate column. Most performance measures must be marked "Go" for the task step to be successfully performed.

● **Supporting collective tasks.** This is a clearly defined, discrete, and measurable activity, action, or event (for example, task) that requires organized or unit performance and leads to accomplishment of a mission.

USE

2-8. The T&EOs can be used for many purposes. For example, a T&EO may be used by an observer controller as an evaluation outline, or by a commander as a training outline.

TASK: Develop the Intelligence, Surveillance, and Reconnaissance Plan (Brigade - Corps) (71-8-2321)
(FM 2-0)   (FM 3-0)   (FM 2-01.3)

CONDITIONS: The unit is conducting or preparing to conduct operations. Communications are established with subordinate and adjacent units, and higher headquarters. Command and Control (C2) Information Systems (INFOSYS) are operational and passing information in accordance with Tactical Standing Operating Procedures (TACSOP). The command has received a Warning Order/Operations Plan/Operations Order/Fragmentary Order (WARNO/OPORD/OPLAN/FRAGO) from higher headquarters and is exercising mission command. Some iterations of this task should be performed in MOPP4.

TASK STANDARDS: The Intelligence section develops the collection management plan to support priority intelligence requirements, and recommends intelligence, surveillance, and reconnaissance collection assets to answer the commander's priority intelligence requirements and information requirements. The collection management plan synchronizes requirements with resources.

Note: Task steps and performance measures may not apply to every unit or echelon. Prior to evaluation, coordination should be made between evaluator and the evaluated units' higher headquarters to determine the task steps and performance measures that may be omitted.

TASK STEPS AND PERFORMANCE MEASURES	GO	NO-GO
1. The Intelligence section analyzes requirements and develops a validated and prioritized list of Information Requirements (IR) by:		
a. Participating in the war gaming process, including:		
(1) Receiving Commander's Critical Information Requirements (CCIR).		
(2) Reviewing IR and assessing Priority Intelligence Requirements (PIR).		
b. Analyzing collection requirements to determine the most effective use of collection assets.		
(1) Records and validates collection requirements.		
(2) Consolidates and prioritizes collection requirements.		
(3) Identifies all organic, adjacent, and higher Intelligence, Surveillance, and Reconnaissance (ISR) assets and availability.		
(4) Recommend Priority Intelligence Requirements (PIR).		
(5) Develop indicators.		
c. Developing the Specific Information Requirements (SIR) that answers each of the intelligence requirements.		
d. Converting SIR into ISR tasks.		
2. The Intelligence section develops the collection plan that effectively answers the commander's PIR by:		
a. Identifying and evaluating ISR collection assets available to support the collection plan including unique support requirements.		
b. Developing a collection strategy based on ISR capability, evaluation, and synchronizing collection requirements through the development of an Intelligence Synchronization Matrix (ISM).		
c. Developing and prioritizing the ISR tasks for SIR and reporting criteria for the collection assets based on required analysis.		

TASK STEPS AND PERFORMANCE MEASURES	GO	NO-GO
(1) Forms directive ISR task reporting requirements.		
(2) Focuses ISR tasks on developed Named Area of Interest (NAI).		
(3) Provides Latest Time Information of Value (LTIOV) for each ISR task.		
(4) Tailors each ISR task to the selected collection assets or organization.		
3. The Intelligence section verifies the dissemination of intelligence information by ensuring the flow is directly from the collectors and processors to requesters by:		
a. Direct dissemination.		
b. Determining perishability.		
c. Determining how much to disseminate.		
d. Disseminating intelligence products.		
4. The Intelligence section evaluates intelligence reporting to confirm all ISR tasks are fully satisfied and that the collection management plan remains fully synchronized by:		
a. Monitoring operations against the ISM confirming linkage with PIR and SIR.		
b. Determining perishability.		
c. Screening reports to verify that ISR tasks are being satisfied.		
d. Providing feedback to ISR collectors and exploiters on the success of the collection effort and ISR tasks that still need to be satisfied.		
5. The Intelligence section updates the collection management plan, verifying that synchronization is maintained by:		
a. Eliminating satisfied intelligence requirements.		
b. Redirecting collection assets to unsatisfied intelligence requirements.		
c. Cueing collection assets to collection opportunities and new requirements that develop during operations and as PIR change.		
d. Maintaining situational awareness and synchronization of changing intelligence requirements during operations.		

* indicates a leader task step.

SUPPORTING COLLECTIVE TASKS

Task Number	Task Title
71-8-2300	Perform Intelligence, Surveillance, and Reconnaissance (Battalion - Corps)
71-8-2210	Perform Intelligence Preparation of the Battlefield (Battalion – Corps)
11-6-8065	Direct Intelligence, Surveillance, and Reconnaissance Operations (ISR)

TASK: Plan Multifunctional Team Missions (34-4-0823)

<u>(FM 3-90.15)</u>   (FM 2-0)   (FM 2-19.4)

CONDITIONS: The Multifunctional Team (MFT) is preparing to support a Site Exploitation mission. The mission was received through a Warning Order (WARNO), Operations Order (OPORD), Fragmentary Order (FRAGO), or verbal order. A target for exploitation has been identified and an objective has been located. The team has the unit Tactical Standing Operating Procedures (TACSOP). The team has received guidance on the rules of engagement (ROE) and the rules of interaction (ROI). Coalition partners, civilians, government agencies, nongovernmental organizations (NGO), private voluntary organizations (PVO), organizations of the international community (IC), and news media may be present in the area. Performance of this task may occur in an asymmetric environment containing imbalanced ideological, cultural, technological and/or military threat capabilities. Team leaders conduct Composite Risk Management (CRM) and take into account environmental considerations during mission planning. Some iterations of this task should be performed in MOPP4.

TASK STANDARDS: The elements of the MFT conduct SIGINT and HUMINT collection and analysis in coordination with supported collection and analysis elements. The MFT conducts necessary coordination with the supported maneuver element and other supporting units providing required assistance. The team integrates all collected information and required support into the mission planning. The MFT team receives the mission brief and conducts rehearsals with the supported maneuver element.

TASK STEPS AND PERFORMANCE MEASURES	GO	NO-GO
1. The team begins mission planning after receipt of mission from G2/S2 of supported unit.		
a. The team leader issues an initial Warning Order to the team members.		
NOTE: The MFT team leader may issue multiple WARNOs or FRAGOs as additional information or changes from the S2/S3 are received.		
(1) Usually within one hour of receipt of mission.		
(2) Establishes task organization of the MFT for the mission, to include:		
(a) Formation.		
(b) Personnel.		
(c) Equipment.		
(3) Includes timeline of events required prior to mission start.		
b. The Human Intelligence (HUMINT) element is dispatched to coordinate with local HUMINT Collection Teams (HCT) and analysis elements.		
(1) Conducts collection, analysis, and continuing target development in coordination with the supported unit Operations Management Team (OMT), HCTs, Fusion Cell, and G2X/S2X.		
(a) Utilizes information collected by Intelligence, Surveillance, and Reconnaissance (ISR) assets.		
(b) Includes information from military source operations.		
(2) Provides up-to-date HUMINT collection and analysis results to the MFT team leader to assist in mission planning.		
(3) Develops products for use at the objective.		
(a) A target-specific questioning plan.		
(b) Smart cards for the recording of HUMINT screening information.		

TASK STEPS AND PERFORMANCE MEASURES	GO	NO-GO
c. The Signals Intelligence (SIGINT) element is dispatched to coordinate with local SIGINT collection elements and the SIGINT Fusion Cell.		
(1) The SIGINT element provides continuing collection, analysis, and target development in coordination with the supported unit and SIGINT Fusion Cell to:		
(a) Determines what communications equipment the threat is using.		
(b) Determines the frequency ranges of threat communications gear.		
(c) Determines the bandwidth/modulation of the communications channels and the tuning step size of threat communications gear.		
(d) Analyzes radio line of sight (RLOS) within the area.		
(e) Predicts the time and location of where threat emitters are active in the area.		
(f) Confirm that emitter signals belong to the target(s) of interest.		
(g) Determine the best location for electronic attack enroute to the objective.		
(2) The SIGINT element provides up-to-date collection and analysis results to the MFT team leader to assist in final mission planning		
* 2. The team leader coordinates with the following local elements for additional support and information about the objective:		
a. Maneuver elements conducting the mission to the objective.		
b. Counterintelligence Coordination Authority (CICA).		
c. Psychological Operations element.		
d. Civil Affairs.		
e. Military Police.		
f. Translators/Interpreters.		
g. Administration and Logistics.		
* 3. The team leader determines amount of time to spend on the objective based upon METT-TC, TACSOP, and supported unit requirements.		
* 4. The team leader develops a Fragmentary Order (FRAGO) based on the TACSOP, information collected, and supported unit's mission requirements as necessary.		
* 5. The team leader conducts the pre-mission brief to team members.		
a. Briefs the mission, and FRAGOs, if applicable.		
b. Establishes reporting procedures for use during mission execution.		
(1) What reports and products will be produced.		
(2) How and where reports will be transmitted.		
c. Receives back brief from subordinate element leaders.		
6. The team conducts rehearsals with supported/supporting maneuver elements, which includes-		
a. Conducting battle drills.		
b. Establishing site security at the objective.		

TASK STEPS AND PERFORMANCE MEASURES	GO	NO-GO
c. Conducting MFT actions while at the objective.		
7. The team conducts precombat checks on vehicles and equipment.		

* indicates a leader task step.

SUPPORTING COLLECTIVE TASKS

Task Number	Task Title
34-5-0221	Synchronize the HUMINT Collection Effort (S2X)
34-5-0820	Manage Prophet Sensor Missions

TASK: Manage Prophet Sensor Missions (34-5-0820)

(FM 2-19.4)   (FM 2-22.3)   (FM 2-0)

CONDITIONS: The Prophet Control Team is operational. The team has received the OPORD/FRAGO and the commander's priority intelligence requirements (PIR). The team has been given a clear mission tasking. An active target signals environment exists. Communications are established for tasking and reporting with ASAS-Light and the combat net radio (CNR). Hazards such as a nuclear, biological, or chemical environment, limited visibility, night, inclement weather, and opposing force can exist. Performance of this task may occur in an asymmetric environment containing imbalanced ideological, cultural, technological and/or military threat capabilities. Unit leaders conduct Composite Risk Management (CRM) and take into account environmental considerations during mission planning. Some iterations of this task should be performed in MOPP4.

TASK STANDARDS: The element manages SIGINT technical taskings to Prophet Sensor teams, enabling teams to report combat information that supports priority intelligence requirements and information requirements to higher headquarters in accordance with the unit TACSOP. Reports are passed in time to influence the supported commander's decisions.

TASK STEPS AND PERFORMANCE MEASURES	GO	NO-GO
1. The team conducts mission planning.		
a. Obtains IPB products from the S2/S3.		
b. Conducts Electronic Preparation of the Battlefield (EPB).		
(1) Determines what threat communications equipment the threat is using.		
(2) Determines the frequency ranges of threat communications gear.		
(3) Determines the bandwidth/Modulation of the communications channels and the tuning step size of threat communications gear.		
(4) Analyzes radio line of sight (RLOS) within the area of operations (AO).		
c. Predicts the time and location of where enemy emitters are in the area of operations (AO).		
2. Task organizes platoon assets to best accomplish the mission.		
NOTE: Prophet Control should, when tactically feasible and Force Protection measures allow, perform system tests of the Prophet systems when they reach their operational site or while in an assembly area. This will provide the analysts with an idea of how the system will perform in the area and establish a rough idea of distance to Signal-to-Noise-Ratio (SNR).		
a. Assigns general sensor locations to each Prophet sensor team.		
b. Ensures Prophet sensor locations have RLOS to both Prophet Control and the target area of interest.		
c. Ensures Prophet sensors are connected to appropriate national systems as required.		
d. Considers mission, enemy, terrain, troops-time and civilian considerations.		
e. Considers the unit and supported unit commander's intent.		
3. Develops Prophet technical taskings.		
a. Determines taskings from the SORs in the OPORD/FRAGO.		
b. Ensures taskings are prioritized based upon the commander's intent and PIR.		

TASK STEPS AND PERFORMANCE MEASURES	GO	NO-GO
c. Assigns taskings to Prophet sensor teams.		
NOTE: When tasking a system to perform a band sweep, the search should be limited to 25Mhz.		
(1) Sends known frequencies of interest.		
(2) Sends known frequency range of emitters.		
(3) Sends signal characteristics of target emitters.		
(4) Delineates areas of interest (AOI).		
(5) Outlines expected enemy activity within the AOI.		
(6) Sends a time-line of expected events.		
d. Ensures Prophet sensor teams acknowledge receipt of taskings IAW the TACSOP.		
e. Develops an event matrix or synchronization matrix to track technical SIGINT taskings IAW the unit TACSOP.		
4. Processes Prophet sensor team reports.		
NOTE: All reports from the Prophet sensor teams will be sent to Prophet Control via the digital reporting link (ASAS-Light) or via voice communications over the CNR IAW the unit's TACSOP.		
a. Receives TACREP from the Prophet sensor teams that include:		
(1) Frequency of the signal.		
(2) Bandwidth/Modulation used.		
(3) Line of Bearing (LOB) to the emitter.		
(4) Signal to Noise Ratio (SNR).		
(5) Time up.		
(6) Time down.		
(7) Gisted voice intercept information IAW the TACSOP (if proper linguists are manning the Prophet sensor teams).		
b. Performs limited analysis of reported information. (34-5-0702)		
c. Performs analysis on the signal intercepted.		
(1) Determines if the intercepted communication is from a possible threat.		
(2) Determines if the transmission originated from where the threat was expected to be.		
(3) Roughly estimates the distance from the Prophet team to the transmitter		
(4) Determines if the information received answers the IR.		
d. Directs other Prophet sensor teams to develop a cut or fix on the transmitter by sending the following information:		
NOTE: Prophet Control can also tip-off higher headquarters when their analysis indicates that an intercepted signal is of high importance and can be exploited by other IEW systems.		
(1) Modulation used.		
(2) Bandwidth.		
(3) Frequency.		

TASK STEPS AND PERFORMANCE MEASURES	GO	NO-GO
(4) Rough location of the transmitter		
e. Performs LOB analysis on cut or fix information reported to determine the transmitter's location.		
5. Prophet Control reports combat information gathered to the supported S2.		
6. Maintains resource status reports from Prophet sensor teams.		
a. Evaluates all reports received from all Prophet sensor teams.		
b. Coordinates with appropriate staff element to correct reported equipment or personnel deficiencies.		
c. Maintains status report board.		
d. Reports consolidated status to the supported S2 and platoon leader IAW the unit TACSOP		
NOTE: Prophet Control should periodically provide SITREPs to the Prophet sensor teams on the status of SIGINT missions conducted.		

* indicates a leader task step.

SUPPORTING COLLECTIVE TASKS

Task Number	Task Title
34-5-0702	Process Incoming Signals Intelligence (SIGINT) Information
34-5-0470	Provide Situational Awareness of the Company Area of Operations

TASK: Perform Intelligence Preparation of the Battlefield (battalion - Corps) (71-8-2210)

(FM 2-01.3)   (FM 2-0)   (FM 2-19.4)

CONDITIONS: The unit is conducting or preparing to conduct operations. Communications are established with subordinate and adjacent units, and higher headquarters. Command and Control (C2) Information Systems (INFOSYS) are operational and passing information in accordance with Tactical Standing Operating Procedures (TACSOP). The command has received a Warning Order/Operations Plan/Operations Order/Fragmentary Order (WARNO/OPORD/OPLAN/FRAGO) from higher headquarters and is exercising mission command. The commander has issued planning guidance. Some iterations of this task should be performed in MOPP4.

TASK STANDARDS: The staff, led by the Intelligence section, performs Intelligence Preparation of the Battlefield by defining the operating environment; describing the battlefield's effects; evaluating the enemy; and determining enemy courses of action. The staff refines higher headquarters intelligence products and/or develops their own intelligence products producing a modified combined obstacle overlay and enemy courses of action which include doctrinal templates, situational templates, identification of high-value targets, an event template, initial priority intelligence requirements and intelligence requirements to support the unit decision-making process. The staff shares Intelligence Preparation of the Battlefield products with subordinate and adjacent units to facilitate parallel or collaborative planning.

Note: Task steps and performance measures may not apply to every unit or echelon. Prior to evaluation, coordination should be made between evaluator and the evaluated units' higher headquarters to determine the task steps and performance measures that may be omitted.

TASK STEPS AND PERFORMANCE MEASURES	GO	NO-GO
NOTE: Step 1 - Define the battlefield environment.		
1. The staff, led by the Intelligence section:		
NOTE: Battle space is the environment, factors, and conditions, commanders must understand to successfully apply combat power, protect the force, or complete the mission. This includes the air, land, sea, space, and the enemy and friendly forces, facilities, weather, terrain, the electromagnetic spectrum, and the information environment within the Area of Operation (AO) and Area of Interest (AOI). The limit of the AO is normally the boundaries specified in the Operations Order (OPORD) or Contingency Plan (CONPLAN) from higher HQs that defines the commander's mission.		
a. Directs the staff to import higher Headquarters (HQs) unit overlays and graphics using their Information Systems (INFOSYS).		
b. Directs the staff to use the maneuver overlays as the starting point for analysis of the unit area of operational intelligence.		
c. Determines the maximum capabilities of the unit to acquire targets and physically dominate the threat.		
d. Anticipates future and on order missions.		
2. The staff, led by the Intelligence section, determines if the amount of detail required is feasible within the time available by:		
a. Identifies the amount of detail required on each area of the battlefield/operation or each threat force to support planning.		
b. Prioritizes efforts to produce the amount of detail within the available time.		

TASK STEPS AND PERFORMANCE MEASURES	GO	NO-GO
c. Determines the amount of time that can reasonably be devoted to each step to meet the commander's time line by backwards planning the IPB process.		
d. Advises the commander if time allotted is insufficient to complete the directed analysis and provides a recommended solution.		
e. Identifies information gaps necessary to define the operational environment.		
f. Submits Request for Information (RFI) to higher headquarters.		
g. Uses the commander's initial intelligence requirements and intent to identify and prioritize gaps in the current holdings.		
h. Evaluates existing databases for information.		
i. Informs the commander of gaps not expected to be filled during the time allotted for IPB.		
3. The staff, led by the Intelligence section, gathers the following overlays and reports to establish a start point for AOI and operational environment analysis by:		
a. Unit Area of Operations (AO) overlay.		
b. Initial Combined Obstacles Overlay (COO) and other geospatial engineering products.		
c. Reports that identify the significant characteristics of the environment (electromagnetic, geography, terrain, weather, demographics, Rules of Engagement [ROE]).		
4. The Intelligence section, in conjunction, with Geospatial Information Service (GI&S) section and Engineer Planner, identifies significant characteristics of the environment that influence friendly and threat operations, by:		
a. Focusing the IPB effort on the areas and characteristics of the battlefield/operation that will influence the commander's mission.		
b. Considering aspects of the environment that have an effect on accomplishing the unit's mission, including:		
(1) Geographical, terrain and weather of the area.		
(2) Population demographics (ethnic groups, religious groups, age distribution, income groups).		
(3) Infrastructures, such as transportation and telecommunications.		
(4) ROE or legal restrictions including international treaties or agreements.		
5. The staff, develops their individual warfighting function portions of the unit AOI on an operational overlay by:		
a. Following guidance from the commander and higher HQs that addresses the establishment of the AOI.		
b. Evaluating the limit of the AOI on the ability of the threat to project power or move forces into the AO including:		
(1) Commander's intent.		
(2) Mission, tasks, constraints, risks, available assets, and specified AO.		
(3) Concept of the operation, and the deception plan.		
(4) Time line for mission execution.		

TASK STEPS AND PERFORMANCE MEASURES	GO	NO-GO
(5) Missions of the adjacent units.		
(6) Assigned AO.		
c. Determining amount of time to accomplish the friendly mission.		
d. Considering the following:		
(1) Geographical locations of other activities or characteristics of the environment that influence Courses of Action (COA) of the commander's decision.		
(2) Anticipate future mission and on-order-missions identified during mission analysis.		
(3) Changes in the unit's operational environment.		
(4) Dividing the AOI into several components, example; ground AOI, air AOI, and political AOI.		
(5) Further identifies significant characteristics of the environment that influence friendly and threat operations.		
6. The staff, led by the Intelligence section, defines the operational environment, by:		
a. Defining the operational environment with parameters that include:		
(1) Access of the opposing threat force to the intelligence assets of higher echelons.		
(2) Access of the opposing threat force to Human Intelligence (HUMINT), Imagery Intelligence (IMINT), Signals Intelligence (SIGINT), and other collection capabilities.		
(3) Fixed Electronic Surveillance (ES), or Electronic Attack (EA) sites that support threat operations.		
(4) Airfields that support ES, or EA aircraft.		
(5) Weather effects and light data using the Integrated Meteorological System (IMETS) web client.		
b. The Plans section, defines the operational environment and develops the maneuver overlay, by:		
(1) Retrieving higher maneuver overlay and graphics.		
(2) Identifying significant characteristics of the environment.		
(3) Integrating the commander's initial guidance and input from the staff.		
(4) Presenting the complete unit maneuver overlay to the commander for approval.		
(5) Posting the maneuver overlay in a shared folder or other location where the other staff sections can access it, notifies the staff of the location.		
c. The Aviation (AVN) section, In Accordance With (ICW) the Air Missile Defense (AMD) section, defines the operational environment with parameters that include:		
(1) Airfields and air avenues of approaches for threat air assault, airborne, and air interdiction forces.		
(2) All threat radars, air defense weapons that can affect flight operations within the AO.		

TASK STEPS AND PERFORMANCE MEASURES	GO	NO-GO
(3) Possible friendly and threat flight routes outside the AO.		
(4) Probable Airspace Coordination Areas (ACA).		
d. The Field Artillery Intelligence Officer (FAIO), ICW the Fires planner, the Electronic Warfare Officer (EWO), and the G6/S6 section evaluate the capabilities of the threat, by:		
(1) Identifying areas that threat fire support Target Acquisition (TA) and delivery systems are capable of ranging the unit AO.		
(2) Determining the maximum capabilities of the unit to acquire targets and physically dominate targets.		
(3) Identifying the area of influence that friendly Direct Support (DS), TA, and delivery systems are able to influence.		
NOTE: The AO and AOI for fire support will normally be the same as those of the supported force.		
e. The AMD section, defines the operational environment with parameters that include:		
(1) Location of tactical ballistic missiles.		
(2) Location of threat airfields.		
(3) Location of Forward Area Arming and Refueling Points (FAARP).		
(4) Location of aids to navigation.		
(5) Range capabilities of threat aircraft.		
(6) Altitude capabilities of threat aircraft.		
(7) Range capabilities of tactical ballistic missiles.		
(8) Flight profiles of tactical ballistic missiles.		
f. The Sustainment section, defines the operational environment with parameters that include:	'	
(1) Operational reserves capable of penetrating the main battle/operating area.		
(2) Insurgent forces are capable of operating within the rear area, or that can affect sustainment operations in the main operating area.		
(3) Terrorist organizations that can interfere with sustainment operations.		
(4) Hostile forces that could affect sustainment units moving in the AO.		
g. The Engineer section defines the operational environment with parameters that include:		
(1) Traffic ability and mobility.		
(2) Survivability.		
(3) Line of sight.		
(4) Obstacle placement.		
(5) Breaching.		
h. The Chemical, Biological, Radiological, Nuclear, and High-Yield Explosives (CBRNE) section, defines the operational environment with parameters that include:		

TASK STEPS AND PERFORMANCE MEASURES	GO	NO-GO
(1) Threat missile, and artillery weapons that can deliver CBRNE weapons into the AO.		
(2) Threat aircraft capable of delivering CBRNE weapons into the AO.		
i. The Signal section, defines the operational environment with parameters that include:		
(1) Required links with higher and adjacent commands.		
(2) Threat jamming assets capable of affecting communication.		
(3) Threat SIGINT collection assets that may target friendly systems.		
(4) Line of Sight characteristics of terrain, to include communications and noncommunication emitters.		
(5) Vegetation and its effects on radio wave absorption and antenna height requirements.		
(6) Large objects including buildings and cliffs that will influence radio waves.		
j. The Civil Military Operations (CMO) section, defines the operational environment with parameters that include:		
(1) Areas affecting the civil component, not normally associated as militarily significant.		
(2) Structures of civil significance: critical infrastructure, culturally significant sites, and sites of practical civil-military applications.		
(3) Capabilities: ability of the civil populace to sustain itself, shortfalls of critical services, availability of contract resources and services.		
(4) Organizations: include Indigenous Populations and Institutions (IPI), Intergovernmental Organizations (IGO), Nongovernmental Organizations (NGO), and Other Government Agencies (OGA).		
(5) People: both individually and collectively that can influence the AO demographic information (historical, cultural, ethnic, political, economic, religious, and humanitarian factors).		
(6) Events: civil or military activities that may influence operations.		
7. The staff, conceptually develops the maneuver portion of the unit operational environment by:		
a. Considering physical dimensions of width, depth, and height; as well as the operational factors of time, tempo, and synchronization.		
b. Including elements of social-political importance.		
c. Considering reach-back and reach-out capabilities of its communications systems to include:		
(1) Areas that reach back to log bases that support the unit's operations.		
(2) Forward to the limit of airborne sensors feeding information to it about the movement and location of an enemy unit approaching it.		
(3) Frequencies and bandwidth sufficiency for supporting sensors, communications platforms, and electronic warfare systems.		
(4) Areas that allow for operation of attack helicopters, and tactical aircraft that are a part of the units operations.		

TASK STEPS AND PERFORMANCE MEASURES	GO	NO-GO
8. The staff, gathers the following overlays and reports, share folders, web servers and File Transfer Protocol (FTP) sites, to establish a start point for AOI and operational environment analysis, including:		
a. Maneuver overlay.		
b. Initial Combined Obstacles Overlay (COO), and other geospatial engineering products.		
c. Reports that identify the significant characteristics of the environment (geography, terrain, weather, demographics, Rules of Engagement [ROE]).		
9. The staff notifies the Intelligence section upon completing their portions of the AOI maneuver overlay, which allows the Intelligence planner to consolidate the individual staff overlay portions.		
10. The Plans and Maneuver sections consolidate the AO, AOI, and operational environment overlays to establish the unit operational environment overlay.		
11. The Plans and Maneuver sections present the unit operational environment overlay to the commander for approval.		
12. The Current Operations section, completes the following, by:		
a. Disseminating the approved unit operational environment overlay to higher HQs and subordinate units as part of a Warning Order (WARNO).		
b. Notifying the staff that the approved unit operational environment overlay has been posted.		
c. Displaying the unit operational environment operations overlay as part of the Common Operational Picture (COP).		
d. Notifying the staff that the approved division battlefield environment overlay has been posted to the MCS server or share folder using the Common Message Processor (CMP) application or the Microsoft Outlook application and /or publishes and distributes thru Publish and Subscribe Service (PASS).		
e. Displaying the battlefield environment OPS overlay as part of the Common Operational Picture (COP).		
13. The staff, continues to update their running estimates and other current critical information as the operational environment changes, by:		
a. Validating significant facts, events, and conclusions based on analyzed data.		
b. Recommending how to best use available resources to the commander.		
NOTE: Step 2 Describe the Battlefield Effects.		
14. The staff, led by the Intelligence section, describes the operational environment's effects on:		
a. Friendly capabilities:		
(1) Maneuver.		
(2) Intelligence.		
b. Threat capabilities:		
(1) Maneuver.		
(2) Intelligence.		

TASK STEPS AND PERFORMANCE MEASURES	GO	NO-GO
c. The staff, analyzes critical Operating Environment (OE) variables including:		
(1) How wind speed and turbulence will affect target acquisition and intelligence collection activities.		
(2) Impact of military operations on the civil populace/activities.		
(3) Restricting effects of low ceilings in air axis of advance.		
(4) Impact of the civil populace/activities on military operations.		
(5) Probability of icing.		
15. The staff, led by the Intelligence section, analyzes the operational environment by consolidating information from the following:		
a. The AMD element analyzes and evaluates the environmental effects on operations by considering:		
(1) Probable target installations or areas.		
(2) Likely air axis of advance, Landing Zones (LZ) or Drop Zones (DZ).		
(3) Likely standoff attack orbits.		
(4) Line of Sight (LOS) from proposed Air Defense Artillery (ADA) locations.		
(5) Limiting and success-inducing effects of weather on air operations.		
(6) Expected times on targets based on weather effects or light data.		
b. The Fires section, analyzes and evaluates the environmental effects on operations by considering:		
(1) Areas best suited to artillery deployments, including:		
(a) Accessibility to ammunition carriers.		
(b) Defilading and masking effects of terrain.		
(c) Security from Levels I, II, and III rear area threats.		
(2) Potential sites for target acquisition assets, both threat and friendly.		
(3) Effects of terrain on munitions effectiveness, including soft sand, dense trees, or shallow bedrock.		
(4) Areas suitable for delivery of special purpose munitions including artillery delivered mines.		
(5) When conducting weather analysis, consider effects on target acquisition systems, target activity, and munitions accuracy.		
c. The AVN section, analyzes and evaluates the environmental effects on operations by considering:		
(1) Potential engagement areas.		
(2) "Danger areas" that optimize threat AMD system fields of fire.		
(3) Areas that mask threat radar and air defense systems.		
(4) Areas that provide good terrain background (ground clutter) effects.		
(5) Terrain shadowing effects.		
(6) Areas where birds gather.		

TASK STEPS AND PERFORMANCE MEASURES	GO	NO-GO
(7) Areas that gives threat air defense systems distinct advantages in covering air axis of advance.		
(8) Concealed and covered routes into potential battle positions.		
(9) Routes that provide for ease of navigation.		
(10) Potential safe areas for downed pilots (also evaluate infiltration corridors).		
(11) Other effects on Airspace Command and Control (AC2) planning.		
(12) Conditions that affect flight in general and aircraft systems in particular.		
(13) Density altitude effects on performance and payload.		
(14) Weather effects on threat air defense systems.		
(15) Effects of wind speed and turbulence on flight operations, especially in close terrain.		
(16) Weather effects on target acquisition systems.		
(17) Conditions that may cause "white out" or "brown out."		
(18) Precipitation effects on FARP activities.		
(19) Restrictions imposed by air space managers.		
(20) High intensity radiation transmission areas.		
d. The Intelligence section analyzes and evaluates the environmental effects on operations for weather by identifying:		
(1) Locations that best support collection coverage by threat collection systems.		
(2) Assets that are ground based (observation or equipment positions) and airborne (standoff positions or orbits).		
(3) Approach routes for each type of system. Consider the unique needs of each type.		
(4) Areas within the AO that offer friendly forces concealment from threat collection systems.		
(5) Populated areas that would facilities special or clandestine HUMINT operations.		
(6) Friendly units, locations, and information vulnerable to collection through the threat capture of U.S. prisoners of war.		
(7) Effects of weather upon collection systems.		
(8) Political, legal, and moral constraints upon collection efforts.		
(9) Effects of local culture upon collection.		
(10) Evaluating the terrain's effects on threat communication, by:		
(a) LOS characteristics of the terrain, including affects on both communications and noncommunications emitters.		
(b) Vegetation and its effects on radio wave absorption and antenna height requirements.		
(c) Locations of high power lines and their interference with radio waves.		
(d) Large vertical objects, such as buildings or cliffs that will influence radio waves.		

TASK STEPS AND PERFORMANCE MEASURES	GO	NO-GO
(e) Effects of soil types on the electric grounding of equipment.		
(11) Evaluating effects of extreme weather conditions on threat sensitive electronic equipment considering:		
(a) Electronic storms and other electromagnetic phenomenon.		
(b) Effects of high winds or obscurants, such as precipitation or blowing dust, on antennas and LOS systems.		
(c) Weather effects on flight operations of electronic surveillance or electronic attack aircraft.		
e. The CBRNE section analyzes and evaluates the environmental effects on operations by identifying:		
(1) Critical terrain features (for example, defiles, choke points, rivers, key terrain for possible threat CBRNE attacks).		
(2) Avenue of Approach (AA) and mobility corridors developed by the Plans cell for areas of vulnerability to CBRNE weapons or areas that is especially suitable for the use of obscurants.		
(3) Critical weather information needed to determine the effects of weather on CBRNE weapons or obscurants.		
(4) Local sources of water suitable for decontamination operations. Including natural and industrial or civic sources.		
f. The Signal Section analyzes and evaluates the environmental effects on operations by identifying:		
(1) Location of customers and communication density.		
(2) Best LOS for required communication links.		
(3) Locations that provide LOS defilade from potential threat collection or jamming systems.		
(4) Site access and escape routes.		
(5) Sites for tenability.		
(6) Effects for forecasted weather on frequencies, optimal frequencies for use, communication degradation from high winds or rain.		
(7) Frequency deconfliction.		
(8) Host Nation (HN) frequency restrictions.		
(9) HN restrictions on terrain use.		
g. The Sustainment section, analyzes and evaluates the environmental effects on operations by identifying:		
(1) Ground AA that can affect sustainment operations.		
(2) Air AA, Landing Zones (LZ), and Drop Zones (DZ) that can effect resupply operations.		
(3) Infiltration lanes that can support the movement of insurgents, light infantry, or Unconventional Warfare (UW) units.		
(4) Terrain that can support hide positions for these type forces.		
(5) Likely ambush locations along main supply routes.		

TASK STEPS AND PERFORMANCE MEASURES	GO	NO-GO
(6) Effects of weather upon forces hostile to sustainment operations.		
(7) Population groups that is sympathetic, neutral, and hostile to U.S. operations.		
(8) Sources of potable and nonpotable water.		
(9) Local communication systems (categorize by degree of Operational Security [OPSEC] allowed).		
(10) Local transportation means and systems.		
(11) Local sources for all classes of supply.		
(12) Location, type, and status of power production facilities.		
(13) Projects to support the local population including:		
(a) Medical assistance programs.		
(b) Food distribution.		
(c) Transportation, shelter, and care of displaced persons.		
NOTE: Treaties, agreements, and legal restrictions might regulate the relationship between sustainment activities and local businesses and organizations.		
h. The Engineer section analyzes and evaluates the environmental effects on operations by identifying:		
(1) Defensible terrain within each avenue of approach to determine locations, which lend themselves to the use of obstacles.		
(2) Breach operations by:		
(a) Concealed and covered routes towards the breach site.		
(b) Cross country mobility.		
(c) Vegetation type and distribution.		
(d) Surface drainage and configuration.		
(e) Surface soils.		
(f) Ground water.		
(g) Obstacles.		
(3) Streams and rivers within the AO. Focus on bridges, ford sites, and areas that lend themselves to river-crossing operations.		
(4) Other manmade or natural obstacles within the AO, such as railroad tracks with steep embankments.		
(5) Effects of obstacles upon the friendly movement.		
(6) Locations where obstacles can be easily traversed or crossed.		
(7) Visibility constraints for each obstacles system, particularly around areas likely to be beached.		
(8) Weather that affects the performance of each type of obstacles for the local terrain, including:		
(a) Effects of weather upon survivability positions.		
(b) Effects of precipitation upon rivers and streams.		

TASK STEPS AND PERFORMANCE MEASURES	GO	NO-GO
(c) Estimate the degree to which each water source would be frozen and its subsequent load capacity during winter.		
(9) Local sources of potable water.		
(10) Local sources of barrier material.		
(11) Ability of the local road network to support anticipated traffic.		
NOTE: When considering local economics, identify the engineer projects, which would most help the local population if time permits. Such projects are especially pertinent for nation assistance and counterinsurgency operations. Projects could include building roads, schoolhouses, power generation facilities, water sanitation, or other public buildings and services.		
16. The staff, led by the Intelligence section, creates tactical decision aids related to their specific areas of responsibility.		
17. The Intelligence section consolidates tactical decision aids and other products and posts them to a designated location(s).		
18. The Intelligence section articulates the intelligence analysis information as the unit conducts its mission analysis and IPB by:		
a. Approving intelligence products.		
b. Consolidating information concerning the battlefield effects products received from all staff sections.		
c. Producing a consolidated MCOO, demographics information, and weather and light data.		
d. Intelligence leader presents the consolidated MCOO to the commander for approval.		
e. Displaying all or portions of the consolidated unit MCOO when approved.		
f. Notifying the intelligence community upon notification of approval of the MCOO.		
g. Disseminating all or key portions of the approved MCOO to higher HQs and subordinate units.		
h. Consolidating input from cells and elements concerning gaps in terrain data.		
i. Recommending Intelligence, Surveillance, and Reconnaissance (ISR) plan.		
j. Submitting Request for Information (RFI) to higher and adjacent subordinate units.		
NOTE: Step 3 Evaluate the Threat		
19. The staff, led by the Intelligence section, identifies and evaluates threat capabilities by identifying:		
a. Threat Decision-Making process to include:		
(1) Provides descriptions of threat counterparts including:		
(a) IPB process.		
(b) Command running estimate or decision-making process, particularly wargaming.		
(c) Techniques for selecting intelligence requirements.		
(d) Collection planning and collection management.		

TASK STEPS AND PERFORMANCE MEASURES	GO	NO-GO
(2) Standard lengths of the threat decision cycle for both anticipated and unanticipated decisions.		
(3) Collection systems available to each threat unit.		
(4) Signature items of equipment that are easily identified by your collection assets.		
(5) Threat's normal operational and communication security procedures.		
(6) Systems that are direct threats to friendly collectors.		
(7) Threat ability to locate and destroy friendly assets.		
b. The FAIO, ICW the Fires section, describes the threat by:		
(1) Evaluating the threat ability to fight the counterfire battle by identifying:		
(a) Target acquisition assets; describe their normal deployment patterns and tactics.		
(b) Capability of each target acquisition system in terms of accuracy and timeliness.		
(c) C2 and information systems that moves target acquisition information to decision makers or weapon systems.		
(2) Describe the threat's ability to locate and destroy friendly target acquisition assets.		
(3) Evaluate rear area threat to artillery units.		
(4) Describe the threats ability to conduct Electronic Attack (EA).		
c. The AMD section, ICW the AVN section, describes the threat by:		
(1) Evaluate threat posed including:		
(a) Unmanned aerial vehicles.		
(b) Missiles (cruise and ballistic).		
(c) Fixed-wing aircraft.		
(d) Rotary-wing aircraft.		
(e) Airborne and air assault forces.		
(2) Evaluate Order of Battle (OB) factors that include:		
(a) Flight operations tactics.		
(b) Ordnance types and availability.		
(c) Ordnance delivery techniques such as standoff ranges, release speeds and altitudes, and guidance systems.		
(d) Technical capabilities of aircraft including all-weather or night capability as well as maximum and minimum speeds, ceiling, range, payloads (in terms of ordnance, numbers and types of equipment, or passengers), and aerial refueling capability.		
(e) Target selection priorities for air strikes or attack by air assaults.		
(f) Air strike allocation procedures.		
(g) Threats to friendly AMD assets, including threat ground forces and EW assets.		

TASK STEPS AND PERFORMANCE MEASURES	GO	NO-GO
d. The AMD section, ICW the AVN section, describes the threat by identifying:		
(1) Units supported by AMD assets.		
(2) Types of AMD systems and their capabilities including:		
(a) Maximum and minimum ranges.		
(b) Maximum and minimum engagement altitudes.		
(c) Minimum engagement times.		
(3) Other threats including lasers or artillery fire zones.		
(4) Artificial illumination effects on target acquisition and night vision devices.		
(5) Target characteristics including:		
(a) Normal deployment patterns in march or attack order.		
(b) Capability to detect attacking aircraft.		
(c) Typical reactions when attacked by aviation.		
e. The EN section describes the threat by:		
(1) Evaluating organization, equipment, and standard operations of threat engineer units that include:		
(a) Mobility.		
(b) Countermobility.		
(c) Survivability.		
(d) Obstacle placement.		
(e) Breaching.		
(2) Evaluating capabilities of engineer unit measured in time that is:		
(a) Required to lay each type of obstacle system.		
(b) Needed to breach obstacles.		
(c) Required to entrench a mechanized infantry company.		
(d) Needed to bridge different size rivers and streams.		
(3) Evaluating tactics that threat engineers employ while conducting each of the above operations.		
(4) Evaluating engineer capabilities of threat infantry, armor, and other non-engineer units.		
f. The CBRNE section evaluates threat capabilities by:		
(1) Ability to employ CBRNE weapons and obscurants.		
(2) Types of delivery systems, including minimum and maximum ranges.		
(3) Threat CBRNE weapons employment doctrine and TTP.		
(4) Threat CBRNE protection capabilities.		
(5) Indicators of preparations to employ CBRNE weapons.		
g. The Signal section evaluates the capabilities of the threat to disrupt or intercept communications by identifying:		
(1) Ability to locate or intercept friendly systems.		

TASK STEPS AND PERFORMANCE MEASURES	GO	NO-GO
(2) Targeting accuracies of collection systems.		
(3) Speed with which the threat can collect, process, and then target communication sites.		
(4) Collection systems to indirect fire assets.		
(5) Ability of threat to influence/affect/impact Indigenous Populations and Institutions (IPI), Intergovernmental Organization (IGO), and Nongovernmental Organization (NGO).		
(6) Ability of threat to influence/affect/impact friendly operations by, through, and with IPI, IGO, and NGO.		
20. The staff, led by the Intelligence section, constructs threat models that accurately portray how threat forces execute operations by:		
a. Consolidating threat model input from staff sections, and constructs initial doctrinal templates overlays, including:		
(1) Retrieving the historical doctrinal template from the Intelligence Database.		
(2) Displaying enemy doctrinal template overlay on the COP.		
(3) Establishing warfighting function doctrinal template overlays and recommends updates to the doctrinal templates.		
(4) Converting threat doctrine or current patterns of operations to graphics including operations overlays.		
(5) Determining how threat normally organizes for combat and how he deploys and employs his units.		
(6) Constructing doctrinal templates overlays through an analysis of intelligence database and evaluation of the threat's past operations.		
b. The Intelligence section, ICW the Fires section, develops the initial HVT list, by:		
NOTE: HVT value usually varies over the course of an operation.		
(1) Receiving staff proposed HVT that are critical to the completion of the threat commander's mission.		
(2) Identifying HVT from an evaluation of the database, the doctrinal templates, and use of tactical judgment.		
(3) Determining how the threat reacts to each identified HVT.		
(4) Creating a rank order of the sets of HVT.		
(5) Recording the sets of HVT as part of the threat model.		
21. The staff, led by the Intelligence section, provides the commander a consolidated staff assessment of threat capabilities and vulnerabilities, by:		
a. Describing threat tactics.		
b. Identifying those HVT critical to the completion of the threat commander's operations.		
c. Identifying threat capabilities, vulnerabilities, supporting missions and other actions that can influence friendly operations.		
d. Refining doctrinal templates as required.		
NOTE: Step 4 Determine Threat Capabilities		

TASK STEPS AND PERFORMANCE MEASURES	GO	NO-GO
22. The staff, led by the Intelligence section, identifies the threat's most likely objectives and desired end state by:		
a. Identifying most likely objectives and desired end state of threat command forces at least one level higher and two levels lower of command.		
b. Ensuring that each echelon's objective will accomplish the likely objectives and desired end state of its parent command.		
c. Ensuring Intelligence section confirm that each level's objective will accomplish the likely objectives and desired end state of its parent command.		
d. Establishing initial Situation Template (SITTEMP) overlay by overlaying the template on the products that depict the operating environment's effects on operations as presented in the MCOO.		
e. Ensuring Intelligence section establishes initial Situation Template (SITTEMP) overlay by overlaying the template on the products that depict the battlefield environment's effects on operations as presented in the Modified Combined Obstacles Overlay (MCOO).		
f. Establishing initial threat COA overlays by integrating the threat models from "Evaluate the Threat" with the analysis from "Describe Battlefield Effects" of the IPB process to portray potential threat COA.		
g. Ensuring Intelligence section establishes initial threat COA overlays by integrating the threat models from "Evaluate the Threat" with the analysis from (Describe Battlefield Effects" of the IPB process to portray potential threat COA.		
h. Refining and develops additional COA overlays based on the threat perception of friendly actions and dispositions (reverse IPB).		
i. Intelligence section refines and develops additional COA overlays based on the threat perception of friendly actions and dispositions (reverse IPB).		
j. Reviewing the initial SITTEMP and threat COA overlays and provide input as necessary.		
k. Staff sections review initial SITTEMP and threat COA overlays and provide input as necessary.		
23. The staff, led by the Intelligence section, identifies and develops the full set of COA available to the threat, in the level of detail time allows, by:		
NOTE: Each developed threat COA has three parts: A situation template, a description of the COA and options, and a listing of HVT. Each threat COA should meet five criteria: suitability, feasibility, acceptability, uniqueness, and consistency with doctrine. A threat COA must have the potential for accomplishing the threat's likely objective or desired end state.		
a. Replicating the COA that the threat commander and staff may be considering.		
b. Identifying all COA that will influence the commander's mission.		
c. Identifying those areas and activities that, when observed, will discern which COA the threat commander has chosen.		
d. Evaluating and identifies threat COA, by:		
(1) Intelligence evaluation, include:		
(a) Determine the targets of friendly collection operations.		
(b) Estimate disposition of threat target acquisition assets.		

TASK STEPS AND PERFORMANCE MEASURES	GO	NO-GO
(c) Estimate rear area threats to friendly units.		
(d) Evaluate and identifying threat insurgent or partisan COA that include: Enemy assembly and hide areas, movement through infiltration lanes, actions on the objective, and exfiltration.		
(e) Evaluate and identify terrorist COA.		
(2) Counterintelligence and counter reconnaissance evaluation including:		
(a) Using the basic friendly maneuver COA model as a start point to determine threat intelligence requirements.		
(b) Estimating the threat's intelligence requirements and attempt to recreate that version of the event template and matrix (NAI and indicators), and the collection plan.		
(c) Identifying locations and activities (indicators) that will confirm or deny key elements of the assumptions that were made about the threat collection effort.		
(d) Depicting range fans for each threat system.		
(e) Describing the type activity that can be collected against within each range fan.		
(f) Highlighting the weakness of the overall threat collection plan including gaps in overage, non-redundant coverage, single-source coverage, or collection coverage vulnerable to deception.		
(g) Highlighting the strengths of the threat collection plan including the coverage that is balanced, redundant, and less vulnerable to deception.		
(h) Developing a friendly event template to support counterintelligence and counter reconnaissance efforts.		
(3) Electronic Warfare evaluation, including:		
(a) Estimating the threat electromagnetic profiles.		
(b) Estimating reactions to Electronic Warfare Support (ES) at critical junctures in the battle.		
(c) Estimating threat use of ES and Electronic Attack (EA) to support their own operations.		
(d) Estimate friendly platforms, facilities, and units vulnerable to EW threat.		
(e) Identify threat attack capabilities known to be neutralized by friendly offensive/defensive Electronic Attack (EA).		
(f) Estimate friendly EW capability gaps.		
(g) Estimate combat effectiveness of friendly Electronic Protection (EP).		
e. The Plans section evaluates and identifies threat COA, by:		
(1) Line of contact.		
(2) Lines of operation.		
(3) Phase of operations.		
(4) Operational objectives.		

TASK STEPS AND PERFORMANCE MEASURES	GO	NO-GO
(5) Movement and employment of large forces.		
f. The AMD section, ICW the AVN section evaluates and identifies threat COA with regards, by:		
(1) Threat air defense system range fans.		
(2) Determining where threat radars or weapon systems are masked by terrain.		
(3) Identifying areas with the least amount of threat air defense coverage.		
(4) Identifying likely threat air approaches to friendly engagement areas and battle positions.		
(5) Developing situation templates for threat actions within the engagement area, including reactions to aviation attack.		
(6) Identifying threat units along flight paths and their reactions to friendly air and develop the appropriate situation templates.		
(7) Considering threat reactions to downed pilots.		
g. The Sustainment section evaluate and identify threat COA, by:		
(1) Areas of threat penetration for ground forces.		
(2) Threat objectives in the rear area that will facilitate the threat main attack or defense.		
(3) Threat HVT and HPT in the rear area that support their concepts of operations including key terrain in the rear area or specified sustainment activities.		
(4) Threat air assault and airborne operations in the rear area, to include:		
(a) Air avenues to landing zones and drop zones.		
(b) Infiltration lanes to the objective.		
(c) Exfiltration lanes.		
h. The AMD section, ICW the AVN section, evaluate and identify threat COA, by:		
(1) Likely locations of threat Forward Area Arming and Refueling Points (FAARP).		
(2) Likely timing of threat air strikes or air assault operations.		
(3) Likely threat targets and objectives.		
(4) Likely threat air corridors and air avenues of approach.		
(5) Likely threat strike package composition, flight profiles, and spacing in time and space, including altitudes.		
(6) Location of friendly air defense assets that may fit into the threat COA.		
(7) Threat ground COA that might require movement of friendly AMD assets.		
i. The Fires section evaluates and identifies threat COA, by:		
NOTE: The COA you focus on should deal primarily with counterfire against your assets, other aspects of force protection, and threat activities that will require the unit to displace.		
(1) Possible threat High Value Targets (HVT).		
(2) Disposition and activity of threat fire support assets.		
(3) Disposition of threat target acquisition assets.		

TASK STEPS AND PERFORMANCE MEASURES	GO	NO-GO
(4) Rear area threat to friendly units.		
j. The EN section evaluates and identifies threat COA, by:		
(1) Developing multiple engineer COA for each maneuver COA available to the threat, that include:		
(a) An estimate of the engineer status of each threat COA for the defense, measured in the percentage of combat vehicles with entrenched primary, alternate, supplementary, and deception positions and the likely extent of obstacles systems.		
(b) Likely locations and extent of obstacles systems required to support each defense system. Categorize the systems by effect (disrupt, turn, fix, or block).		
(c) An estimate of the mobility support for each threat COA for the offense, measured in the breaching and fording capabilities of both the maneuver and the support engineer detachments.		
(2) Developing threat Decision Points (DP) for engineer units that focus on decisions, by:		
(a) Forward deployment of breaching teams.		
(b) The employment of artillery scatterable mines.		
(c) Shift the priority of engineer missions (for example, mobility to counter mobility).		
(d) Redirect Direct Support (DS) or General Support (GS) engineer assets.		
(e) Close lanes in obstacle systems to support battle handover during a rearward passage of lines.		
(f) Forward deployment of obstacle teams to close breeches between the first and second echelons.		
k. The CRBATTALIONE section evaluates and identifies threat COA including:		
(1) Likely area of ground force penetration of forward lines that would be a suitable CBRNE target.		
(2) Friendly assets the threat is likely to consider High Payoff Targets (HPT) for engagement by CBRNE weapons.		
(3) Potential requirements to move sites or replace destroyed sites.		
(4) Existing contaminated areas that may indicate the COA adopted by the threat.		
(5) Threat ability to locate or intercept the systems.		
(6) Threat targeting accuracies of collection systems.		
(7) Threat speed with which the threat can collect, process, and then target communication sites.		
l. The Signal section evaluates and identifies threat COA, including:		
(1) Direct threat to communication due to the expected flow of battle (over running of sites).		
(2) Probability of Levels I, II, or III rear area threats.		

TASK STEPS AND PERFORMANCE MEASURES	GO	NO-GO
(3) Potential requirements to move sites or replace destroyed sites.		
(4) Threat ability to locate or intercept the systems.		
(5) Threat targeting accuracies of collection systems.		
(6) Threat speed with which the threat can collect, process, and then target communication sites.		
(7) Threat EA effectiveness (equipment and techniques).		
(8) Threat ability to link collection systems to indirect fire assets.		
(9) Threat range capabilities of supporting indirect fire systems.		
(10) Threat ability to conduct deep strikes or operations.		
m. Develop each COA into as much detail as the situation requires and time available allows.		
n. The CMO section evaluates and identifies threat COA, including:		
(1) Determine WHAT type of operation, such as attack, defend, reinforce, or conduct retrograde.		
(2) Threat ability to mass civilians to conceal threat operations.		
(3) Determine WHEN the action will begin in terms of the earliest time that the threat can adopt the COA under consideration.		
(4) Threat ability to use civilians to conduct threat operations.		
(5) Determine WHERE the COA will take place to include:		
(6) Threat ability to use civilians to disrupt friendly operations:		
(a) Sectors.		
(b) Zones.		
(c) Axis of attack.		
(d) Avenues of approach.		
(e) COA objectives.		
(7) Determine HOW the threat will employ assets, such as dispositions, location of main effort, the scheme of maneuver, and how it will be supported.		
(8) Likely routes for Dislocated Civilian (DC) movement.		
(9) Determine WHY the objective or end state the threat intends to accomplish is the most appropriate.		
(10) Increased demand for resources to support DC in the AO.		
NOTE: Consider threat forces available to at least one level of command above the unit's own when developing each COA. Time permitting, work to a degree of resolution at two levels of command below the unit's own.		
24. The staff, led by the Intelligence section, evaluates and prioritizes each COA, by:		

TASK STEPS AND PERFORMANCE MEASURES	GO	NO-GO
NOTE: The resulting set of COA depicts the full set of options available to the threat. Remember that the threat COA identified are assumptions about the threat, not facts. Because of this, the staff cannot predict with complete accuracy which of the COA the threat will employ. However, the commander and staff still need to develop a plan that is optimized to one of the COA, while still allowing contingency options if the threat chooses another COA. The staff must evaluate each COA and prioritize it according to how likely it is that the threat will adopt that option. Establish an initial priority list to allow the staff to plan for friendly COA. Once the commander selects a friendly COA, the unit may need to reorder the list of threat COA. Consider especially any changes in the threat's perception of friendly forces.		

    a. Analyzing each COA to identify its strength and weaknesses, centers of gravity, and decisive points.

    b. Evaluating how well each COA meets the criteria of suitability, feasibility, acceptability, and consistency with doctrine.

    c. Evaluating how well each COA takes advantage of the operational environment.

    d. Comparing each COA to the others and determine if the threat is more likely to prefer one over the others.

    e. Considering the possibility that the threat may choose the second or third "best" COA while attempting a deception operation, portraying acceptance of the "best" COA.

    f. Analyzing the threat's recent activity to determine if there are indicators that one COA is already being adopted.

    g. Ranking the threat's COA in their likely order of adoption.

    h. Modifying the list as needed to account for changes in the current situation.

    i. Reprioritizing the initial list of threat COA to reflect changed friendly dispositions and activities once the commander has selected the friendly COA.

25. The staff, led by the Intelligence section, identifies initial collection requirements, by:

NOTE: After identifying the set of potential threat COA, the battle staff must determine which one the enemy will actually adopt. Initial collections requirements are designed to assist in determine this. Identifying initial collection requirements revolves around predicting specific areas and activities, which, when observed, will reveal which COA the threat has chosen. The areas where the unit expects key events to occur are called Named Areas of Interest (NAI). The activities that reveal the selected COA are called indicators.

    a. Creating an Event Template including:

        (1) Evaluate each COA to identify its associated NAI.

        (2) Wargame execution of the COA and note places where activity must occur if that COA is adopted.

        (3) Determine times and places where the threat's HVT are employed or enter areas where they can be easily acquired and engaged.

        (4) Determine places the unit expects the threat to take certain actions or make certain decisions, including the adoption of a branch plan or execution of a counterattack.

        (5) Compare and contrast the NAI and indicators associated with each COA against the others and identify their differences.

    b. Creating an Event Matrix, including:

TASK STEPS AND PERFORMANCE MEASURES	GO	NO-GO
(1) Determine details on the type of activity expected in each NAI.		
(2) Determine the times the NAI is expected to be active.		
(3) Determine the NAI relationship to other events on the battlefield.		
(4) Restate the events associated with each NAI in the form of indicators.		
(5) Enter the indicators into the event matrix along with the times they are likely to occur.		
(6) Record the "Latest-Time-Information-of-Value" (LTIOV) time line into the matrix as a guide for the collection manager.		
(7) Refine the event matrix during staff wargaming and the targeting process.		

* indicates a leader task step.

SUPPORTING COLLECTIVE TASKS

Task Number	Task Title
71-8-2300	Perform Intelligence, Surveillance, and Reconnaissance (battalion - Corps)
71-8-2410	Provide Intelligence Support to Targeting (Battalion - Corps)
71-8-5315	Process Relevant Information to Create a Common Operational Picture (Battalion - Corps)

TASK: Develop Information Requirements (Division - Corps) (71-8-2311)

<u>(FM 2-01.3)</u>   (FM 3-0)   (FM 5-0)
(FM 6-0)

CONDITIONS: The unit is conducting or preparing to conduct operations. Communications are established with subordinate and adjacent units, and higher headquarters. Command and Control (C2) Information Systems (INFOSYS) are operational and passing information in accordance with Tactical Standing Operating Procedures (TACSOP). The command has received a Warning Order/Operations Plan/Operations Order/Fragmentary Order (WARNO/OPORD/OPLAN/FRAGO) from higher headquarters and is exercising mission command. The commander has issued planning guidance. Some iterations of this task should be performed in MOPP4.

TASK STANDARDS: The Collection Management element develops a prioritized list of what information needs to be collected and produced into intelligence. The list is compared against the latest-time-intelligence-is-of-value to ensure intelligence and information are reported to meet operational requirements.

Note: Task steps and performance measures may not apply to every unit or echelon. Prior to evaluation, coordination should be made between evaluator and the evaluated units' higher headquarters to determine the task steps and performance measures that may be omitted.

TASK STEPS AND PERFORMANCE MEASURES	GO	NO-GO
1. The Collection Management element analyzes and combines intelligence and information about the threat's capabilities, friendly vulnerabilities, and the operational environment by:		
a. Sorting collected information by relevance.		
b. Comparing collected information which pertains to the Commander's Critical Information Requirements (CCIR) and Request for Information (RFI).		
2. The Collection Management element validates and prioritizes information and intelligence requirements by:		
a. Converting relevant information into a suitable format to conduct intelligence analysis, production, or immediate use by the commander.		
b. Prioritizing information and intelligence collection requirements by:		
(1) CCIR, Priority Information Requirements (PIR) and Friendly Forces Information Requirements (FFIR).		
(2) Enemy action or inaction.		
c. Forwarding Specific Information Requirements (SIR) that cannot be answered by available assets to higher or lateral organizations as RFI.		
3. The Collection Management element recommends to the commander those Information Requirements (IR) produced during the Military Decision-Making Process (MDMP) that meet the criteria for PIR by:		
a. Developing prioritized list that reflects the commander's intent.		
b. Verifying the commander's IR.		
c. Refining PIR to specific questions that are linked to operational decisions.		
4. The Collection Management element develops SIR and indicators by:		

TASK STEPS AND PERFORMANCE MEASURES	GO	NO-GO
a. Identifying the activities that will confirm specified events as they relate to the SIR and indicators.		
b. Identifying sets of specific information that will provide an answer to each intelligence requirement.		
c. Breaking requirements into smaller, more specific questions which, when answered, can satisfy the larger intelligence requirement.		
d. Confirming SIR describe what information is required, where in the operational area it can be obtained, and when it is to be answered.		
e. Verifying SIR are as detailed as possible.		

* indicates a leader task step.

SUPPORTING COLLECTIVE TASKS

Task Number	Task Title
34-6-2035	Manage Requests for Information (RFI) (brigade)
34-6-2042	Process Specific Information Requirements (SIR)
71-8-2210	Perform Intelligence Preparation of the Battlefield (Battalion - Corps)

TASK: Perform Intelligence, Surveillance, and Reconnaissance (Battalion - Corps) (71-8-2300)

(FM 2-01)   (FMI 2-01)   (FM 5-0)   (FM 6-0)

CONDITIONS: The unit is conducting or preparing to conduct operations. Communications are established with subordinate, adjacent units, and higher headquarters. Command and Control (C2) Information Systems (INFOSYS) are operational and are passing information in accordance with Tactical Standing Operating Procedures (TACSOP). The command has received a Warning Order/Operations Plan/Operations Order/Fragmentary Order (WARNO/OPLAN/ OPORD/FRAGO) from higher headquarters and is exercising mission command. The commander has issued guidance. Some iterations of this task should be performed in MOPP4.

TASK STANDARDS: The Staff led by the Intelligence, Surveillance, and Reconnaissance section develops the Intelligence, Surveillance, and Reconnaissance plan; tasks and directs available Intelligence, Surveillance, and Reconnaissance assets to answer the commander's priority intelligence requirements and information requirements, and obtains the required information.

Note: Task steps and performance measures may not apply to every unit or echelon. Prior to evaluation, coordination should be made between evaluator and the evaluated units' higher headquarters to determine the task steps and performance measures that may be omitted.

TASK STEPS AND PERFORMANCE MEASURES	GO	NO-GO
1. The commander issues initial Intelligence, Surveillance, and Reconnaissance (ISR) planning guidance, by providing:		
a. ISR intent.		
b. Initial Priority Intelligence Requirements (PIR).		
c. Risk assessment guidance.		
2. The staff led by the Intelligence, Surveillance, and Reconnaissance Operations (ISR OPS) section, including representative from the Fires, Plans, and Current Operations sections develops the initial ISR requirements as part of mission analysis, by identifying:		
a. Initial PIR.		
b. Higher Headquarters (HQ) PIR that require unit assets to collect.		
c. Specific Information Requirements (SIR) from the commander's PIR.		
d. Named Areas of Interest (NAI) and Target Areas of Interest (TAI) for the unit; Battlefield Surveillance Brigades and Battalions (Battlefield Surveillance Brigade.)		
3. The staff led by the ISR OPS section converts the Serious Incident Reports (SIR) to production and collection requirements. Develops SIR for each NAI for each collection asset.		
4. The staff led by the ISR OPS section develops the initial ISR concept, by confirming:		
a. Evaluating resources.		
b. Collection assets required.		
c. Equipment required:		
(1) Identifies the proximity of the collection assets to the NAI, environmental conditions, and signature provided by the target.		

TASK STEPS AND PERFORMANCE MEASURES	GO	NO-GO
(2) Determines availability of ISR assets. (higher and two levels down).		
(3) Determines capabilities of ISR assets.		
(4) Matches resources to requirements.		
d. Develops ISR scheme of support in coordination with the Plans, Fires, and Maneuver sections.		
e. Develops and prioritizes Specific Orders and Requests (SOR).		
f. Distribution of the Warning Order (WARNO), through Current Operations, to subordinate units not later than completion of the draft concept of ISR.		
5. The ISR OPS section assisted by the staff completes the initial ISR plan, by:		
a. Developing initial event template matching NAI against Commander's Critical Information Requirements (CCIR) and decision points.		
b. Developing initial ISR plan guidance in order to answer the What, Where, When, Why, and Who should collect.		
c. Drafting the order for an ISR mission in the form of a collection emphasis message and submits to the Maneuver section for approval.		
d. Creating the initial ISR concept, notional overlay, and collection matrix (Intelligence Synchronization Message).		
e. Integrating Electronic Warfare (EW) into the ISR plan.		
6. The ISR OPS section, In Conjunction With (ICW) Current Operations, determines the appropriate unit in the form of a mission tasking order (OPORD or FRAGO) and disseminates ISR order to higher, adjacent, and subordinate units, by:		
a. Assigning tasking and NAI to each asset.		
b. Integrating the ISR assets into the ISR concept.		
c. Integrating air reconnaissance assets into the ISR concept.		
d. Refining the Rules of Engagement (ROE) for direct fire, Strikers, Air Defense Artillery (ADA), and Close Air Support (CAS).		
7. The staff led by the ISR OPS section identifies collection gaps and submits Requests for Information (RFI) to higher HQ.		
8. The ISR OPS section develops a refined ISR concept as part of staff wargaming, by:		
a. Receiving refined staff products to include updated PIR, IR, High Value Targets (HVT), and High Payoff Target List (HPTL).		
b. Using the commander's CCIR and situation and event templates and associates them with enemy Course of Action (COA) in order to define collection requirements of decided COA.		
c. Refining the ISR plan by integrating the scheme of maneuver, fires, and engineers.		
d. Providing engineer plan to support ISR concept and establishes engineer collection requirements		
e. Developing AMD and early warning plan to integrate into the ISR concept.		
f. Assisting with the identification of Chemical, Biological, Radiological, Nuclear, High-Yield Explosives (CBRNE) with in the NAI, and integrates CBRNE operations and CBRNE defense into the ISR concept.		

TASK STEPS AND PERFORMANCE MEASURES	GO	NO-GO
g. Completing associated fires and effects plan to support the ISR concept.		
h. Coordinating aspects of maneuver, by:		
(1) Planning for the infiltration and exfiltration of collection assets and resupply routes through friendly force sectors and or zones.		
(2) Establishing collection assets relationship with security force.		
(3) Establishing ISR control measures including: battle handover line, limits of advance, limits of reconnaissance, restrictive fire lines, no fire areas, and area "limits" of responsibility to deconflict troops and terrain.		
(4) Performing terrain management.		
i. Coordinating with the Sustainment section, develops the sustainment support plans to support ISR, by:		
(1) Verifying the Sustainment, Health Services, and Personnel Services Support Plans.		
(2) Verifying required resources to necessary to evacuate casualties, wounded personnel and unserviceable equipment.		
j. Identifying changes in factors of Mission, Enemy, Terrain and Weather, Troops and Support available, Time available, Civil considerations (METT-TC) and make appropriate adjustments and changes.		
9. The staff led by the ISR OPS section ICW the Plans and Maneuver sections, completes the final ISR plan, by:		
a. Updating the ISR plan, notional overlay, ISR collection matrix, and Situation Template (SITTEMP).		
b. Issue WARNO 2 with following information including:		
(1) Area of operation for Reconnaissance, Surveillance, and Target Acquisition (RSTA) units.		
(2) Mission statement.		
(3) ISR Task Organization (TO).		
(4) Reconnaissance objective.		
(5) PIR and IR to be answered.		
(6) Line of Departure (LD) or Line of Contact (LC) time.		
(7) Initial NAI.		
(8) Routes to Area of Operation (AO) and passage of lines instructions.		
(9) Fire Support Coordinating Measures (FSCM) and Airspace Control Measures (ACM).		
(10) Communications and logistics support.		
(11) Medical Evacuation (MEDEVAC) procedures.		
(12) Frequency deconfliction measures.		
c. Uses approved ISR plan to coordinate the final Decision Support Template (DST) with the staff.		
d. Produces the ISR annex, including ISR notional overlay and SITTEMP, for inclusion in the order.		

TASK STEPS AND PERFORMANCE MEASURES	GO	NO-GO
10. The Staff led by the ISR OPS section prepares for ISR operations, by.		
a. Verifying cross attachment of ISR assets.		
b. Verifying logistic readiness of assets.		
c. Requesting special equipment.		
d. Providing recovery time for assets and units.		
e. Positioning forces to support infiltration of ISR assets.		
f. Conducting confirmation briefs with subordinate and supporting elements.		
g. Conducting crosswalks between subordinate unit plans and the order.		
h. Reviewing subordinate unit orders to insure confirmation of ISR planning.		
11. The Staff led by the ISR OPS section updates the ISR plan as the tactical situation necessitates.		

* indicates a leader task step.

SUPPORTING COLLECTIVE TASKS

Task Number	Task Title
71-8-2321	Develop the Intelligence, Surveillance, and Reconnaissance Plan (brigade - Corps)
71-8-5139	Maintain Synchronization (Battalion - Corps)
71-8-5112	Integrate Requirements and Capabilities (Battalion – Corps)

Note: Task steps and performance measures may not apply to every unit or echelon. Prior to evaluation, coordination should be made between evaluator and the evaluated units' higher headquarters to determine the task steps and performance measures that may be omitted.

TASK: Conduct ISR Synchronization and Integration (Battalion - Brigade) (17-6-1007)

(FM 3-0)   (FMI 2-0)   (FMI 2-01.3)

CONDITIONS: The brigade combat team (BCT)/battalion (BN) is conducting or preparing to conduct operations and has issued a reconnaissance plan as an annex to an operation order (OPORD). Reconnaissance assets have deployed in accordance with (IAW) the order and are conducting operations. The BCT/BN has communications with higher, adjacent, subordinate, and supporting elements. The BCT/BN received guidance on the rules of engagement (ROE). Military, civilian, joint, and multinational partners, and news media may be present in the operational environment (OE). Some iterations of this task should be performed in mission-oriented protective posture 4 (MOPP) 4.

TASK STANDARDS: The BCT/BN staff directs the reconnaissance effort and achieves the reconnaissance objectives. The BCT/BN staff evaluates and analyzes information collected by ground and air assets; coordinates and monitors reconnaissance handover IAW the commander's desires; coordinates target acquisition (TA); and coordinates reconnaissance asset resupply. The BCT/BN staff monitors execution of reconnaissance tasks and issues fragmentary orders (FRAGO) to reposition or refocus reconnaissance assets, exploit developing information, and achieve objectives. All communication and reporting is IAW applicable standing operating procedures (SOPs).

TASK STEPS AND PERFORMANCE MEASURES	GO	NO-GO
Plan/Prepare		
1. The BCT/BN staff gain and/or maintain situational understanding (SU) using available communications equipment, maps, intelligence summaries, situation reports (SITREPs), and other available sources. Intelligence sources include human intelligence (HUMINT), signal intelligence (SIGINT), and imagery intelligence (IMINT) to include unmanned aircraft systems (UASs).		
* 2. The BCT/BN commander and staff utilize the planning process IAW the military decision-making process. (Refer to Task 71-8-5110, Plan Operations using the Military Decision-Making Process [Battalion – Corps].)		
3. The BCT/BN staff, led by the Intelligence cell, develops the ISR plan and tasks and directs available reconnaissance and Military Intelligence (MI) units. (Refer to Task 71-8-2321, Develop the Intelligence, Surveillance, and Reconnaissance Plan [Brigade – Corps] and Task 71-8-2300, Perform Intelligence, Surveillance, and Reconnaissance [Battalion – Corps].)		
Execution		
4. The BCT/BN staff coordinates deployment of air and ground elements and other reconnaissance assets as necessary. They take the following actions:		
a. Coordinate repositioning of reconnaissance assets to assist maintaining control during all phases of the operation.		
b. Identify weaknesses and gaps in enemy defenses and/or dispositions and:		
(1) Coordinate employment of higher headquarters (HQ) SIGINT and IMINT assets to gain first contact, locate, and identify threat defensive positions, obstacles, and local reserves.		
(2) Disseminate information to subordinate elements that confirms threat dispositions and identifies potential infiltration/exfiltration lanes and/or zones.		

TASK STEPS AND PERFORMANCE MEASURES	GO	NO-GO
c. Assess routes, areas and/or zones using available intelligence.		
d. Employ ground units, aviation, or UASs to reconnoiter routes, areas and/or zones.		
e. Conduct deception operations.		
f. Coordinate for passage of lines by reconnaissance assets with subordinate units.		
g. Coordinate with adjacent units to assist or support the deployment, as necessary.		
5. The BCT/BN staff evaluates combat information and intelligence reports. They take the following actions:		
a. Extract and collate essential intelligence information from messages and reports.		
b. Determine the usability of the information.		
b. Determine the accuracy of the information.		
b. Determine the timeliness of the information.		
c. Determine the completeness of the incoming information.		
d. Determine the precision of the incoming information.		
e. Determine the relevancy of the incoming information to other staff sections or higher HQ specific orders or requests (SOR).		
d. Determine the security of the incoming information.		
6. The BCT/BN staff analyzes combat information and intelligence reports. They take the following actions:		
a. Identify highly perishable combat information.		
b. Compare information with information requirements (IR) and priority intelligence requirements (PIR).		
c. Compare information with commander's list of high-payoff targets (HPT).		
d. Compare information with situation map (SITMAP).		
e. Determine if information has targeting potential by:		
(1) Determining the currency of the information.		
(2) Conducting source evaluation.		
(3) Determining the apparent impact on friendly and threat operations in conjunction with the current operations and fires element if the target in question was destroyed or suppressed by friendly fire.		
(4) Passing highly perishable and targeting quality combat information to the current operations cell, fires cell, and higher HQ for immediate action IAW unit SOP.		
(5) Determining the exact location IAW unit SOP of the prospective target.		
(6) Disseminating targeting locations to the fires cell.		
f. Pass highly perishable data to subordinate units' S-2 immediately after analysis IAW unit SOP.		
g. Analyze data based on predetermined key terrain, avenues of approach, trafficability data, and lines of communication (LOC) to determine how new activity fits into the entire intelligence picture.		

TASK STEPS AND PERFORMANCE MEASURES	GO	NO-GO
h. Determine if incoming data meets the criteria for a decision point (DP), line, or event.		
i. Collate incoming information with existing intelligence to determine if new activities are indicators of a specific enemy course of action (ECOA).		
j. Request additional information from higher and subordinate units to fill gaps in intelligence IAW unit SOP.		
k. Project future threat dispositions based on potential ECOA.		
l. Frequently populate the joint common database and common operating picture (COP) with correlated enemy information during mission execution.		
7. The BCT/BN staff monitors internal reconnaissance handovers to ensure that specified ISR plan criteria are met. They take the following actions:		
a. Monitor repositioning of air and ground to ensure contact is maintained contact during handover.		
b. Monitor fire support control measures (FSCM) and criteria for activation:		
(1) Coordinated fire lines.		
(2) Restricted fire line.		
(3) No fire areas.		
(4) Restricted fire areas.		
c. Monitor control measures to support handover, passage of lines, and/or bypasses between units.		
d. Ensure that all BCT/BN elements acknowledge changes to FSCM.		
e. Ensure that spot reports (SPOTREP) and other intelligence information continue to be transmitted during reconnaissance handover.		
f. Confirm reconnaissance handover between elements is complete when specified criteria are met IAW ISR plan.		
8. The BCT/BN staff coordinates TA, as necessary. They take the following actions:		
a. Analyze targets and calls-for-fire to ensure they meet the higher commander's intent and/or essential fire support tasks (EFST).		
b. Direct Strikers and/or laser-equipped observation posts (OP) to designate specified targets.		
c. Move and/or shift air and ground elements either to account for potential and/or actual enemy/threat actions or to replace losses at the decisive point.		
d. Coordinate electronic warfare (EW) and other nonlethal attacks against HPTs based on reports.		
e. Assess effects of attacks on targets based on reports.		
9. The BCT/BN staff coordinates resupply of reconnaissance assets, as necessary. They take the following actions:		
a. Obtain logistics requests.		
b. Consolidate and prioritize the requests.		
c. Determine probable logistics package (LOGPAC) and logistics release point (LRP) times and locations.		

TASK STEPS AND PERFORMANCE MEASURES	GO	NO-GO
d. Determine main supply route, if not already designated.		
e. Prioritize specific quantities of Classes I through X to be transported to each unit.		
f. Identify number of personnel to go forward with LOGPAC to units they will be assigned.		
g. Identify units requiring evacuation of personnel who are killed in action (KIA), wounded in action (WIA), and contaminated.		
h. Coordinate requirements such as back haul recovery of KIAs and captured material.		
i. Coordinate for LOGPAC time and location.		
10. The BCT/BN staff coordinates with higher HQ for reconnaissance handover as necessary. (Refer to Task 17-1-4025, Conduct Reconnaissance Handover [Battalion – Brigade].)		
Assess		
11. The BCT/BN staff updates the ISR plan as necessary based on information reported by the reconnaissance assets. They take the following actions:		
a. The XO monitors the deployment of air and ground elements and other reconnaissance assets.		
b. Reconnaissance planning team recommends repositioning of collection assets.		
c. Reconnaissance planning team evaluates reports for accuracy and answers to commander's critical information requirements (CCIR).		
d. S-2 section and analysis control element (ACE) analyze reports and passes information to subordinate units.		
e. Reconnaissance planning team updates collection plan and identifies if more information is needed to answer CCIR.		
f. Reconnaissance planning team issues FRAGOs to reposition or refocus air and ground assets as information and evolving courses of action (COA) identify other considerations.		
12. The BCT/BN staff maintains synchronization. (Refer to Task 71-8-5139, Maintain Synchronization [Battalion – Corps].)		

* indicates a leader task step.

Task Number	Task Title
17-1-4025	Conduct Reconnaissance Handover (Battalion – Brigade)
17-6-9225	Conduct a Screen (Battalion - Brigade)
71-8-2300	Perform Intelligence, Surveillance, and Reconnaissance (Battalion - Corps)
71-8-5110	Plan Operations using the Military Decision Making Process (Battalion – Corps)
71-8-5139	Maintain Synchronization (Battalion – Corps)

TASK: Perform Intelligence Synchronization (34-4-1723)

(FMI 2-01)   (FM 2-0)   (FM 2-01.3)

CONDITIONS: Given the unit intelligence collection assets, an initial entry intelligence package in either digital or hard copy format, intelligence preparation of the battlefield (IPB), weather products, and the commander's initial planning guidance in accordance with (IAW) FM 2-01 and unit standard operating procedure (SOP). Performance of this task may occur in an asymmetric environment containing imbalanced ideological, cultural, technological and/or military threat capabilities. Unit leaders conduct Composite Risk Management (CRM) and take into account environmental considerations during mission planning. Some iterations of this task should be performed in MOPP4.

TASK STANDARDS: The element develops an intelligence collection plan that makes the best use of collection assets available to answer the commander's priority intelligence requirements and the intelligence requirements of other intelligence users IAW FM 2-01 and unit Standard Operating Procedure (SOP).

TASK STEPS AND PERFORMANCE MEASURES	GO	NO-GO
1. Develops collection requirements that identify, prioritize, and refine uncertainties concerning the threat and battlefield environment.		
a. Participates in wargaming.		
(1) Role plays the threat using threat courses of action developed during the intelligence preparation of the battlefield process.		
(2) Determines whether normally available collection assets can cover each named area of interest.		
b. Analyzes collection requirements to ensure the most effective use of assets.		
(1) Records requirements, in the form of specific orders, from higher headquarters.		
(2) Records requests for information from higher and adjacent units.		
(3) Validates collection requirements.		
(a) Determines the feasibility of collecting intelligence to satisfy the requirement.		
(b) Determines whether the requirement adequately specifies what is to be collected, where it is to be collected, when the collection should occur, why the intelligence is important, and who needs the results.		
(c) Determines the necessity for collection by checking the database to see if the information has already been collected.		
(4) Consolidates collection requirements by merging similar requirements.		
(5) Prioritizes collection requirements according to their importance to mission success.		
c. Develops specific information requirement sets to provide an answer to each intelligence requirement.		
2. Develops the collection plan to produce the intelligence required to effectively answer the commander's intelligence requirements.		
a. Evaluates collection resources available to support the collection plan.		

TASK STEPS AND PERFORMANCE MEASURES	GO	NO-GO
(1) Determines the availability of collectors and processors at G2/S2, S6 levels.		
(2) Evaluates the capabilities of available collection assets against collection targets.		
(3) Determines the vulnerability of collection assets to threat forces.		
(4) Evaluates the performance history of available collection assets.		
b. Develops a collection strategy based upon the evaluation of available resources.		
(1) Selects resources to support the collection strategy.		
(a) Tasks organic resources.		
(b) Requests collection support from higher headquarters' assets.		
(c) Includes cueing, redundancy, mix, and integration of selected resources in the collection strategy.		
(2) Synchronizes collection requirements through the development of the intelligence synchronization matrix.		
c. Develops specific order and request (SOR) sets from the developed specific information requirements.		
(1) Forms directive SOR reporting requirements.		
(2) Focuses SORs on developed named areas of interest.		
(3) Provides last time information of value for each SOR.		
(4) Tailors each SOR to the selected collection system or organization.		
d. Prioritizes SORs for collection assets.		
3. Tasks or requests collection with all necessary data to execute the mission.		
a. Determines the proper tasking or request format.		
(1) Uses fragmentary orders to task assets, if appropriate.		
(2) Uses paragraph three "Intelligence Acquisition Tasks" of the intelligence annex to the operations order.		
(3) Transmits requests for information to the next higher or adjacent headquarters to address requirements that exceed organic capabilities.		
b. Implements intelligence tasking.		
4. Disseminates intelligence information.		
5. Evaluates intelligence reporting to ensure all SORs are fully satisfied and the collection plan remains fully synchronized.		
a. Maintains collection synchronization by tracking the flow of operations against the intelligence synchronization matrix.		
b. Correlates reports to requirements.		
(1) Identifies the original SOR and requirement the reported information satisfies.		
(2) Develops templates to match incoming reports to outstanding SORs.		
c. Screens reports to determine whether the SOR has been satisfied using the following criteria:		
(1) Determines the pertinence of information in addressing the tasked SOR.		

TASK STEPS AND PERFORMANCE MEASURES	GO	NO-GO
(2) Determines the completeness of reported information.		
(3) Determines whether the information was reported by the last time information of value established in the original SOR.		
(4) Evaluates whether the information can be used to cue other collection assets.		
d. Provides feedback to collectors and exploiters on the success of the collection effort and SORs that still need to be satisfied.		
6. Updates collection planning to ensure SORs are updated and synchronization is maintained.		
a. Eliminates satisfied collection requirements.		
b. Redirects assets to unsatisfied requirements.		
c. Cues assets to collection opportunities that develop during operations.		
d. Maintains synchronization as the need for change in the collection plan becomes apparent.		
e. Adds new collection requirements as planning or execution of the course of action evolves and the threat situation develops.		

* indicates a leader task step.

SUPPORTING COLLECTIVE TASKS

Task Number	Task Title
34-5-0221	Synchronize the HUMINT Collection Effort (S2X)
34-5-0820	Manage Prophet Sensor Missions

TASK: Synchronize the HUMINT Collection Effort (S2X) (34-5-0221)

(FM 2-22.3)   (FM 2-19.4)

CONDITIONS: The S2X team is deployed as part of the brigade Combat Team (BCT) brigade Headquarters. Communications with the operational management team, S2, national and theater level assets, and other intelligence elements have been established. The Counterintelligence and Interrogation Operations Workstation (CI&I OPS WS), the Counterintelligence/Human Intelligence (HUMINT) Automated Tool Set (CHATS) or approved communications system for the correlation and analysis of reported combat information from the HUMINT and CI collectors is operational. HUMINT and CI collection teams are dispersed throughout the area of operations. The commander's priority Intelligence requirements are known. The team has the rules of engagement (ROE), the rules of interaction (ROI), the tactical standing operating procedures (TSOP) and is familiar with the Laws of War including the Geneva Convention. Performance of this task may occur in an asymmetric environment containing imbalanced ideological, cultural, technological and/or military threat capabilities. Unit leaders conduct Composite Risk Management (CRM) and take into account environmental considerations during mission planning. Some iterations of this task should be performed in MOPP4.

TASK STANDARDS: Develops HUMINT and CI specific orders or requests (SORs) based on the brigade commander's priority intelligence requirements and transmits them to the operational management teams. Synchronizes and deconflicts the HUMINT and CI collection effort with higher, adjacent and lower elements. Consolidates and analyzes incoming reports. Answers priority intelligence requirements in time to influence the commander's Decision-Making process. Provides technical guidance to the operational management teams as needed. All is done IAW the ROE, ROI, TSOP, and the Laws of War including the Geneva Convention.

TASK STEPS AND PERFORMANCE MEASURES	GO	NO-GO
1. The S2X or the Intelligence Requirements team advises and assists the commander and the S2 on human intelligence (HUMINT) and counterintelligence (CI) collection.		
a. Provides discipline (liaison, screening operations, investigation, etc) expertise on how teams can best satisfy priority intelligence requirements (PIRs).		
b. Deconflicts all HUMINT and CI operations in the area of operations (AO).		
c. Assists in developing HUMINT and CI specific requirements and orders (SOR) for information based on commander's PIRs.		
d. Creates intelligence products such as link diagrams, pattern analysis, and association matrixes to answer PIRs.		
e. Provides oversight and/or manage the Intelligence Contingency Funds (ICF) and Source Incentive Program (SIP) for HUMINT and CI teams.		
f. Coordinates technical support, as needed, for HUMINT and CI assets in the AO to accomplish the mission.		
g. Establishes a subversion and espionage directed against the army (SAEDA) reporting program for the brigade.		
2. Collaborates with the operational management team (OMT).		
Note: Normally, the HUMINT Operation Cell (HOC) and Counterintelligence Coordinating Authority (CICA) in the *2X work directly with the OMT. However, the BCT Brigade S2X does not have an HOC. Therefore, the S2X collaborates with the OMT thru the CICA and performs the function of the HOC.		

TASK STEPS AND PERFORMANCE MEASURES	GO	NO-GO
a. Transmits new tasking, changes to tasking, orders and other information to the OMT, as necessary, and verify receipt.		
b. Receives combat information and reports from the OMT.		
(1) Executes control mechanisms to ensure quality reporting.		
Note: Authorized systems/suite of systems such as CI/HUMINT automated tool set/individual tactical reporting tool/CI and Interrogation Operations Workstation/ (CHATS/ITRT/CI&I OPS WS) should be used for reporting to ensure compatibility with other communication systems.		
(2) Establishes reporting guidance requiring reports be processed in a timely manner (Latest Time Information Is Of Value (LTIOV))		
(3) Serves as the approval authority for release of HUMINT reports.		
c. Coordinates with the CICA to provide CI support to HUMINT operations.		
d. Coordinates with brigade S2 and other units for movement and to facilitate mission accomplishment and avoid fratricide.		
e. Enforces reporting of HUMINT collector contact with an adversary intelligence service to support Information Operations (IO) and Force Protection.		
f. Serves as the main link between the OMT and other intelligence elements.		
g. Advises and assist the OMT on operational planning and tactics when requested.		
3. The S2X or the Intelligence Requirements team reviews HUMINT and CI collection tasking.		
a. Collaborates with the intelligence, surveillance, and reconnaissance requirements team, the OMT, and other elements, as necessary, to ensure current collection tasking and requests for information support the commander's PIRs.		
b. Performs liaison and coordination with the host nation and other government agencies (mainly the defense intelligence agency (DIA)) for national level taskings and requirements.		
c. Performs liaison with organic and non-organic sections/units as necessary in response to requests for information from the teams.		
d. Reviews tasking from higher to identify if it is within the capability and purview of the teams.		
e. Provides team feedback to focus and validate collection efforts.		
f. Revises tasking, as necessary, to answer current and new PIRs.		
g. Provides updated PIRs to OMTs enabling teams to have the most current PIRs		
4. The S2X or the Intelligence Requirements team synchronizes and control collection.		
a. Oversees collection activities for compliance with DOD Directive 5240-1, Intelligence Activities.		
b. Maintains a database of all incoming and outgoing tasking.		
c. Establishes and maintain a collection requirements list.		
d. Avoids tasking teams operating in the same geographical area with the same collection requirement, unless necessary.		
e. Maintains the brigade consolidated source database (for source operations).		
(1) Develops the source registry for the AO.		

TASK STEPS AND PERFORMANCE MEASURES	GO	NO-GO
(2) Coordinates with the CICA to ensure registration of CI sources and the deconfliction of source operations.		
f. Requires duplicate dossiers be maintained for all sources and contacts.		
g. Ensures different HUMINT and CI personnel are not using the same source to obtain the same information.		
h. Establishes a quality control program to review incoming reports for format, clarity, completeness, and relevance to the collection requirement.		
i. Corroborates or establishes procedures to corroborate information from HUMINT and CI collection.		
Note: It is essential the information is corroborated before it is acted on. Ways to corroborate are by queuing other intelligence disciplines or requesting information from national level agencies.		
j. Establishes and enforces a foreign disclosure policy for the multinational forces.		
5. The S2X or the Intelligence Requirements team pulls national and theater information as needed.		
a. Acts as a system administrator for HUMINT and CI specific automation systems to ensure connectivity with higher and adjacent entities.		
b. Accesses the national source database via migration defense intelligence threat data system or its replacement.		
c. Accesses national and theater HUMINT and CI reports and products through the supporting army force analysis elements.		
* 6. OIC/NCOIC monitors the overall operation of the S2X.		

* indicates a leader task step.

SUPPORTING COLLECTIVE TASKS

Task Number	Task Title
34-5-0470	Provide Situational Awareness of the Company Area of Operations
34-5-0471	Support Company Level Intelligence, Surveillance, and Reconnaissance
34-5-0472	Provide Intelligence Support Team Input to Targeting

TASK: Coordinate HUMINT Operations (OMT) (Battlefield Surveillance Brigade) (34-5-0331)

(FM 2-22.3)   (FM 2-19.4)

CONDITIONS: The Operational Management Team (OMT) is deployed as part of the Collection and Exploitation Company or the Counterintelligence (CI)/Human intelligence (HUMINT) Company supporting the Battlefield surveillance Brigade (BfSB). Communications with the *2X, CI Coordinating Authority (CICA), HUMINT Operations Cell (HOC), national and coalition HUMINT organizations (when applicable), and HUMINT Collection Teams (HCTs) are established. Approved communications systems for the correlation and analysis of reported combat information are operational. Biometric tools and databases, as well as various other intelligence databases, are available. The OMT has the unit's Tactical Standing Operating Procedure (TACSOP), HUMINT Appendix to Annex B, the current Rules of Engagement (ROE), Rules of Interaction (ROI) and is familiar with the Laws of War including the Geneva Convention. The commander's Priority Intelligence Requirements/Information Requirements (PIRs/IRs) are known. Performance of this task may occur in an asymmetric environment containing imbalanced ideological, cultural, technological and/or military threat capabilities. Unit leaders conduct Composite Risk Management (CRM) and take into account environmental considerations during mission planning. Some iterations of this task should be performed in MOPP4.

TASK STANDARDS: The OMT coordinates with the *2X and HOC on HUMINT collection requirements. The OMT provides focus, management, and operational control of the HCTs ensuring information is obtained to identify elements, intentions, compositions, strength, dispositions, tactics, equipment, personnel, and capabilities. The OMT augments the *2X when not controlling HUMINT collection teams and performs all operations IAW the commander's guidance, FM 2-22.3, the TACSOP, HUMINT Appendix to Annex B, the ROE, ROI and Laws of War including the Geneva Convention. The OMT performs limited analysis of incoming information and reports per TACSOP and Operations Order (OPORD).

TASK STEPS AND PERFORMANCE MEASURES	GO	NO-GO
1. Coordinates with the supported *2X to establish tasking and reporting procedures.		
2. Manages subordinate Human intelligence (HUMINT) Collection Team (HCT)s.		
3. Receives HUMINT collection tasking from the *2X.		
4. Develops HCT requirements using available HUMINT assets.		
5. Tasks HCTs with collection requirements and focus.		
6. Provides guidance and technical control of operational activity to synchronize collection efforts and enhance the Common Operational Picture.		
7. Coordinates specific HUMINT collection missions with *2X and HUMINT Operations Cell (HOC) to limit redundancies or plan redundant area of coverage.		
8. Maintains situational awareness:		
a. Communicates with organizations that potentially interact with HUMINT sources (Civil Affairs, CICA, Psychological Operations, Special Forces, national and coalition HUMINT organizations.)		
b. Maintains rapport with organizations with HUMINT sources.		
c. Reviews Vulnerability Assessments and Force Protection information.		
9. Coordinates with CICA:		
a. Reports HCT contact with adversary intelligence service to CICA.		

TASK STEPS AND PERFORMANCE MEASURES	GO	NO-GO
b. Requests CI support to HUMINT operations.		
10. Creates and maintains a system to record the status of HCTs.		
a. Records the location of each team and update their location as necessary. Ideally, team locations should be posted on both a digital and paper map.		
Note: HCTs may be required to conduct their own coordination for locations and movement within a supported unit's Area of Operations (AO).		
b. Records the collection mission(s) tasked to each team.		
c. Advises the *2X and the HUMINT collection platoon of the status of the HCTs.		
11. Maintains communications with HCTs.		
12. Provides feedback to HCTs regarding collection activities.		
13. Redirects team's focus based on current collection requirements, as needed.		
Note: If a team is tasked to move to a new location, it can take weeks to months before an HCT develops a source network in the new location.		
14. Provides OMT personnel to augment HCTs briefly during critical missions.		
15. Conducts initial quality control of reports for accuracy, clarity, completeness, format, and relevance to collection requirements.		
16. Performs initial analysis of incoming reports and information ensuring correct lines of debriefing and interrogation.		
NOTE: Initial analysis should include any Priority Intelligence Requirements/Information Requirements (PIRs/IRs) the reports may answer, and any HUMINT trends or patterns discovered.		
17. Correlates reports and information received.		
Note: Use authorized collection and reporting systems to ensure compatibility with other communication systems.		
18. Disseminates reports to *2X along with any initial analysis.		
19. Maintains files including:		
a. Source information and other reports in a systematic electronic or hard copy filing system.		
b. Duplicate dossiers for all sources and contacts.		
20. Provides the same direction and control as above to any attached HCTs not organic to the military intelligence company but under the control of the OMT.		
21. Coordinates with supported element for tasking when teams are in direct support of another element.		
22. Informs the *2X of any collection requirements requested by the supported element.		
23. Assists the *2X as a conduit between subordinate HCTs, the HUMINT Operations Cell (HOC), supported unit headquarters, and *2X.		
24. Reports mission and equipment status to the HOC and supported headquarters.		
25. Integrates HCTs directly into the maneuver commander's intelligence, surveillance, and reconnaissance planning.		
26. Manages support to interrogations.		

TASK STEPS AND PERFORMANCE MEASURES	GO	NO-GO
27. Manages military source contact operations.		
a. Continuously monitors HUMINT operations to ensure proper source handling.		
b. Validates source ability to satisfy requirements.		
c. Determines value for continuing the operation.		
d. Documents source's ability to satisfy information requirements in order to facilitate source validation and evaluation.		
e. Manages use of intelligence contingency funds and incentives.		
28. Manages Document Exploitation (DOCEX) operations.		
29. Manages debriefing program of friendly force personnel.		
30. Manages interpreter/linguist support.		
*32. Monitors the overall operation of the OMT.		

    * indicates a leader task step.

SUPPORTING COLLECTIVE TASKS

Task Number	Task Title
34-5-0470	Provide Situational Awareness of the Company Area of Operations
34-5-0471	Support Company Level Intelligence, Surveillance, and Reconnaissance
34-5-0472	Provide Intelligence Support Team Input to Targeting

TASK: Process Incoming Signals Intelligence (SIGINT) Information (34-5-0702)

(FM 2-19.4)   (FM 2-22.3)   (FM 2-0)

CONDITIONS: The Signals Analysis or Prophet Control team is given a clear mission tasking. The team may be collocated with the supported G2/S2. Connectivity exists between the analysis element and national level databases. Combat information is provided by the Collection Teams. Performance of this task may occur in an asymmetric environment containing imbalanced ideological, cultural, technological and/or military threat capabilities. Unit leaders conduct Composite Risk Management (CRM) and take into account environmental considerations during mission planning. Unit leaders conduct Composite Risk Management (CRM) and take into account environmental considerations during mission planning. Some iterations of this task should be performed in MOPP4.

TASK STANDARDS: The team analyzes incoming SIGINT, identifies information meeting intelligence requirements, and provides combat intelligence to the supported G2/S2 in time to influence the supported commander's decision. The team computes locational data and incorporates into intelligence reporting and mission planning.

TASK STEPS AND PERFORMANCE MEASURES	GO	NO-GO
1. Processes incoming tactical reports (TACREP).		
a. Prioritizes incoming tactical reports (TACREP)		
b. Identifies reportable combat information.		
(1) Compares intercept material to tasking.		
(2) Converts grid and time data in accordance with (IAW) reporting criteria.		
(3) Reports all information that directly answers a PIR/SOR to the supported G2/S2 within 15 minutes of receipt.		
(4) Reports all critical intelligence IAW the TACSOP and appropriate USSID within 10 minutes of recognition.		
(5) Obtains existing intelligence/information from local and national databases.		
(6) Collates all combat information by activity, target set.		
(7) Forwards combat information to the supported G2/S2.		
c. Identifies information requiring further exploitation to include:		
(1) Information that may answer an adjacent unit's PIR/IR		
(2) New or unknown signals		
(3) Signals requiring further processing unavailable locally		
d. Forwards exploitable target/signal data to the appropriate unit/agency IAW the unit TACSOP.		
e. Adjusts Prophet tasking if required.		
2. Establishes and maintains net and station continuity on assigned targets.		
a. Establishes a target history file.		
b. Records target procedures, locations, or any data corresponding to targets.		
c. Incorporates target data from existing local and national databases.		

TASK STEPS AND PERFORMANCE MEASURES	GO	NO-GO
d. Performs basic link analysis.		
e. Provides updated target data to the Prophet Teams.		
f. Refines tasking as appropriate.		
3. Locates target using radio direction finding (RDF) data.		
Note: If less than three lines-of-bearing (LOB) are available, go to step d.		
a. Determines fix location.		
b. Determines circular error probability (CEP).		
c. Forwards location data to the targeting section of the supported G2/S2. (Go to step g)		
d. Determines cut or LOB location.		
e. Uses terrain analysis and signal strength/quality to further define target location.		
f. Requests RDF support, from other intelligence assets (GSS, Guardrail, and UGS etc.) to fix target location.		
g. Plots fixes on the overlay and initiate threat warning as required.		
h. Reports fix data to the supporting unit's G2/S2 targeting section.		
i. Maintains RDF/LOB overlays to track enemy locations and movement and assist in maintaining enemy situational awareness.		
j. Analyzes fix quality and make adjustments to Prophet Team deployment as needed.		
* 4. Recommends adjustments to tasking.		
a. Compares combat information to tasking.		
b. Notes any intelligence gaps, duplication of effort, or special items.		
c. Transmits recommendations to the supported G2/S2.		

* indicates a leader task step.

SUPPORTING COLLECTIVE TASKS

Task Number	Task Title
34-5-0470	Provide Situational Awareness of the Company Area of Operations
34-5-0471	Support Company Level Intelligence, Surveillance, and Reconnaissance
34-5-0472	Provide Intelligence Support Team Input to Targeting

TASK: Perform Analysis (Brigade/Battalion) (34-6-2034)

(FM 2-19.4)   (FM 2-0)

CONDITIONS: The section, which may be augmented, is established and operational. The section is receiving combat information and intelligence reports from collection assets which must be analyzed to support the commander's concept of operations, and the unit's planning, preparation, and execution of decisive actions in the area of operations. Performance of this task may occur in an asymmetric environment containing imbalanced ideological, cultural, technological and/or military threat capabilities. Unit leaders conduct Composite Risk Management (CRM) and take into account environmental considerations during mission planning. Some iterations of this task should be performed in MOPP4.

TASK STANDARDS: Receives and analyzes combat information and produces intelligence products to meet the commander's Decision-Making and planning requirements. The section develops the current threat situation for the common operating picture, common understanding of current and future situation, target nominations, and imagery products.

TASK STEPS AND PERFORMANCE MEASURES	GO	NO-GO
1. The S2 section establishes communications via the ASAS, DCGS-A MFWS with collection assets, and other organic and nonorganic elements as necessary. OIC and NCOIC monitor overall operation of the S2 section.		
2. Receives and analyzes combat information and develops products.		
a. The S2 section develops the current threat portion of the common operating picture. The four situation development steps are:		
(1) Record information into text or graphic format and arrange into groups of related items.		
(2) Evaluate information as to the relevance to operations, the reliability of the source, and the accuracy of the information.		
(3) Analyze information to draw conclusions and establish its relevance to forecasted threat courses of action and the commander's priority intelligence requirements.		
(a) Determine the impact of the information on the unit's mission.		
(b) Make recommendations based upon the information to assist the commander in the Decision-Making process.		
(4) Update current intelligence databases and graphics as combat information is received.		
b. Develops a common understanding of the current and future situation.		
(1) Fuses products received from collection assets.		
(2) Conducts trend and pattern analysis.		
c. Conducts continuous intelligence preparation of the battlefield using the four step intelligence preparation of the battlefield process:		
(1) Defines the battlefield environment.		
(2) Describes the battlefield's effects.		
(3) Evaluates the threat.		

TASK STEPS AND PERFORMANCE MEASURES	GO	NO-GO
(4) Determines threat courses of action.		
d. Produces products such as visual overlays and maps with icons linked to photos or video. Some sources of their combat information are:		
(1) Digital camera photos from reconnaissance scouts;		
(2) Unmanned aerial system video;		
(3) Imagery databases at theater and national level.		
e. Conducts limited electronic support (ES) and signals intelligence (SIGINT) analysis:		
(1) Conducts emitter mapping.		
(2) Performs net/node analysis and platform capability association.		
(3) Correlates SIGINT information for population into the all-source intelligence ASAS, DCGS-A MFWS databases.		

* indicates a leader task step.

SUPPORTING COLLECTIVE TASKS

Task Number	Task Title
71-8-2321	Develop the Intelligence, Surveillance, and Reconnaissance Plan (Brigade - Corps)
71-8-2210	Perform Intelligence Preparation of the Battlefield (Battalion - Corps)
71-8-5112	Integrate Requirements and Capabilities (Battalion – Corps)

TASK: Process Specific Information Requirements (SIR) (34-6-2042)

(FMI 2-01)   (FM 2-0)   (FM 2-01.3)

CONDITIONS: The section is located at the Tactical Operations Center and understands the commander's guidance. The section has the operation order (OPORD) and fragmentary order (FRAGO) available. Elements are operational and intelligence information is being received. Coalition forces and noncombatants may be present in the operational environment. Performance of this task may occur in an asymmetric environment containing imbalanced ideological, cultural, technological and/or military threat capabilities. Unit leaders conduct Composite Risk Management (CRM) and take into account environmental considerations during mission planning. Some iterations of this task should be performed in MOPP4.

TASK STANDARDS: The S-2 Section processes intelligence and combat information critical in determining enemy dispositions and intentions to 100 percent accuracy. The S-2 section develops this information in timely and accurate manner enabling the commander to identify and take appropriate action at a decisive point in the battle. The time required to perform this task in MOPP4 and/or blackout conditions is increased.

TASK STEPS AND PERFORMANCE MEASURES	GO	NO-GO
1. The appropriate section determines Specific Information Requirements (SIR), with a focus on responding to Priority Intelligence Requirements (PIR) and Intelligence Requirements (IR).		
a. Identifies threat and characteristics that will provide an answer to each IR.		
b. Identifies information and intelligence gaps.		
c. Develops SIRs into specific/detailed questions such as:		
(1) When will threat reconnaissance teams move east of PL Ford in TF 1-1 IN sector?		
(2) Where is more than one platoon of threat mine clearing units (two or more sapper squads or two or more BAT-Ms) in brigade sector?		
(3) Will threat elements interfere with the regional power plant repair?		
d. Provides SIR for integration into the Intelligence Synchronization plan and Intelligence, Surveillance, and Reconnaissance (ISR) requesting matrix.		
e. Incorporates lower-level PIR/IR into the SIR and ISR plan as necessary.		
2. The appropriate section processes incoming intelligence data.		
a. Determines the reliability of the source or agency.		
b. Determines the credibility of incoming information.		
c. Compares incoming data with the intelligence estimate.		
d. Compares incoming data with intelligence products developed during the Intelligence Preparation of the Battlefield process against the:		
(1) List of intelligence indicators.		
(2) Intelligence workbook.		
(3) PIR, IR and SIR.		
(4) Situation Map.		

TASK STEPS AND PERFORMANCE MEASURES	GO	NO-GO
Note: The appropriate section determines the validity of incoming data based on preceding standards.		
e. Analyzes the threat:		
(1) Composition.		
(2) Disposition (recent, current, and projected location and how they are deployed).		
(3) Strength.		
(4) Tactics and operations (strategy, methods of operation, and doctrine).		
(5) Training.		
(6) Logistics support (internal and external).		
(7) Combat/Operational effectiveness:		
(a) Ability to replace personnel and equipment losses.		
(b) Ability to obtain necessary logistical supplies.		
(c) Ability to conduct operations a various levels of expertise.		
(d) Level of operational Improvised Explosive Device experience.		
(e) Level of morale of the leaders/members of the organization.		
(8) Electronic technical data including HF short-wave, cellular phone, Internet, mail, courier, ham radio and citizen band-sets.		
(9) Miscellaneous data such as family history and genealogy, false unit identification, names or designators, political and military goals, propaganda, and demographics.		
(10) Other factors to consider such culture, finance, intelligence, internal organizational processes, personalities, recruitment, and support.		
3. The appropriate section provides the chemical officer an estimate of the threat's ability and likeliness to initiate Chemical, Biological, Radiological and Nuclear (CBRN) operations.		
4. The appropriate section estimates, with the chemical officer, the effects of threat smoke munitions and CBRN weapons on friendly operations.		
5. The appropriate section provides input to assist in the development of:		
a. Command information analysis for information operations.		
b. Operations security analysis.		
c. Electronic Warfare analysis.		
d. Tactical deception plan.		

    * indicates a leader task step.

SUPPORTING COLLECTIVE TASKS

Task Number   **Task Title**

34-6-2040   Conduct Intelligence Preparation of the Battlefield (IPB)

TASK: Disseminate Combat Information and Intelligence (34-6-2044)

(FMI 2-01)   (FM 2-0)   (FM 2-19.4)

CONDITIONS: The unit is deployed and supporting combat operations. The operation order (OPORD) or fragmentary order (FRAGO) has been published. The unit has the tactical standing operating procedures, completed intelligence products, an initial entry intelligence package from higher headquarters in digital or hard copy, brigade or other intelligence gathering assets supporting the unit. Coalition forces and noncombatants may be present in the operational environment. Performance of this task may occur in an asymmetric environment containing imbalanced ideological, cultural, technological and/or military threat capabilities. Unit leaders conduct Composite Risk Management (CRM) and take into account environmental considerations during mission planning. Some iterations of this task should be performed in MOPP4.

TASK STANDARDS: The section disseminates combat information and intelligence to the appropriate units and staff elements. The information accurately portrays weather, terrain, and the enemy's current and probable future courses of action, capabilities, vulnerabilities, and order of battle. This is done in accordance with the tactical standing operating procedures. The section provides information in time for commanders and staff to plan and mass forces at the proper time and place to successfully influence the battle.

TASK STEPS AND PERFORMANCE MEASURES	GO	NO-GO
1. Arranges for direct (point-to-point) dissemination of information from collector to requestor.		
a. Writes the requirement for direct dissemination into ISR task whenever possible.		
b. Tracks the status of each request through use of information copies or similar means.		
Note: Use the All Source Analysis System-Light (ASAS-L) and Distributed Common Ground System-Army Multi-Functional Workstation (DCGS-A MFWS) message auto generate/auto fill as required.		
2. Determines perishability of information.		
a. Identifies users and checks information against outstanding requirements to determine who requested it.		
b. Checks to determine if the information satisfies, completely or partially, the requests of other users.		
3. Determines quantity of information to disseminate.		
a. Ensures compartmented information is not disseminated to unauthorized users.		
b. Prevents overwhelming commanders and overloading communication devices by sending only information necessary to satisfy user requests.		
4. Determines dissemination methods.		
a. Intelligence Officer in coordination with the Operations Officer and Signal Officer determines available dissemination methods. As a minimum, plans for a primary and alternate method.		
b. Monitors the dissemination means for effectiveness.		
5. Identifies dissemination media.		
a. Uses a combination of voice, graphics, and text to disseminate small amounts of information.		

TASK STEPS AND PERFORMANCE MEASURES	GO	NO-GO
b. Uses voice communications to disseminate information when speed of transmission is critical.		
c. Uses graphics to disseminate information on disposition, composition, and strength; use text to disseminate other order of battle information.		
6. Develops audit trail to ensure information has been received by intended recipient.		
7. Manages database to automatically parse and disseminate information.		
a. Creates new databases IAW unit SOP.		
b. Ensures database entries are accomplished by standardized conventions.		
c. Establishes security protocols that allow only authorized personnel access to the database.		
d. Develops procedures to minimize redundancy of data to ensure effective use of limited space, speed up database queries, and reduce analyst confusion caused by duplicate data entries.		
e. Utilizes standardized procedures of exporting/importing databases across unit lines that ensure the information will be immediately available for use.		
f. Protects the database from loss or corruption.		
(1) Establishes plan to backup database information to prevent its irrevocable loss.		
(2) Regularly updates database software to incorporate the latest changes fixing glitches or security holes.		

* indicates a leader task step.

SUPPORTING COLLECTIVE TASKS

Task Number   **Task Title**

34-6-2041   Produce Intelligence Products

TASK: Conduct Long Range Surveillance (LRS) Staff Planning (brigade) (34-6-2050)

(FM 3-55.93)   (FM 2-0)   (FM 5-0)

CONDITIONS: The Battlefield surveillance Brigade (BfSB) is conducting operations independently or as part of a division, corps, or Army forces (ARFOR) and has received an operation order (OPORD) or fragmentary order (FRAGO) with a mission at the location and time specified. The mission requires the planning, coordination for, and use of LRS assets as part of the intelligence, surveillance, and reconnaissance (ISR) plan to answer the commander's critical information requirements (CCIR) and priority intelligence requirements (PIR). The order includes all applicable overlays and or graphics. All necessary personnel and equipment are available. The brigade has communications with higher, adjacent, subordinate, and supporting elements. The brigade has been provided guidance on the rules of engagement (ROE) and rules of interaction (ROI). Performance of this task may occur in an asymmetric environment containing imbalanced ideological, cultural, technological and/or military threat capabilities. Unit leaders conduct Composite Risk Management (CRM) and take into account environmental considerations during mission planning. Some iterations of this task should be performed in MOPP4.

TASK STANDARDS: The brigade staff conducts LRS planning and coordination in accordance with (IAW) the tactical standing operating procedures (TSOP), the order, and or higher commander's guidance. The brigade staff integrates and employs LRS assets as part of the brigade ISR plan to answer the CCIR and PIR. The LRS commander or senior representative advises the commander, S-2 and/or S-3 on the proper employment and missions for LRS unit. The brigade LRS unit conducts necessary coordination with the brigade staff and complies with the ROE and ROI. Operations security (OPSEC) is strictly enforced throughout the planning process.

TASK STEPS AND PERFORMANCE MEASURES	GO	NO-GO
NOTE: Only select key battle staff leaders have the need to know for specific LRS missions and surveillance locations. Maintain strict OPSEC measures at all times for the conduct and planning of LRS missions due to the vulnerability of the teams and sensitivity of the missions.		
1. Brigade leaders maintain situational understanding using digital command and control (C2) information systems (INFOSYS), frequency modulated (FM) communications, maps, intelligence summaries, situation reports (SITREPs), and other available information sources.		
2. Brigade S-3, S-2, and ISR section leader begin ISR planning based upon the mission and the commander's CCIRs and PIRs.		
a. Identify named areas of interest (NAI) and target area of interest (TAI) for surveillance by military intelligence battalion signals intelligence (SIGINT), imagery intelligence (IMINT), and human intelligence (HUMINT) assets and capabilities.		
b. Identify NAI and TAI that can be collected on by the Reconnaissance & Surveillance Squadron's Recce Troops.		
c. Identify NAI and TAI that can be collected on by other attached, OPCON, or TACON units supporting the BfSB.		
d. Identify NAI and TAI locations that could best be surveilled by human intelligence LRS assets such as:		
(1) Critical points along an avenue of approach.		
(2) Key terrain and choke points in urban or complex areas to:		

TASK STEPS AND PERFORMANCE MEASURES	GO	NO-GO
(a) Counter the IED threat and attacks.		
(b) Counter threat ambush attempts.		
(c) Counter sniper attacks.		
(d) Counter indirect fire attacks.		
(e) Determine threat patterns.		
(3) Critical points along key lines of communications (LOC) or major supply routes (MSR).		
(4) Known or suspected border crossing points and routes.		
(5) Suspected troop or insurgent infiltration routes, supply bases, training bases, or assembly areas.		
(6) Suspected insurgent or criminal safe houses.		
(7) Persistent area or target surveillance sites in support friendly operations to:		
(a) Collect information to plan/prepare for an attack or assault.		
(b) Trigger a planned attack or assault.		
(c) Conduct post assault surveillance to determine its effects.		
(8) River fording sites.		
(9) Bridges and railway junctions.		
(10) Airfield traffic and activities.		
(11) Mountain passes or valleys.		
(12) Missions in support of protecting critical points of host nation infrastructure vulnerable to threat activities such as:		
(a) Oil and natural gas pipelines or facilities.		
(b) Water treatment facilities.		
(c) Electric and hydroelectric facilities, stations, and substations.		
e. Ensure that potential LRS locations are not already included in other BCT, Division, Corps, or ARFOR ISR collection plans.		
3. S-3 determines, in conjunction with the S-2 and LRS commander, the appropriate type of LRS mission(s) to be conducted, such as:		
a. Surveillance of the target area.		
b. Limited reconnaissance of an area, zone, or route.		
c. Target acquisition, identification, and location.		
d. Damage assessment of a target or potential target.		
e. Terrain and weather reporting of a location.		
f. Collateral activities such as:		
(1) Conduct disaster relief.		
(2) Conduct coalition support.		
(3) Combat search and rescue.		
(4) Pathfinder operations.		

TASK STEPS AND PERFORMANCE MEASURES	GO	NO-GO
4. S-3 determines, in conjunction with the S-2 and LRS commander, the most advantageous means of insertion and extraction such as:		
a. Ground insertion.		
b. Air insertion by helicopter.		
c. Airborne insertion.		
d. Waterborne insertion.		
e. Remaining in stay behind positions after friendly forces depart an area.		
5. S-3 and S-2 nominate the selected LRS mission(s) to the commander for approval.		
6. S-3 coordinates, as necessary, with the MI battalion, USAF TACP, BAE/ADAM, FSC, and HCS for:		
a. Support to the LRS mission.		
b. LRS support to USAF, army aviation, fire support, SIGINT, or HUMINT missions.		
7. S-3, S-2, and LRS commander prepare the warning order and mission planning folder, with input from other elements of the brigade staff, to be issued to the LRS team(s) NLT 72 hours prior to the execution of the mission. The mission folder provides:		
a. An overview of the operation that includes:		
(1) Enemy or threat road to war.		
(2) The division or corps mission and intent.		
(3) The division or corps concept of operations.		
b. NAI target area data:		
(1) NAI number and location with grid coordinates.		
(2) The task, purpose, and intent while in the target area.		
(3) Description, location, and significance of the NAI.		
(4) Operational graphics.		
(5) The PIR, SIR, and SOR to be answered.		
(6) Timeline of key events while in the target area:		
(a) Time of insertion.		
(b) When surveillance of NAI is to begin and end.		
(c) Time of extraction.		
c. Terrain, weather, and light data.		
(1) Climatology of the area.		
(2) Solar and lunar tables for the period of the mission.		
(3) Current and extended weather forecast.		
(4) Terrain description and relief data of the area.		
(5) Vegetation surrounding the target area.		
(6) Built up areas.		
(7) The effects of OAKOC in the area.		
(a) Observation and fields of fire.		

TASK STEPS AND PERFORMANCE MEASURES	GO	NO-GO
(b) Avenues of approach.		
(c) Key terrain.		
(d) Obstacles.		
(e) Cover and concealment.		
(8) Landing and pickup zone information.		
(9) Locations and potability of water sources in the target area.		
d. Enemy/threat force information.		
(1) Composition and disposition.		
(2) Capabilities.		
(a) Night vision devices.		
(b) Radio direction finding and jamming.		
(c) Reaction times to events.		
(d) Morale and motivation.		
(3) Strengths and weaknesses.		
(4) Recent activities.		
(5) Expected activities and indicators.		
e. Civilian population around the target area.		
(1) Language and dialects spoken.		
(2) Political views and tendencies.		
(3) Religious affiliation(s).		
(4) Security or police organizations.		
(5) Economic considerations.		
(a) Local currency.		
(b) Means of local economic support.		
(6) Population control measures within the AO.		
(a) Identification cards.		
(b) Passports and visas.		
(c) Work papers or identification.		
(d) Ration cards.		
(e) Security checkpoints.		
(7) Details of any recent population movement in, around, or through the target area.		
(8) Industrial infrastructure and facilities in the target area.		
(9) Transportations routes in and around the target area.		
(10) Civilian gathering places such as auditoriums, stadiums, and places of worship.		
(11) Agricultural areas in and around the target area.		
(12) Border crossing points and avenues of approach.		

TASK STEPS AND PERFORMANCE MEASURES	GO	NO-GO
(a) Locations.		
(b) Border structures and facilities.		
(c) Border crossing security measures.		
(d) Border security personnel types, numbers, weapons, ordnance, and vehicles.		
f. Friendly forces in and around the target area.		
(1) Locations.		
(2) Missions and characteristics.		
g. Operational coordinating instructions.		
(1) Critical planning and operating time tables.		
(2) Necessary fire support details coordinated through the Fire Support Cell.		
(3) Concept for aerial insertion and extraction, if required, coordinated through the ADAM/BAE Section.		
(4) Concept for vehicle or ground insertion, if required.		
(5) Warterborne insertion and extraction operational information, if required.		
(6) Host nation or partisan forces support details.		
h. Communications information.		
(1) Signal Operating Instructions (SOI).		
(2) Tactical satellite (TACSAT) frequencies and availability.		
(3) High frequency (HF) propagation charts.		
(4) HF frequency list.		
(5) LRS reporting schedule and procedures to higher headquarters.		
(6) Internet protocol (IP) addresses.		
i. Intelligence requirements:		
(1) The CCIR, PIR, and the specific information request (SIR) to be answered.		
(2) Essential elements of friendly information (EEFI).		
(3) Friendly force information requirements (FFIR).		
(4) Radio direction finding capabilities of the threat.		
(5) Threat rear area security capabilities and reaction time.		
j. Required maps and imagery to conduct the mission:		
(1) Area orientation maps.		
(a) 1:250,000 scale maps minimum for planning.		
(b) 1:50,000 scale maps for planning and operations.		
(c) Joint operational graphics of the area for planning.		
(2) Line of sight graphics or matrix of the area.		
(3) 1:5,000 scale low oblique photos of the area within 5km of the NAI.		
(4) IPB products, to include:		
(a) Modified combined obstacle overlay.		

TASK STEPS AND PERFORMANCE MEASURES	GO	NO-GO
(b) Situation template.		
(c) Event template.		
(5) GI&S terrain products.		
k. Evasion plan information.		
(1) Safe route or area for evasion to a designated place of recovery.		
(2) Survival, civilian population, medical, and border information.		
(3) Sources for sustenance in the area.		
(4) Any necessary orders or special instructions for evasion.		
l. Coordinating instructions:		
(1) Insertion and extraction information.		
(2) Link up procedures with friendly, partisan, or contact point personnel.		
(3) Movement by other than air.		
(4) Departure from and return through forward friendly lines.		
(5) Available fire support.		
(6) Resupply by cache or air resupply.		
(7) Friendly and/or coalition force boundaries.		
(8) Brigade staff element available for support and planning.		
(9) Required special weapons and equipment.		
(10) Data necessary to maintain communications.		
m. Current intelligence estimate.		
n. Intelligence Annex to the OPORD.		
8. S-2 Section updates the LRS teams regularly on the current threat situation as the teams prepare for mission execution.		

* indicates a leader task step.

SUPPORTING COLLECTIVE TASKS

Task Number	Task Title
71-8-2300	Perform Intelligence, Surveillance, and Reconnaissance (Battalion - Corps)
71-8-2410	Provide Intelligence Support to Targeting (Battalion - Corps)
71-8-5315	Process Relevant Information to Create a Common Operational Picture (Battalion - Corps)

TASK: Conduct Unmanned Aircraft System (UAS) Surveillance Missions (01-4-7927)

(FM 3-04.155)   (TC 1-600)

CONDITIONS: The aviation element is conducting assigned missions in a simulated-live, virtual, or constructive-combat environment. The UAS unit receives an operations order/fragmentary order (OPORD/FRAGO), directing it to conduct UAS surveillance missions. The unit's mission planning system (Falcon View or equivalent system) is available, operational, contains all enemy and friendly locations, and graphic control measures provided by the higher headquarters. The unit conducts flight operations within safe flight parameters with associated equipment, personnel, applicable operational references, and the commanders' intent. The UAS unit's surveillance missions may occur independently or in conjunction with other manned aircraft, ground maneuver elements or intelligence systems performing surveillance during day, at night, and in limited adverse weather in support of decisive or shaping operations. Performance of this task may occur in an asymmetric environment containing imbalanced ideological, cultural, technological and/or military threat capabilities. Some iterations of this task should be performed in MOPP4.

TASK STANDARDS: The unit conducts UAS surveillance missions in accordance with (IAW) published directives and regulations, unit's tactical standing operation procedure (TACSOP) and the commander's guidance. The unit conducts assigned missions within safe flight parameters with associated equipment, personnel, and applicable operational references without safety violations or incidents. The UAS unit's sensor and laser employment; and level of interoperability support surveillance missions IAW the supported commander's intent. The unit reports tactical information concerning the location and movement of threat elements, and any commander's critical information requirements (CCIR) to higher/supported headquarters and/or other targeting or intelligence systems in an expeditious manner and without error.

TASK STEPS AND PERFORMANCE MEASURES	GO	NO-GO
* 1. The unit commander/leader receives the pre-mission or en route warning order/OPORD/FRAGO for mission analysis and troop-leading procedures.		
a. Determines specified, implied, and essential tasks.		
b. Conducts a mission, enemy, terrain and weather, troops and support available, time available, and civil considerations (METT-TC) analysis.		
c. Determines a tentative plan for UAS support.		
d. Conducts a common operational picture (COP)/map and Falcon View reconnaissance of the area of operations (AO) for UAS support.		
e. Initiates any mission planning and control (MPLC) ground control station (GCS) movements or handover of unmanned aircraft (UA), as required.		
* 2. The unit commander/leader and mission commander (MC) continue collaborative mission analysis to coordinates mission requirements and a common situational awareness of the surveillance missions.		
a. Review the COP, higher/supported unit intelligence preparation of the battlefield, intelligence summaries, and any pre-mission joint/national asset intelligence imagery products provided.		
b. Conduct mission planning/preparation IAW TACSOP.		
c. Coordinate mission planning/preparation with supporting and supported units in work groups and planning sessions, dependent on time available.		
* 3. The UAS platoon leader and/or MC conduct pre-mission or en route preparation		

TASK STEPS AND PERFORMANCE MEASURES	GO	NO-GO
a. Conduct pre-mission or en route air mission briefs between air mission commander (AMC) or ground commander/leaders IAW TACSOP.		
b. Brief the mission and AMC/ground commander's intent and scheme of maneuver to GCS unmanned aircraft crewmembers (UACs).		
c. Conduct pre-mission UAS unit rehearsal and combined arms rehearsal with supported units, if time is available.		
d. Conduct en route brief-backs between the AMC/ground commanders in lieu of rehearsals during dynamically re-tasked surveillance missions.		
e. Supervise installation of applicable surveillance sensor payloads and communications relay payloads (CRP), as required.		
f. Perform pre-combat or en route GCS inspections and pre-combat or en route aircraft checks IAW TACSOP and mission brief.		
g. Provide company flight operations and UAS platoon mission planning products from Falcon View and other airspace planning systems to the GCS MC and UACs.		
h. Load or change GCS presets for the UA routes, loiter positions, and altitudes and any handover waypoints for level of interoperability (LOI) support of the surveillance missions.		
i. Launch or divert mission essential UAS and readied stand-by UA for departure.		
4. The unmanned aircraft operator employs cleared flight routes to the surveillance objective to avoid fratricide or threat engagement.		
a. Unmanned aircraft operator follows approved routes and altitudes at prescribed times in compliance with airspace control measures identified in the airspace control order or coordinated through the division airspace command and control (AC2) cell or air defense airspace management/brigade aviation element (ADAM/BAE) .		
b. Unmanned aircraft operator or MC confirms identification, friend, or foe settings and air defense coordination with the ADAM/BAE.		
c. Unmanned aircraft operator conducts aerial passage of lines, as required.		
d. Unmanned aircraft operator avoids/reports known or suspected enemy air defenses except to conduct surveillance operations outside their engagement envelope for targeting purposes.		
e. Unmanned aircraft operator and MC conduct actions on contact Hellfire engagements, if applicable, and/or air combat maneuvers to avoid threat air defense engagement.		
5. The unit conducts surveillance operations in support of the battlefield surveillance Brigade, fires brigade, and maneuver elements.		
a. Conducts surveillance of specified named areas of interest (NAIs) and targeted areas of interest (TAI) using electro-optical/infrared (EO/IR) and/or synthetic aperture radar/ground moving target indicator radar (SAR/GMTI) sensors.		
b. Mission payload operator (PO) and MC conduct sensor cueing, and LOI support when conducting cooperative surveillance with other air and ground reconnaissance, surveillance, and target acquisition (RSTA) assets.		

TASK STEPS AND PERFORMANCE MEASURES	GO	NO-GO
c. MC conducts reconnaissance handover/target handover with supported/supporting elements when conducting cooperative surveillance with other manned and unmanned air and ground RSTA assets.		
d. PO conducts terrain surveillance using terrain analysis.		
(1) Identifies areas where the enemy has observation and fields of fire.		
(2) Monitors avenues of approach into NAI/TAI, likely enemy axis of advance or infiltration routes, and routes where ambushes and improvised explosives may be employed by the threat.		
(3) Identifies key terrain, such as hills, intersections/overpasses, bridges and gap crossings, and complex terrain creating chokepoints.		
(4) Locates enemy obstacles or monitors friendly ones.		
(5) Determines areas the enemy may use for cover and concealment, to include urban canyons, sensitive sites (such as schools, churches, hospitals), and infrastructure.		
e. PO determines critical man made terrain features and urban areas where collateral damage could occur.		
f. MC assesses the enemy situation.		
g. PO tracks enemy forces, locations, assets and resources to establish hostile intent of personnel appearing to be civilians, or positive identification of threat elements.		
h. MC employs CRP or satellite data link, as required, to support surveillance in conjunction with supported battlefield surveillance Brigade, fires brigade, or maneuver brigade elements for shaping operations.		
* 6. The MC reports critical information obtained from the surveillance missions.		
a. Reports information requested by the maneuver commander (CCIR) or identified in the OPORD/FRAGO and mission briefings.		
b. Reports information by voice or text radio, military internet relay chat, or data link with supported/supporting elements using approved LOI.		
c. Reports information to supported/supporting RSTA elements for cueing purposes, and reconnaissance handover/target handover.		
d. Employs CRP, as required, for required reporting.		
7. Unmanned aircraft operator and MC return/divert the UA to the launch and recovery site (LRS) or alternate mission, as required.		
a. Ground control section uses planned/updated flight routes and techniques to return to the LRS when low on fuel or ammunition.		
b. As supplies permits, instead of returning to the LRS, diverted to new preplanned or dynamically re-tasked mission, to include other surveillance, as part of route, area, or zone reconnaissance or security missions.		
c. MC debriefs missions, consolidate videos, tapes, compact disks, UAS maintenance status, and submits the appropriate closing reports to higher echelon headquarters.		
* 8. Commander/Leader performs or delegates performance of the steps in the composite risk management (CRM) process for each step in troop leading procedures.		

* indicates a leader task step.

SUPPORTING COLLECTIVE TASKS

Task Number	Task Title
01-3-7904	Conduct Unmanned Aircraft System (UAS) Launch
01-2-7922	Coordinate Countermeasures to Protect Unmanned Aircraft Systems (UAS) against Enemy Air Defense (AD)

TASK: Conduct Zone Reconnaissance (17-6-9314)

<u>(FM 3-20.96)</u>   (FM 3-90)   (FM 3-90.6)
(FM 17-95)

CONDITIONS: The brigade combat team (BCT) or battalion (BN) is conducting operations independently or as part of a division or Army forces, and receives an operation order (OPORD) or fragmentary order (FRAGO) to conduct a zone reconnaissance. The higher commander's order(s) detail the need for information regarding the enemy situation and/or information about cross-country trafficability within the zone. Included in this order is the specific zone(s) to be reconnoitered, line(s) of departure (LD), limit(s) of advance (LOA) or objective(s), the higher commander's critical information requirements (CCIR), and higher commander's intent. Adequate time to accomplish the mission and gather critical information has been allocated by higher headquarters (HQ). All necessary personnel and equipment are available. The BCT/BN has communications with higher, adjacent, subordinate, and supporting elements. The BCT/BN has been provided guidance on the rules of engagement (ROE). Military and civilian, joint and multinational partners, and news media may be present in the operational environment (OE). Some iterations of this task should be conducted during limited visibility conditions. Some iterations of this task should be performed in mission-oriented protective posture (MOPP) 4.

TASK STANDARDS: The BCT/BN conducts the zone reconnaissance in accordance with (IAW) the standing operating procedures (SOP), the order, and/or higher commander's guidance. The BCT/BN finds and reports all threat forces within the zone(s), reconnoiters specific terrain within the zone(s), reports areas of chemical, biological, radiological, and nuclear (CBRN) contamination, renders route reports on major routes, reports details of the population in the zone, and reports CCIR. If time permits, the BCT/BN also reconnoiters all terrain; inspects and evaluates all bridges; locates fords or crossing sites near all bridges; inspects and evaluates all overpasses, underpasses, and culverts; locates and clears all mines, obstacles, and barriers within capability; and locates bypasses around urban areas, and routes through urban areas, obstacles, and contaminated areas. The BCT/BN complies with the ROE.

TASK STEPS AND PERFORMANCE MEASURES	GO	NO-GO
Plan		
* 1. The BCT/BN leaders gain and/or maintain situational understanding (SU) using available communications equipment, maps, intelligence summaries, situation reports (SITREPs), and other available information sources. Intelligence sources include human intelligence (HUMINT), signal intelligence (SIGINT), and imagery intelligence (IMINT) to include unmanned aircraft systems (UASs).		
* 2. The commander and staff receive an order or anticipate a new mission, and begin the military decision-making process (MDMP). (Refer to task 71-8-5110, Plan Operations using the Military Decision-Making Process.) They take the following actions:		
a. Issue a warning order (WARNO) to subordinates as appropriate.		
b. Initiate movements that facilitate reconnaissance.		
* 3. The commander and staff plan zone reconnaissance. They take the following actions:		
a. Coordinate with higher headquarters (HQ) and adjacent units to obtain required intelligence products and other terrain products.		
b. Conduct a map reconnaissance.		
c. Update the joint common database and common operational picture (COP), providing current SU to provide timely and accurate information for intelligence preparation of the battlefield (IPB) and the planning process.		

TASK STEPS AND PERFORMANCE MEASURES	GO	NO-GO
d. Conduct IPB. (Refer to task 34-6-2040, Conduct Intelligence Preparation of the Battlefield.)		
(1) Define the battlefield environment using terrain analysis tools.		
(2) Describe the battlefield effects on operations in terms of the military aspects of terrain using observations and fields of fire, avenues of approach, key terrain, obstacles, concealment and cover (OAKOC).		
(3) Evaluate the enemy.		
(4) Produce a modified combined obstacle overlay (MCOO) and disseminates to subordinate elements.		
(5) Determine enemy courses of action (ECOA).		
e. Implement and integrate higher HQ reconnaissance plan.		
f. Integrate the following seven reconnaissance fundamentals. Take the following actions:		
(1) Ensure continuous reconnaissance.		
(2) Do not keep reconnaissance assets in reserve.		

(3) Orient on the reconnaissance objective(s), such as:
      • Threat oriented.
      • Terrain oriented.
      • Society oriented.
      • Infrastructure oriented.
      • A combination of threats.		

(4) Report information rapidly and accurately.		
(5) Retain freedom to maneuver.		
(6) Gain and maintain threat contact.		
(7) Develop the situation rapidly.		
g. Define reconnaissance objectives and assigns tasks to subordinate elements. Even though the unit is assigned a zone reconnaissance mission, subordinate units could be assigned a zone, area, or route reconnaissance mission. (Refer to Task 71-8-5123, Task Organize for Operations.)		
h. Determine speed of the reconnaissance effort and locations where more deliberate reconnaissance is required.		
i. Integrate and synchronize air and ground operations. Take the following actions:		
(1) Determine mission command relationship of the air and ground elements.		
(2) Assign zones for subordinate units and determines essential on-station times for the air elements.		
(3) Prioritize critical tasks to be performed by air and ground elements.		
j. Integrate and synchronize warfighting functions based on the mission variables of mission, enemy, terrain and weather, troops and support available, time available and civil considerations (METT-TC). Take the following actions:		
(1) Plan fire support. Take the following actions:		
(a) Assign priority of fire or nonlethal effects and priority of targets.		

TASK STEPS AND PERFORMANCE MEASURES	GO	NO-GO
(b) Establish fire support coordination measures (FSCM) that supports the reconnaissance mission.		
(c) Synchronize movement of mortars, artillery, and attached fires support assets to scheme of maneuver.		
(2) Plan engineer support. Take the following actions:		
(a) Plan for priority of support to the reconnaissance objective.		
(b) Integrate obstacle intelligence (OBSTINTEL) requirements into the priority intelligence requirements (PIR) and reconnaissance plan.		
(c) Plan adequate mission command to rapidly shift priority of effort and support in order to reinforce success or respond to a changing situation.		
(d) Plan for emplacement of situational obstacles, as needed.		
(3) Plan air and missile defense (AMD) support (if support has been provided by higher HQ). Take the following actions:		
(a) Coordinate for adequate coverage of the unit during the mission.		
(b) Shift assets as required by phase of the operation.		
(c) Plan for increased air defense (AD) coverage of areas where the unit is most vulnerable to air attacks.		
(d) Coordinate AMD coverage with air defense airspace management (ADAM)/brigade aviation element (BAE), if required.		
(4) Plan chemical, biological, radiological and nuclear (CBRN) defense. Take the following actions:		
(a) Integrate CBRN reconnaissance assets into reconnaissance plan.		
(b) Ensure CBRN assets are positioned to quickly detect enemy use of CBRN.		
(c) Coordinate immediate and thorough decontamination based on the commander's priorities and vulnerability analysis.		
(5) Plan sustainment operations. Take the following actions:		
(a) Integrate movement and positioning of sustainment assets with the scheme of maneuver.		
(b) Anticipate timely resupply of class I, III, and V.		
(c) Support a rapid reorganization by providing immediate forward support once BCT/BN elements reach the LOA.		
(d) Plan and coordinate medical support and casualty evacuation.		
k. Determine the tempo of the reconnaissance effort and link it to execution information.		
l. Determine the engagement and bypass criteria.		
m. Prepare and disseminate orders and graphics.		
n. Conduct composite risk management. (Refer to Task 71-8-5145, Conduct Composite Risk Management [Battalion – Corps].)		

TASK STEPS AND PERFORMANCE MEASURES	GO	NO-GO
* 4. The BCT/BN commander and staff conduct confirmation briefings with subordinates immediately after the OPORD is issued to ensure subordinates understand commander's intent and concept.		
Prepare		
* 5. The BCT/BN prepare for the mission. They take the following actions:		
a. Refine the plan based on continuously updated intelligence.		
b. Conduct precombat checks.		
c. Supervise subordinate MDMP and/or troop-leading procedures to ensure planning and preparations are on track and consistent with the unit commander's intent.		
d. Conduct rehearsals during day and limited visibility, if possible.		
e. Position forces.		
6. Unit begins movement to the area of operations (AO).		
Execute		
7. The unit conducts passage of lines, as required. (Refer to Task 07-6-1081, Conduct a Passage of Lines as Passing Unit [Battalion–Brigade] and/or Task 07-6-1082, Conduct a Passage of Lines as a Stationary Unit [Battalion–Brigade].)		
8. Subordinate units conduct zone reconnaissance to find and report all threat forces within the zone, reconnoiter specific terrain within the zone, and report CCIR. They take the following actions:		
a. Confirm or deny intelligence estimates at reconnaissance objectives, named areas of interest (NAI), or target areas of interest (TAI).		
b. Identify civilian unrest or resistance and/or reports on other significant civilian factors.		
c. Report progress continually, informing higher HQ of all relevant information concerning terrain, threat, and population(s).		
d. Use graphic control measures and COP to control progress through the zone, assist in coordinating reconnaissance, assure security, and coordinate air and ground operations. Take the following actions:		
(1) Use contact points with adjacent elements along boundaries and mission command systems to assist in coordinating reconnaissance and assure security.		
(2) Use checkpoints (or other graphic control measures and COP) to indicate critical terrain features, control reconnaissance, or coordinate air and ground operations.		
(3) Use additional control measures, as necessary.		
e. Air elements reconnoiter forward or to the flanks of the ground element to provide early warning. They take the following actions:		
(1) Reconnoiter open terrain and areas not easily accessible to vehicles.		
(2) Check key points.		
(3) Locate the flanks of enemy forces encountered.		
(4) Reconnoiter gaps or close terrain between ground unit zones or AOs.		

TASK STEPS AND PERFORMANCE MEASURES	GO	NO-GO
(5) Screen open flanks.		
(6) Locate bypasses around obstacles and threat positions.		
(7) Provide security on the far side of obstacles.		
(8) Locate and maintain contact with large threat formations, especially moving ones, before they make contact with ground elements.		
(9) Coordinate joint air attack team (JAAT) or attached attack helicopter operations when a hasty attack is necessary.		
f. Reconnoiter all terrain within the zone (to include urban areas) and render route reports on major routes in the zone.		
g. Inspect and evaluate all bridges within the zone.		
h. Locate suitable fording and crossing sites near all bridges and send bridge report to update the COP.		
i. Inspect and evaluate all overpasses, underpasses, and culverts.		
j. Locate and clear all mines, obstacles, and barriers in the zone, within its capability.		
k. Locate and report bypasses around all urban areas, obstacles, and contaminated areas.		
l. Find and report all threat or factional forces within the zone; send and update spot report (SPOTREP).		
m. Collect and report detailed information rapidly, to include CCIR.		
n. Conduct breaching or crossing operations, as required.		
9. Subordinate elements make contact with threat forces. They take the following actions:		
a. Element in contact deploys and reports situation to higher command, as required.		
b. Commander of element in contact evaluates and develops the situation.		
c. Commander of element in contact chooses a course of action (based on commander's intent) to eliminate or contain the enemy. He takes the following actions:		
(1) Conducts a hasty attack.		
(2) Establishes a hasty defense in order to maintain contact with the enemy.		
(3) Conducts a bypass of threat force.		
d. Commander of element in contact recommends course of action to higher HQ.		
e. Maintain reconnaissance contact with threat elements it cannot destroy.		
f. Maintain mission command.		
g. Sustain reconnaissance/combat capability.		
Assess		
10. The BCT/BN commander and staff assess the situation. They take the following actions:		
a. Conduct mission command and report the developing situation to higher HQ.		
b. Reposition main and tactical command posts (CPs) to sustain constant monitoring and tracking of subordinate units, and to evaluate information that impacts on decision points.		

TASK STEPS AND PERFORMANCE MEASURES	GO	NO-GO
c. Staff tracks the operation, updates the COP, and updates higher, adjacent and subordinate unit's SU.		
d. Provides complete reconnaissance report, to include sketch or overlay, to higher HQ.		
11. The BCT/BN consolidates as necessary. (Refer to task 07-6-5037, Conduct Consolidation.)		
12. The BCT/BN reorganizes as necessary. (Refer to task 07-6-5082, Conduct Reorganization.)		
13. The BCT/BN continues operations as directed.		

* indicates a leader task step.

Task Number	Task Title
07-6-5037	Conduct Consolidation (Battalion – Brigade)
07-6-5082	Conduct Reorganization (Battalion – Brigade)
17-6-1007	Control Intelligence, Surveillance, and Reconnaissance (ISR) Operations (Battalion - Brigade)
17-6-1272	Conduct Area Security (Battalion - Brigade)
17-6-9315	Conduct Area Reconnaissance (Battalion - Brigade)
17-6-9320	Conduct Reconnaissance in Force (Battalion - Brigade)
63-6-2036	Develop the Operational Areas Security Plan
71-8-2210	Perform Intelligence Preparation of the Battlefield (Battalion – Corps)
71-8-2300	Coordinate Intelligence, Surveillance, and Reconnaissance ISR Effort (Battalion – Corps)
71-8-5110	Plan Operations using the Military Decision-Making Process (Battalion – Corps)
71-8-5145	Conduct Composite Risk Management (Battalion – Corps)

TASK: Conduct a Reconnaissance Handover (17-1-4025)

(FM 3-20.96)   (FM 3-90.6)   (FM 3-90)

CONDITIONS: The brigade combat team (BCT) or battalion (BN) is conducting tactical operations and is required to conduct reconnaissance handover (RHO) with another unit. The BCT/BN either accepts reconnaissance and surveillance (R&S) responsibilities from a forward unit or is relieved of these responsibilities by a rearward unit. The RHO may be a single event associated with a terrain feature and/or change of mission or a series of continuous events conducted to enable the BCT/BN to continue its reconnaissance mission uninterrupted. The BCT/BN has communications with higher, adjacent, subordinate, and supporting elements. The BCT/BN receives guidance on the rules of engagement (ROE). Military, civilian, joint and multinational partners, and news media may be present in the operational environment (OE). Some iterations of this task should be performed in mission-oriented protective posture (MOPP) 4.

TASK STANDARDS: The BCT/BN planned and conducted RHO with a forward force, with a follow-on force, and/or with a security force. The BCT/BN provided the link between units to ensure that continuous observation was maintained of all the assigned named areas of interest (NAI), target areas of interest (TAI), targets, and/or enemy forces in contact. The BCT/BN provided information that answered the higher commander's information requirements (IR) and enabled combat units to maneuver to a position of advantage prior to contact. The commander ensured that critical information was transmitted between elements using the communications system that most effectively allowed timely decisions by his higher headquarters (HQ). All communication and reporting are in accordance with (IAW) applicable standing operating procedures (SOP).

TASK STEPS AND PERFORMANCE MEASURES	GO	NO-GO
Plan		
* 1. BCT/BN leaders gain and/or maintain situational understanding (SU) using available communications equipment, maps, intelligence summaries, situation reports (SITREPs), and other available information sources. Intelligence sources include human intelligence (HUMINT), signal intelligence (SIGIT), and imagery intelligence (IMINT) to include unmanned aircraft systems (UAS).		
* 2. The BCT/BN commander and staff receive an order or anticipate a new mission and begin the military decision-making process (MDMP). (Refer to Task 71-8-5110, Plan Operations using the Military Decision-Making Process.) They take the following actions:		
a. Update the joint common database and common operational picture (COP), providing current SU to provide timely and accurate information for intelligence preparation of the battlefield (IPB) and the planning process.		
b. Coordinate redundant surveillance using available reconnaissance assets to assist in maintaining contact during handover.		
c. Conduct IPB. (Refer to task 71-8-2210, Perform Intelligence Preparation of the Battlefield [Battalion–Corps].)		
d. Coordinate locations and/or criteria for RHO with higher HQ, as applicable.		
e. Identify and coordinate communications plan between units, to include—		
(1) Radio frequencies.		
(2) Net identifications (ID).		
(3) Enhanced Position Location and Reporting System (EPLRS) frequencies.		

TASK STEPS AND PERFORMANCE MEASURES	GO	NO-GO
(4) Maneuver Control System (MCS) host files (if units are from different systems).		
(5) Communications security (COMSEC) variables for communications and establishment of tactical internet (TI) between units.		
f. Establish far- and near-range recognition signals and/or exchange combat identification information to prevent fratricide.		
g. Coordinate indirect fires and exchange fire support (FS) information to include—		
(1) Available assets.		
(2) Preplanned targets, final protective fires (FPF), and smoke missions.		
(3) Fire support coordination measures (FSCM) and criteria for activation and/or shifting of fires with higher HQ.		
(4) Artillery handover with forward/follow-on/security force.		
h. Exchange reconnaissance plan with the other unit.		
i. Identify and coordinate criteria for target handover, as necessary.		
j. Coordinate control measures to support handover, passage of lines (POL), and/or bypasses between units.		
k. Select contact point(s) or linkup points to collocate commanders and/or command posts (CP) as necessary.		
l. Coordinate transfer and/or acceptance of mission command of elements between BCT/BN and another HQ, as necessary. They take the following actions:		
(1) Accept mission command of elements behind the reconnaissance handover line (RHL) from a forward force.		
(2) Transfer mission command of elements behind the RHL to a follow-on force.		
(3) Transfer mission command of elements in front of the RHL to a security force.		
m. Specify responsibilities and procedures for integrating designated units into the network, if necessary.		
n. Conduct composite risk management. (Refer to Task 71-8-5145, Conduct Composite Risk Management [Battalion – Corps].)		
Prepare		
* 3. The BCT/BN command and staff exercise mission command of the reconnaissance handover. They take the following actions:		
a. Refine the plan based on continuously updated intelligence.		
b. Continue to conduct extensive reconnaissance operations.		
c. Conduct pre-combat checks as required.		
d. Supervise subordinate MDMP and or troop-leading procedures to ensure planning and preparations are on track and consistent with the unit commander's intent.		
e. Conduct rehearsals during day and limited visibility if possible,		
Execute		

TASK STEPS AND PERFORMANCE MEASURES	GO	NO-GO
4. The BCT/BN accepts RHO from a forward force IAW the order and/or SOP. It takes the following actions:		
a. Establishes frequency modulation communications and/or digital connectivity to link its higher HQ to the forward force, as necessary.		
b. Maneuvers reconnaissance and surveillance elements and/or coordinates positioning of external assets to accept reconnaissance and/or target handover, from an advantageous position, of the following:		
(1) NAIs.		
(2) TAIs and/or preplanned targets.		
(3) High-payoff targets (HPT) and/or enemy forces in contact.		
c. Establishes surveillance of designated areas and/or acquires enemy forces based on the specific information requirements (SIR), commander's critical information requirements (CCIR), and attack guidance.		
d. Accepts fires handover by submitting calls for fire by the forward force, as necessary.		
e. Accepts target handover from the forward force through acquisition of designated targets IAW the fires plan and/or attack guidance.		
f. Displays correct recognition signal IAW the signal operating instruction (SOI) or SOP, as necessary.		
g. Completes RHO after reconnaissance and surveillance elements acknowledge they have initiated surveillance of designated areas and/or gained contact with identified enemy forces.		
5. The BCT/BN conducts RHO with a follow-on force IAW order and/or SOP. They take the following actions:		
a. Occupy covered and concealed positions and/or establishes observation posts (OP) as necessary to maintain surveillance of areas and/or enemy forces.		
(1) Establish restrictive fire control measures around positions and/or OPs as required.		
(2) Maintain weapons orientation toward the enemy, engaging in self-defense as necessary, or		
b. Bypass enemy, avoiding decisive engagement, to continue reconnaissance while maintaining contact with the enemy forces. They take the following actions:		
(1) Maintain weapons orientation toward the enemy, engaging in self-defense as necessary.		
(2) Use appropriate movement techniques and covered and concealed routes based on mission, enemy, terrain and weather, troops and support available, time available, and civil considerations (METT-TC).		
(3) Employ indirect fires to suppress enemy in contact and screen friendly movement as required.		
(4) Maintain communications with BCT/BN assets until RHO.		
c. Relay follow-on force calls for fire until the force's designated fires cell accepts fire and effects handover.		

TASK STEPS AND PERFORMANCE MEASURES	GO	NO-GO
d. Conduct target handover when the follow-on force acknowledges it has acquired the designated target.		
e. Display correct recognition signal IAW the SOI or SOP, as necessary.		
f. Complete RHO after follow-on force acknowledges it has initiated surveillance of designated areas and/or gained contact with identified enemy forces.		
6. The BCT/BN conducts RHO with a security (stationary) force to its rear IAW order and/or SOP. They take the following actions:		
a. Confirm security force has occupied positions to provide overwatch and assist the BCT/BN's rearward POL.		
b. Employ indirect fires to suppress enemy in contact and to screen friendly movement.		
c. Disengage by element while maintaining contact using BCT/BN and other reconnaissance assets.		
(1) Maintain weapon orientation toward the enemy, engaging in self-defense as necessary.		
(2) Use appropriate movement techniques and covered and concealed routes based on METT-TC to the passage points.		
d. After fires handover, submit calls for fire to the designated security force fires cell, as necessary.		
e. Conduct target handover when the security force acknowledges it has acquired the designated target.		
f. Complete RHO when the security force acknowledges it is observing designated locations and/or has gained contact with designated enemy forces.		
7. The BCT/BN exercises mission command during the RHO. They take the following actions:		
a. Establish communications with the forward/follow-on/security force. They take the following actions:		
(1) Enter command net.		
(2) Enter operations and intelligence (O&I) net.		
(3) Enter FS net.		
(4) Ensure acceptance of task organization and connectivity within the digital network.		
(5) Ensure designated units receive related information and reports that were transmitted.		
(6) Update the COP/situation map (SITMAP).		
b. Commander, or his designated BCT/BN staff representative, moves to a position where he can most effectively maintain communications and coordinate the handover, as necessary. He takes the following actions:		
(1) Identifies areas, targets, and/or enemy forces requiring handover between forces.		
(2) Designates phase line or point for handover, if not previously designated.		
(3) Establishes criteria (trigger) for handover, if not previously identified.		

TASK STEPS AND PERFORMANCE MEASURES	GO	NO-GO
(4) Directs BCT/BN assets to maintain surveillance or accept handover, as required.		
c. Main CP or tactical CP collocates with forward/follow-on/security force CP or command group as necessary.		
d. BCT/BN staff continuously reports information to the forward/follow-on/security force and/or higher HQ, covering, as a minimum—		
(1) Current enemy activity, to include location, size, and composition.		
(a) If enemy is moving, reports direction of movement, formation, and estimated rate of advance.		
(b) If enemy is defending, reports (as applicable) orientation, obstacle locations, perceived engagement areas, flanks, proposed breach sites, and reserves.		
(2) Friendly actions, to include location, size, and activities of sustainment elements.		
(3) Status of area surveillance with respect to observation.		
(4) Positions and status of supporting units, if applicable.		
e. The BCT/BN staff coordinates activation and/or shifting of FSCM, as necessary. They take the following actions:		
(1) Ensure all BCT/BN and supporting elements acknowledge changes to FSCM.		
(2) Ensure higher HQ and/or forward/follow-on/security forces are aware of changes to FSCM.		
f. The BCT/BN staff coordinates transfer of mission command of elements between the BCT/BN and other HQ IAW order and/or SOP. They take the following actions:		
(1) Ensure BCT/BN elements have established communications with the gaining HQ prior to RHO.		
(2) Establish contact with elements for which the BCT/BN is accepting mission command prior to RHO.		
g. S3 tracks the manning of contact or linkup points to coordinate passage or bypass with forward/follow-on/security force. They take the following actions:		
(1) Confirm recognition signals.		
(2) Exchange passage information IAW order or SOP.		
(3) Guide follow-on unit to appropriate location.		
h. The BCT/BN staff confirms RHO is complete when specified criteria are met. They take the following actions:		
(1) Accept handover from forward unit when BCT/BN element has initiated surveillance or acquired enemy force.		
(2) Conduct handover when follow-on or security force confirms surveillance of area or gained contact with enemy force.		
(3) Conducts handover with forward/follow-on/security force when designated RHL is activated.		
Assess		

TASK STEPS AND PERFORMANCE MEASURES	GO	NO-GO

* 8. BCT/BN leaders assess the operation. They take the following actions:
 	
    a. Monitor the situation during all phases of the operation.
 	
    b. Direct adjustments to ensure that operations remain aligned with the commander's intent.
 	
9. The BCT/BN consolidates as necessary. (Refer to Task 07-6-5037, Conduct Consolidation (Battalion-Brigade), for further details.)
 	
10. The BCT/BN reorganizes as necessary. (Refer to Task 07-6-5082, Conduct Reorganization (Battalion-Brigade), for further details.)
 	
11. The BCT/BN continues operations as directed.		

* indicates a leader task step.

Task Number	Task Title
07-6-1092	Conduct an Attack (Battalion - Brigade)
07-6-5037	Conduct Consolidation (Battalion - Brigade)
07-6-5082	Conduct Reorganization (Battalion - Brigade)
07-6-1081	Conduct a Passage of Lines as Passing Unit (Battalion - Brigade)
07-6-1082	Conduct a Passage of Lines as a Stationary Unit (Battalion - Brigade)
17-2-4025	Conduct Reconnaissance Handover (Platoon - Company)
17-3-4025	Conduct Reconnaissance Handover
17-6-1007	Conduct (ISR) Synchronization and Integration (Battalion - Brigade)
17-6-3809	Conduct Battle Handover (Battalion - Brigade)
17-6-9314	Conduct Zone Reconnaissance (Battalion-Brigade)
17-6-9315	Conduct Area Reconnaissance (Battalion-Brigade)
71-8-2210	Perform Intelligence Preparation of the Battlefield (Battalion – Corps)
71-8-2300	Perform Intelligence, Surveillance, and Reconnaissance (Battalion - Corps)
71-8-5110	Plan Operations Using the Military Decision-Making Process (Battalion - Corps)
71-8-5123	Task Organize for Operations (Battalion - Corps)
71-8-5145	Composite Risk Management (Battalion – Corps)

TASK: Conduct Area Reconnaissance (17-6-9315)

(FM 3-20.96)　　　　　　　　(FM 3-90)　　　　　　　　(FM 3-90.6)
(FM 17-95)

CONDITIONS: The brigade combat team (BCT) or battalion (BN) is conducting operations independently or as part of a division or Army forces, and receives an operation order (OPORD) or fragmentary order (FRAGO) to conduct an area reconnaissance. The higher order(s) highlight a great degree of certainty regarding the reconnaissance objective. The area may or may not be contiguous to other friendly areas targeted for reconnaissance. Included in this order are the specific area(s) to be reconnoitered, line(s) of departure (LD), limit(s) of advance (LOA) or an objective, the higher commander's critical information requirements (CCIR), and higher commander's intent. Adequate time to accomplish the mission and gather critical information has been allocated by higher headquarters (HQ). All necessary personnel and equipment are available. The BCT/BN has communications with higher, adjacent, subordinate, and supporting elements. The BCT/BN has been provided guidance on the rules of engagement (ROE). Military, civilian, joint and multinational partners, and news media may be present in the operational environment (OE). Some iterations of this task should be conducted during limited visibility conditions. Some iterations of this task should be performed in mission-oriented protective posture (MOPP) 4.

TASK STANDARDS: The BCT/BN conducts the area reconnaissance in accordance with (IAW) the standing operating procedures (SOP), the order, and/or higher commander's guidance. The BCT/BN finds and reports all threat forces within the area(s), reconnoiters specific terrain within the area(s), reports areas of chemical, biological, radiological, and nuclear (CBRN) contamination, renders route reports on major routes, reports details of the population in the area, and reports CCIR. If time permits, the BCT/BN also reconnoiters all terrain; inspects and evaluates all bridges; locates fords or crossing sites near all bridges; inspects and evaluates all overpasses, underpasses, and culverts; locates and clears all mines, obstacles, and barriers within capability, and locates bypasses around urban areas and routes through urban areas, obstacles, and contaminated areas. The BCT/BN complies with the ROE.

TASK STEPS AND PERFORMANCE MEASURES	GO	NO-GO
Plan		
* 1. The BCT/BN leaders gain and/or maintain situational understanding (SU) using available communications equipment, maps, intelligence summaries, situation reports (SITREPs), and other available information sources. Intelligence sources include human intelligence (HUMINT), signal intelligence (SIGINT), and imagery intelligence (IMINT) to include unmanned aircraft systems (UASs).		
* 2. The commander and staff receive an order or anticipate a new mission, and begin the military decision-making process (MDMP). (Refer to Task 71-8-5110, Plan Operations using the Military Decision-Making Process.) They take the following actions:		
a. Issue a warning order (WARNO) to subordinates as appropriate.		
b. Initiate movements that facilitate reconnaissance.		
* 3. The commander and staff plan area reconnaissance. They take the following actions:		
a. Coordinate with higher HQ and adjacent units to obtain required intelligence products and other terrain products.		
b. Conduct a map reconnaissance.		
c. Update the joint common database and common operational picture (COP), providing current SU to provide timely and accurate information for intelligence preparation of the battlefield (IPB) and the planning process.		

TASK STEPS AND PERFORMANCE MEASURES	GO	NO-GO
d. Conduct IPB. (Refer to task 71-8-2210, Perform Intelligence Preparation of the Battlefield [Battalion – Corps].) Take the following actions:		
(1) Define the battlefield environment using terrain analysis tools.		
(2) Describe the battlefield effects on operations in terms of obstacles, cover and concealment, observation, key terrain, and avenues of approach for air and ground operations.		
(3) Evaluate the enemy.		
(4) Produce a modified combined obstacle overlay (MCOO) and disseminates to subordinate elements.		
(5) Determine enemy courses of action (ECOA).		
e. Implement and integrate higher HQ reconnaissance plan.		
f. Integrate the seven reconnaissance fundamentals.		
(1) Ensure continuous reconnaissance.		
(2) Do not keep reconnaissance assets in reserve.		
(3) Orient on the reconnaissance objective(s), such as:		
• Threat oriented.		
• Terrain oriented.		
• Society oriented.		
• Infrastructure oriented.		
• A combination of these factors.		
(4) Report all information rapidly and accurately.		
(5) Retain freedom to maneuver.		
(6) Gain and maintains threat contact.		
(7) Develop the situation rapidly.		
g. Define reconnaissance objectives and assigns tasks to subordinate elements. Even though the unit is assigned an area reconnaissance mission, subordinate units could be assigned a zone, area, or route reconnaissance mission. (Refer to task 71-8-5123, Task Organize for Operations for further details.)		
h. Determine speed of the reconnaissance effort and locations where more deliberate reconnaissance is required.		
i. Integrate and synchronize warfighting functions based on the mission variables of mission, enemy, terrain and weather, troops and support available, time available and civil considerations (METT-TC).		
(1) Integrate and synchronize air and ground operations. Take the following actions:		
(a) Determine mission command relationship of the air and ground elements.		
(b) Assign areas for subordinate units and determines essential on-station times for the air elements.		
(c) Prioritize critical tasks to be performed by air and ground elements.		
(2) Plan fire support (FS). Take the following actions:		

TASK STEPS AND PERFORMANCE MEASURES	GO	NO-GO
(a) Assign priority of fire or nonlethal effects, and priority of targets.		
(b) Establish fire support coordination measures (FSCM) that support the concept of operation.		
(c) Synchronize movement of mortars, artillery, and attached FS assets to scheme of maneuver.		
(3) Plan engineer support. Take the following actions:		
(a) Plan for priority of support to the reconnaissance objective.		
(b) Integrate obstacle intelligence (OBSTINTEL) requirements into the priority intelligence requirements (PIR) and reconnaissance plan.		
(c) Plan adequate mission command to rapidly shift priority of effort and support in order to reinforce success or respond to a changing situation.		
(d) Plan for emplacement situational obstacles, as needed.		
(4) Plan air and missile defense (AMD) support (if support has been provided by higher HQ). Take the following actions:		
(a) Coordinate for adequate coverage of the unit during the mission.		
(b) Shift assets as required by phase of the operation.		
(c) Plan for increased air defense (AD) coverage of areas where the unit is most vulnerable to air attacks.		
(d) Coordinate AMD coverage with air defense and airspace management (ADAM)/brigade aviation element (BAE) if required.		
(5) Plan chemical, biological, radiological, and nuclear (CBRN) defense. Take the following actions:		
(a) Integrate CBRN reconnaissance assets into the reconnaissance plan.		
(b) Ensure CBRN assets are positioned to quickly detect enemy use.		
(c) Coordinate immediate and thorough decontamination based on the commander's priorities and vulnerability analysis.		
(6) Plan sustainment operations. Take the following actions:		
(a) Integrate movement and positioning of sustainment assets with the scheme of maneuver.		
(b) Plan timely resupply of class I, III, and V.		
(c) Support a rapid reorganization by providing immediate forward support once units reach the LOA.		
(d) Plan and coordinate casualty evacuation.		
k. Determine the tempo of the reconnaissance effort and links it to execution information.		
l. Determine the engagement and bypass criteria.		
m. Prepare and disseminate orders and graphics.		
n. Conduct composite risk management (CRM). (Refer to Task 71-8-5145, Conduct Composite Risk Management [Battalion – Corps].)		

TASK STEPS AND PERFORMANCE MEASURES	GO	NO-GO
4. The BCT/BN commander and staff conduct confirmation briefings with subordinates immediately after OPORD is issued to ensure subordinates understand commander's intent and concept.		
Prepare		
5. The BCT/BN prepare for the mission. They take the following actions:		
a. Refine the plan based on continuously updated intelligence.		
b. Conduct precombat checks.		
c. Supervise subordinate decision-making processes to ensure planning and preparations are on track and consistent with the unit commander's intent.		
d. Conduct rehearsals during day and limited visibility, if possible.		
e. Position forces.		
6. Unit begins movement to the area of operations (AO).		
Execute		
7. Unit conducts passage of lines, as required. (Refer to Task 07-6-1081, Conduct a Passage of Lines as Passing Unit [Battalion – Brigade] and/or 07-6-1082, Conduct a Passage of Lines as a Stationary Unit [Battalion – Brigade].)		
8. The unit conducts area reconnaissance to find and report all threat forces within the area. They take the following actions:		
a. Confirm or denies intelligence estimates at reconnaissance objectives, named areas of interest (NAI), or target areas of interest (TAI).		
b. Identify civilian unrest or resistance and other significant civilian factors.		
c. Report progress continually, informing higher HQ of all relevant information concerning the objective area.		
d. Use graphic control measures and COP to control progress through the area, assist in coordinating reconnaissance, assure security, and coordinate air and ground operations. Take the following actions:		
(1) Use contact points with adjacent elements along boundaries and mission command systems to assist in coordinating reconnaissance and to assure security.		
(2) Use checkpoints (or other graphic control measures and COP to indicate critical terrain features, control reconnaissance, or coordinate air and ground operations.		
(3) Use additional control measures, as necessary.		
e. Air elements reconnoiter forward or to the flanks of ground elements to provide early warning. They take the following actions:		
(1) Reconnoiter open terrain and areas not easily accessible to vehicles.		
(2) Check key points.		
(3) Locate the flanks of enemy forces encountered.		
(4) Reconnoiter gaps or close terrain between ground unit AOs.		
(5) Screen open flanks.		

TASK STEPS AND PERFORMANCE MEASURES	GO	NO-GO
(6) Locate bypasses around obstacles and threat positions.		
(7) Provide security on the far side of obstacles.		
(8) Locate and maintain contact with large threat formations, especially moving ones, before they make contact with ground elements.		
(9) Coordinate joint air attack team (JAAT) or attached attack helicopter operations when a hasty attack is necessary.		
f. Reconnoiter all key terrain within the objective area and renders route reports on major routes in the AO.		
g. Locate and determine extent of all contaminated areas within the AO.		
h. Inspect and evaluate all bridges within the area.		
i. Locate suitable fording and crossing sites near all bridges and sends bridge report to update the COP.		
j. Inspect and evaluate all overpasses, underpasses, and culverts.		
k. Identify and mark obstacles, creates lanes as specified in execution orders.		
l. Locate and report bypasses around all urban areas, obstacles, and contaminated areas.		
m. Identify and report threat or factional forces within the area.		
9. The unit reacts to contact IAW METT-TC, OPORD, and ROE.		
Assess		
10. The BCT/BN commander and staff assess the situation. They take the following actions:		
a. Conduct mission command and report the developing situation to higher HQ.		
b. Reposition command posts (CPs) to sustain constant monitoring and tracking of subordinate units, and to evaluate information that impacts on decision points.		
c. Track the operation; update the COP; and update higher, adjacent, and subordinate unit's SU.		
d. Provide complete reconnaissance report, to include sketch or overlay, to higher HQ.		
10. The BCT/BN consolidates as necessary. (Refer to Task 07-6-5037, Conduct Consolidation [Battalion – Brigade].)		
11. The BCT/BN reorganizes as necessary. (Refer to Task 07-6-5082, Conduct Reorganization [Battalion – Brigade].)		
12. The BCT/BN continues operations as directed.		

* indicates a leader task step.

Task Number	Task Title
07-6-1081	Conduct a Passage of Lines as Passing Unit (Battalion – Brigade)
07-6-1082	Conduct a Passage of Lines as a Stationary Unit (Battalion – Brigade)
07-6-5037	Conduct Consolidation (Battalion – Brigade)
07-6-5082	Conduct Reorganization (Battalion – Brigade)

Task Number	Task Title
71-8-2210	Perform Intelligence Preparation of the Battlefield (Battalion – Corps)
71-8-2300	Coordinate Intelligence, Surveillance, and Reconnaissance ISR Effort (Battalion – Corps)
71-8-5110	Plan Operations using the Military Decision-Making Process (Battalion – Corps)
71-8-5145	Conduct Composite Risk Management (Battalion – Corps)

TASK: Conduct a Screen (Battalion-Brigade) (17-6-9225)

(FM 3-20.96)   (FM 3-90)   (FM 17-95)
(FM 5-0)

CONDITIONS: The brigade combat team (BCT) or battalion (BN) receives an operation order (OPORD) or fragmentary order (FRAGO) directing it to conduct a stationary or moving screen mission for a larger force. The order designates the general trace of the screen, the duration of the screen, and the time it must be established. The BCT/BN may be reinforced with sustainment assets. The BCT/BN has communications and digital connectivity with higher, adjacent, subordinate, and supporting elements. The BCT/BN received guidance on the rules of engagement (ROE). Military, civilian, joint, and multinational partners and news media may be present in the operational environment (OE). Some iterations of this task should be conducted during limited visibility conditions. Some iterations of this task should be performed in mission-oriented protective posture (MOPP) 4.

TASK STANDARDS: The BCT/BN coordinates with the screened force commander, and conducts the screen in accordance with (IAW) doctrine, the order, and/or higher commander's guidance. The BCT/BN does not allow any enemy ground element to pass through the screen undetected and unreported. The BCT/ BN maintains continuous surveillance of enemy reconnaissance and main body avenues of approach (AA), detects all enemy activity in the area of operations (AO), provides early warning of enemy approach to the screened force, and destroys or repels enemy reconnaissance elements within its capabilities until displacement criteria is met as specified in the OPORD. The BCT/BN complies with the ROE. All overlays and graphics are provided and all communication and reporting is IAW applicable standing operating procedures (SOP).

TASK STEPS AND PERFORMANCE MEASURES	GO	NO-GO
Plan		
* 1. The BCT/BN leaders gain and/or maintain situational understanding (SU) using available communications equipment, maps, intelligence summaries, situation reports (SITREPs), and other available information sources. Intelligence sources include human intelligence (HUMINT), signal intelligence (SIGINT), and imagery intelligence (IMINT) to include unmanned aircraft systems (UASs).		
* 2. The BCT/BN commander and staff receive an order of a new mission and begin the military decision-making process (MDMP). (Refer to Task 71-8-5110, Plan Operations using the Military Decision-making Process [Battalion–Corps].)		
* 3. The commander and staff coordinate with the protected force commander. They take the following actions:		
a. Determine if reinforcements are necessary to accomplish the screen mission.		
b. Coordinate the general trace of the screen and effective time, if appropriate.		
c. Reaffirm area of responsibility.		
d. Determine the interval to be maintained between the BCT/BN and the protected force.		
e. Determine battle/target handover criteria, graphic control measures, and procedures.		
f. Coordinate special requirements or constraints, such as observing named areas of interest (NAI) or target areas of interest (TAI).		
g. Confirm focus of screen is oriented towards:		
(1) Terrain.		

TASK STEPS AND PERFORMANCE MEASURES	GO	NO-GO
(2) Threat.		
(3) Friendly unit.		
h. Confirm if tempo of screen is:		
(1) Short Duration.		
(2) Long Duration.		
(3) Extended Duration.		
i. Monitor engagement and displacement criteria during mission.		
* 4. The commander and staff plan the screen mission. They take the following actions:		
a. Coordinate with higher headquarters (HQ) and adjacent units to obtain required intelligence products, and initiates a terrain analysis using digital or analog maps and other terrain products.		
b. Conduct a map reconnaissance that:		
(1) Identifies screen trace, orientation, lateral and rear boundaries, and NAIs.		
(2) Identifies enemy AAs and possible objectives for enemy reconnaissance and infiltrating elements.		
(3) Identifies tentative control measures and dismount and remount points.		
(4) Selects routes or sectors to facilitate rearward displacement.		
(5) Disseminates data to subordinate units.		
c. Integrate the fundamentals of security to:		
(1) Orient on the force, area, or facility to be protected.		
(2) Perform continuous reconnaissance.		
(3) Provide early and accurate warning.		
(4) Provide reaction time and maneuver space.		
(5) Maintain threat contact.		
d. Conduct intelligence preparation of the battlefield (IPB). (Refer to Task 71-8-2210, Perform Intelligence Preparation of the Battlefield [Battalion–Corps].)		
e. Develop and disseminate the situation template (SITEMP).		
f. Develop the reconnaissance and surveillance plan and employ assets to conduct reconnaissance early in the MDMP process. (Refer to Task 71-8-2300, Coordinate Intelligence, Surveillance, and Reconnaissance ISR Effort [Battalion–Corps].) Take the following actions:		
(1) Develop a plan that answers the commander's critical information requirements (CCIR) and accomplishes his intent.		
(2) Integrate use of air assets and unmanned aircraft systems (UASs) if available. Air assets may conduct surveillance:		
(a) Forward of the screen.		
(b) To the rear of the screen.		
(c) To the flanks of ground elements.		
(d) In gaps between ground elements.		

TASK STEPS AND PERFORMANCE MEASURES	GO	NO-GO
(e) To add depth and extend capabilities within sector.		
(f) When continuous observation of threat elements allows ground forces to displace to subsequent positions.		
g. Coordinate employment of the BCT/BN to accomplish the mission. Take the following actions:		
(1) Assign units to observe, identify, and report enemy actions.		
(2) Dispatch liaison officers (LNO) as required.		
(3) Coordinate for additional combat, sustainment assets for augmentation, as required.		
(4) Employ protection elements, such as engineers, to provide support to maneuver elements.		
(5) Designate aviation screen lines for aviation unit(s).		
h. Plan for air and ground integration.		
i. Plan for use of organic and supporting sensor.		
j. Plan for positioning of mission command elements such as command posts and trains.		
k. Designate which unit has responsibility for the area between the screening force rear boundary and the screen forces AO.		
l. Designate graphic control measures that include:		
(1) Initial screen line and forward line of own troops (FLOT).		
(2) Subsequent screen lines as phase lines (PL).		
(3) Passage of lines, graphics, and infiltration lanes.		
(4) Left and right limits of the screen as well as a PL for the rear boundary.		
(5) AOs or boundaries for subordinate elements.		
(6) Rally points, linkup points, contact points, and checkpoints.		
(7) Direct locations for unit(s) observation posts (OP) on approaches of major concern. They take the following actions:		
(a) Designate NAIs and assigns observation responsibilities.		
(b) Position electronic warfare (EW) collection assets, if available.		
(8) Named areas of interest (NAI) and target areas of interest (TAI).		
m. Annotate unit graphic control measures using higher HQ FRAGO overlay as a guide, and disseminates graphics to subordinate units.		
n. Establish engagement criteria according to:		
(1) Size of enemy force.		
(2) Formation or type of enemy unit.		
(3) Location of enemy unit.		
o. Integrate and synchronize warfighting functions based on the mission variables of mission, enemy, terrain and weather, troops and support available, time available and civil considerations (METT-TC). Take the following actions:		
(1) Plan fire support (FS) that:		

TASK STEPS AND PERFORMANCE MEASURES	GO	NO-GO
(a) Synchronizes fires to only report, disrupt, and destroy/delay enemy forces and protect all screen force positions.		
(b) Assigns priority of fires (artillery and mortars) or nonlethal effects and priority of targets.		
(c) Plans direct and indirect fires, attack aviation, and close air support (CAS).		
(d) Plans obscuration fires as required, dependent on mission, enemy, terrain and weather, troops and support available, time available, and civil considerations (METT-TC).		
(e) Plans deception fires, as necessary.		
(f) Develops fire support coordinating measures (FSCM) such as no fire areas (NFA) to facilitate control and prevent fratricide.		
(g) Integrates EW with indirect fires and maneuver to disrupt and deceive the enemy.		
(h) Synchronizes terrain management for the movement and positioning of artillery elements.		
(i) Conducts a time-distance analysis, covering the enemy's probable rate of advance and the time of flight of artillery or mortars, to synchronize indirect fires.		
(2) Develop scheme of engineer operations to support scheme of maneuver, and update engineering overlay data that:		
(a) Ensures terrain visualization products from the higher HQ are available and distributed.		
(b) Integrates obstacle intelligence (OBSTINTEL) requirements into the priority information requirements (PIR) and reconnaissance and surveillance plan.		
(c) Ensures confirmed OBSTINTEL is immediately disseminated to all BCT/BN and supporting elements.		
(d) Designs obstacles forward to delay enemy reconnaissance elements temporarily and assists in their destruction.		
(e) Identifies required mobility tasks throughout the depth of the BCT/BN AO or axis.		
(f) Plans SCATMINE systems for flank security and hasty defense as required.		
(g) Plan engineer mobility operations to maintain MSRs.		
(3) Plan CBRN defense support. Take the following actions:		
(a) Integrate CBRN reconnaissance assets into the reconnaissance and surveillance plan.		
(b) Ensure CBRN reconnaissance assets are positioned to quickly detect enemy use of CBRN at anticipated times and locations.		
(c) Develop a plan or required adjustments to SOP to disseminate CBRN threats to all BCT/BN and supporting elements immediately upon detection.		

TASK STEPS AND PERFORMANCE MEASURES	GO	NO-GO
(d) Integrate and synchronize the use of smoke to support critical actions.		
(e) Coordinate immediate and thorough decontamination plans based on the commander's priorities and vulnerability analysis, and disseminates planned and active sites.		
(f) Plan for alternate routes, collection points, and aid stations for evacuation of contaminated casualties and equipment.		
(4) Plan and coordinate air and missile defense (AMD) support. Take the following actions:		
(a) Integrate short-range air defense (SHORAD) and high-to-medium altitude air defense (HIMAD) employment considerations.		
(b) Ensure adequate AMD coverage of the BCT/BN during movement to screen location.		
(c) Plan for increased AMD coverage of areas where the BCT/BN is most vulnerable to air attacks, such as movements through restrictive terrain.		
(d) Prioritize AMD coverage of the BCT/BN based on the high risk of attack because of criticality, vulnerability, recoupment, and threat. High risk elements include trains, CPs, LOGPACs and AAs.		
(5) Plan logistics to maintain a continuous sustainment during all operations. Take the following actions:		
(a) Integrate the movement and positioning of the BCT/BN support unit(s) and attached sustainment assets with the scheme of maneuver.		
(b) Integrate refueling, rearming, and resupply operations with the scheme of maneuver.		
(c) Ensure adequate support to reconnaissance elements.		
(d) Keep maintenance assets and other support teams well forward.		
(e) Considerations include pre-positioning limited amounts of ammunition, POL, and barrier material in centrally located forward positions and on subsequent positions in depth.		
(f) Plan supply routes to all BCT/BN element's locations.		
(g) Plan immediate support to high-risk operations.		
(h) Plan and coordinates casualty evacuation assets.		
(i) Establish drop points for movement of key supplies.		
(j) Plan on-order control measures, logistics release points (LRP), unit maintenance collection points (UMCP), and ambulance exchange points (AXP).		
p. Develop contingency plan for contact with the enemy prior to reaching initial screen line.		
q. Conduct composite risk management. (Refer to Task 71-8-5145, Conduct Composite Risk Management [Battalion–Corps].)		
r. Plan movement of units performing flank screen.		
s. Plan limited visibility surveillance requirements.		

TASK STEPS AND PERFORMANCE MEASURES	GO	NO-GO
t. Coordinate for air and ground unit(s) passage of lines, if necessary.		
5. The commander and staff publish the order and distribute throughout the BCT/BN.		
Prepare		
6. The BCT/BN prepares for the screening mission. They take the following actions:		
a. Refine the plan based on continuously updated intelligence.		
b. Conduct extensive reconnaissance.		
c. Conduct rehearsal(s) during daylight and periods of reduced visibility, if possible.		
d. Position forces.		
Execute		
7. The BCT/BN executes the screen. They take the following actions:		
a. Move to and occupy initial screen line.		
b. Establish OPs along or slightly forward of the initial screen line as dictated by terrain. Units take the following actions:		
(1) Occupy assigned positions.		
(2) Reconnoiter forward of ground positions or reconnoiters terrain hard to reach by ground vehicles.		
(3) Conduct patrols between OPs and in areas that cannot be observed as the situation permits.		
c. Maintain contact with the protected force.		
d. Maintain continuous surveillance of enemy elements in the AO. Take the following actions:		
(1) Orient units on enemy reconnaissance and main body AAs.		
(2) Report all observed enemy activity.		
e. Detect and report all enemy ground elements attempting to pass through the screen.		
f. Allow no enemy ground element to pass through the screen undetected and unreported.		
g. Provide early warning to the screened force. Take the following actions:		
(1) Impede and harass the enemy with supporting indirect fires.		
(2) Employ indirect fire whenever possible.		
(3) Employ direct fire, if necessary, to accomplish mission.		
(4) Report any activity in the AO by spot reports (SPOTREP).		
(5) Avoid becoming decisively engaged.		
h. Maintain contact with the enemy once contact is made.		
i. Destroy, defeat, or repel all enemy reconnaissance patrols using available systems and support.		
j. Impede and harass the enemy using available systems and support.		
k. Determine the direction of threat movement.		

TASK STEPS AND PERFORMANCE MEASURES	GO	NO-GO
l. Displace units to the subsequent screen lines on order. Take the following actions:		
(1) Maintain enemy contact while displacing.		
(2) Deploy on subsequent screen line and continues to screen.		
(3) Report enemy activities even while displacing.		
m. Ensure units conduct patrols between OPs, and in areas that cannot be observed, as the situation permits.		
n. Use all available night and thermal observation devices and electronic surveillance devices during periods of limited visibility.		
o. If conducting a moving screen, take the following actions:		
(1) For screening a flank of the protected unit, the BCT/BN occupies a series of successive screens that maintain the time and distance factors of the main body commander.		
(2) For advance or rear screens, the BCT/BN moves its units in the AO using extended zone reconnaissance (advance screen) or extended delay (rear screen) techniques.		
(3) Maintain same speed as protected force.		
(4) Maintain same distance from protected force.		
(5) Employ air elements and sensors to assume screen mission during ground movement.		
(6) Use preplanned routes to subsequent position unless prevented by enemy situation.		
p. Maintain continuous communication with subordinate elements and higher HQ.		
q. Comply with ROE.		
Assess		
* 8. The commander and staff maintain SU and control movement of the screen; on order, conduct battle handover and rearward passage of lines with main body; and prepare for subsequent missions. They take the following actions:		
a. Direct elements to move, on order, to successive screen lines.		
b. Use FRAGOs and graphic control measures to direct the moves.		
c. Direct elements to report when they occupy new screen lines or OPs.		
d. Consolidate as necessary. (Refer to Task 07-6-5037, Conduct Consolidation [Battalion–Brigade].)		
e. Reorganize as necessary. (Refer to Task 07-6-5082, Conduct Reorganization [Battalion–Brigade].)		
f. Continue operations as directed.		

* indicates a leader task step.

SUPPORTING COLLECTIVE TASKS

Task Number	Task Title
07-6-1036	Conduct Delay (Battalion-Brigade)
07-6-5037	Conduct Consolidation (Battalion–Brigade)
07-6-5082	Conduct Reorganization (Battalion–Brigade)
17-6-3809	Conduct Battle Handover (Battalion-Brigade)
17-6-9222	Conduct a Guard (Battalion-Brigade)
17-6-9314	Conduct Zone Reconnaissance (Battalion-Brigade)
71-8-2210	Perform Intelligence Preparation of the Battlefield (Battalion–Corps)
71-8-2300	Coordinate Intelligence, Surveillance, and Reconnaissance ISR Effort (Battalion–Corps)
71-8-5110	Plan Operations using the Military Decision-making Process (Battalion–Corps)
71-8-5111	Conduct the Military Decision-making Process (Battalion-Corps)
71-8-5145	Conduct Composite Risk Management (Battalion–Corps)

TASK: Conduct Battle Handover (Battalion - Brigade) (17-6-3809)

(FM 3-90.6)   (FM 3-90)

CONDITIONS: During full spectrum operations, the brigade combat team (BCT) or battalion (BN) is required to conduct a battle handover (BHO) with a force to its front or rear. The BCT/BN may be the moving or stationary force. If stationary, it is positioned to provide security, indirect fire support (FS), and direct FS to the moving force during the BHO. If moving, the BCT/BN will receive security, indirect FS, and sustainment from the stationary force after coordination has been made. The BHO may or may not be conducted under pressure. The BCT/BN has established communications with higher, adjacent, subordinate, and supporting elements. The BCT/BN receives guidance on the rules of engagement (ROE). Military, civilian, joint and multinational partners, and news media may be present in the operational environment (OE). Some iterations of this task should be performed in mission-oriented protective posture (MOPP) 4.

TASK STANDARDS: The BCT/BN coordinates with the other force per higher headquarters (HQ) order, exchanges all required or specified information, and reports any discrepancies to the higher HQ. The BCT/BN conducts BHO in accordance with (IAW) the criteria established by the higher HQ. All communication and reporting are IAW applicable standing operating procedures (SOP). The BCT/BN completes BHO at the location and time specified by the controlling higher HQ.

TASK STEPS AND PERFORMANCE MEASURES	GO	NO-GO
Plan		
* 1. The BCT/BN leaders gain and/or maintain situational understanding (SU) using available communications equipment, maps, intelligence summaries, situation reports (SITREPs), and other available information sources. Intelligence sources include human intelligence (HUMINT), signal intelligence (SIGINT), and imagery intelligence (IMINT) to include unmanned aircraft systems (UASs).		
* 2. The BCT/BN commander and staff receive an order or anticipate a new mission and begin the military decision-making process (MDMP). (Refer to Task 71-8-5110, Plan Operations using the Military Decision-making Process.)		
Note: Each maneuver battalion coordinates the BHO with the security force to their front. This coordination overlaps the coordination for the passage of lines (POL), and so the battalion should conduct the two simultaneously. They take the following actions:		
a. Update the joint common database and common operational picture (COP), providing current SU to provide timely and accurate information for intelligence preparation of the battlefield (IPB) and the planning process.		
b. Confirm the specified tasks, location, and timing of the BHO with common higher HQ.		
c. Coordinate and exchanges information, orders, and control measures, (such as the civilian considerations, battle handover line [BHL], contact points, ROE, routes, and where forces will pass through) with the other HQ.		
d. Conduct IPB, with emphasis on influencing factors (Refer to Task 71-8-2210, Perform Intelligence Preparation of the Battlefield [Battalion–Corps].)		
e. The S-2 coordinates location and criteria for reconnaissance handover with other forces by:		
(1) Coordinating redundant surveillance and an integrated COP to assist maintaining contact during handover.		

TASK STEPS AND PERFORMANCE MEASURES	GO	NO-GO
(2) Coordinating criteria for target acquisition handover.		
(3) Providing the commander with a projection of enemy locations, strength, and activities during the period of the handover.		
(4) Confirming and/or determining terrain, weather, and light factors that will influence the handover and providing the estimate to S-3.		
f. The fires cell coordinates criteria for FS handover with other forces. They take the following actions:		
(1) Exchange FS plans to include:		
(a) Essential fire support tasks (EFST).		
(b) Attack guidance and priority of fires.		
(c) Target lists and overlay.		
(2) Coordinate fire support coordination measures (FSCM) and criteria for activation and/or shifting with other force. Take the following actions:		
(a) Coordinate fire lines (CFL).		
(b) Restrict fire line (RFL).		
(c) Designate no fire areas (NFA).		
(d) Restrict fire areas (RFA).		
(3) Coordinate additional FS requirements as required. Take the following actions:		
(a) Assign priorities, final protective fires (FPF), and requests of preplanned targets.		
(b) Coordinate position areas for artillery (PAA).		
(4) Establish criteria to trigger FS handover.		
(5) Assure adequate FS during the transfer of responsibility and passage of lines or relief operation that occurs during handover.		
g. The S-3 coordinates criteria for BHO with other forces. They take the following actions:		
(1) Coordinate control measures to support handover and passage of lines, to include:		
(a) Contact point(s) location(s) for linkup with other force.		
(b) Passage points, lanes, and routes.		
(c) Air corridors for aviation elements.		
(d) Assembly areas (AAs) or attack positions.		
(2) Prepare a liaison team for collocation with the other unit.		
(3) Assure timely collocation of tactical command posts (CP) or command groups of the BCT/BN and other units if feasible.		
(4) Coordinate far- and near-range recognition signals.		
(5) Coordinate actions on contact.		
(6) If applicable, determine method to break contact and order of withdrawal.		
(7) Coordinate details of the POL or relief operation, including:		

TASK STEPS AND PERFORMANCE MEASURES	GO	NO-GO
(a) Timing for transfer of command and support.		
(b) Exact locations of routes, contact points, passage points, and AAs/attack positions.		
(c) Exact details of command relationships during the handover.		
h. The executive officer (XO) coordinates transfer or acceptance of mission command of elements prior to the BHO between the BCT/BN and other HQ as necessary, including:		
(1) Establishing direct liaison with other units.		
(2) Arranging for reception and briefing of liaison teams from the other unit.		
i. The XO or S-3 determines requirements to collocate CPs or command groups as necessary by:		
(1) Designating CPs to collocate.		
(2) Coordinating location and timing for collocation.		
j. The S-6 establishes communications and exchanges Internet protocol (IP) addresses, frequency modulation (FM) and/or enhanced position location and reporting system (EPLRS) frequencies, communications security (COMSEC) key, and/or signal operation instructions (SOI) with forward/follow-on/security force as necessary.		
k. The S-3 specifies responsibilities and procedures for integrating specific units into the digital network if necessary. They take the following actions:		
(1) Update locations and status of units.		
(2) Provide locations of key elements to those units.		
(3) Provide key information to specific units.		
l. The S-3 reports discrepancies or planning to the higher HQ for resolution.		
m. The S-4 coordinates the movement of sustainment elements to move as early as possible to avoid hampering the movement of combat forces.		
n. The BCT/BN engineer coordinator coordinates to determine the status of obstacles, routes and protected positions in the vicinity of the BHL.		
o. Conduct composite risk management. (Refer to Task 71-8-5145, Conduct Composite Risk Management [Battalion–Corps].) The senior commander specifies the following in the order(s):		
(1) Acceptable risk to the security force.		
(2) Disengagement criteria in quantifiable terms, such as—		
(a) Friendly strength level.		
(b) Time.		
(c) Event.		
Prepare		
* 3. The BCT/BN command and staff exercise mission command of the BHO. They take the following actions:		
a. The staff establishes communications with the forward/rearward force. They take the following actions:		
(1) Dispatch and receive liaison teams.		

TASK STEPS AND PERFORMANCE MEASURES	GO	NO-GO
(2) Enter other unit's nets (such as command, operations and intelligence O[&I], and FS).		
(3) Ensure acceptance of task organization and connectivity within the digital network.		
b. The main CP or tactical CP collocates with forward/rearward force CP or command group as necessary.		
c. The S-3 section uses appropriate systems to update the COP, disseminating information between the forward/rearward force and/or the common higher HQ, and receives as a minimum:		
(1) Current enemy activity to include location, composition, disposition, and feasible courses of action (COA). Take the following actions:		
(a) If moving, report direction of movement, formation, and estimated rate of advance.		
(b) If defending, report orientation; obstacle locations; perceived engagement areas (EA); flanks; proposed breach sites, if applicable; and reserves, if known.		
(2) Answer the forward/rearward commander's critical information requirements (CCIR).		
(3) Friendly actions to include location, size, and activities of combat and sustainment elements.		
(4) Ongoing reconnaissance operations and status of area surveillance with respect to purpose for observation.		
(5) Locations and orientation of fires for stationary units supporting the BHO and POL.		
(6) Fire mission requests, status, and availability.		
(7) Activation of contact points for guides.		
(8) Shifting of additions or modifications to control measures.		
(9) If applicable, locations of obstacles, lanes, and degree of marking IAW order and/or SOP.		
(10) If applicable, tracks and disseminates positions and status of supporting units.		
d. The fires cell coordinates activation and/or shifting of FSCMs as necessary. They take the following actions:		
(1) Ensure all subordinate and supporting elements acknowledge changes to FSCMs.		
(2) Ensure forward/rearward forces and the common higher HQ acknowledge changes to FSCMs.		
e. The BCT/BN engineer coordinator (ENCOORD) establishes contact with the ENCOORD of the other unit, tracks the mobility-countermobility situation, and plans for the use of combat engineer support for the handover.		
f. The staff coordinates transfer of mission command of elements between the BCT/BN and other HQ IAW order and/or SOP. They take the following actions:		

TASK STEPS AND PERFORMANCE MEASURES	GO	NO-GO
(1) Ensure BCT/BN elements have established communications with the gaining HQ prior to BHO.		
(2) Establish contact with elements for which the BCT/BN is accepting mission command prior to BHO.		
g. The S-3 confirms manning of contact or linkup points to coordinate passage or bypass with forward/follow-on/security force.		
h. The liaison officer (LNO) or liaison team coordinates with other HQ, as applicable, to include:		
(1) Establishing voice and digital communications.		
(2) Coordinating with staff sections to answer requests for information (RFI) and providing additional information on BCT/BN operations. Take the following actions:		
(a) Describe the commander's intent.		
(b) Describe CCIR.		
(c) Describe the scheme of maneuver to include sequence and timing of critical events.		
(d) Describe operations security (OPSEC) and deceptive activities.		
(3) Sharing or disseminating enemy and friendly situation updates.		
(4) Alerting the BCT/BN of significant events, changes to the other commander's CCIR, and forwarding intelligence reports and products.		
(5) Conducting linkup procedures at contact points.		
(6) Confirming POLs and/or BHO coordination.		
Execute		
4. The BCT/BN accepts BHO from a forward stationary or moving force IAW the order and/or SOP. They take the following actions:		
a. Prepare for BHO. Take the following actions:		
(1) If applicable, subordinate units occupy defensive or support by fire positions behind the BHL to provide direct FS for the withdrawing forward force.		
(2) If applicable, collocate designated CPs.		
(3) Establish air reconnaissance in the area of the handover, if applicable.		
b. The XO/S-3 accepts reconnaissance handover when criteria are met. They take the following actions:		
(1) Coordinate movement and/or positioning of BCT/BN elements to accept reconnaissance and/or target handover from an advantageous position. They consider the following:		
(a) Name areas of interest (NAI).		
(b) Preplan targets.		
(c) Determine high-payoff targets (HPT) and/or enemy/threat forces in contact.		

TASK STEPS AND PERFORMANCE MEASURES	GO	NO-GO
(2) Establish air and ground surveillance of designated areas and/or acquire enemy/threat forces based on the information requirements, CCIR, and attack guidance.		
c. The XO/S-3 accepts BHO when criteria are met. They take the following actions:		
(1) Ensure the BCT/BN accepts mission command of any forward force elements forward of the BHL until released.		
(2) Report and receive acknowledgement of BHO within the BCT using maneuver control system (MCS), Force XXI battle command brigade and below (FBCB2), and voice communications.		
(3) Report BHO completion to common higher HQ using MCS and voice communications.		
5. The BCT/BN conducts BHO with a follow-on force IAW order and/or SOP. They take the following actions:		
a. Prepare for the BHO. Take the following actions:		
(1) Subordinate units occupy defensive or support by fire positions to provide direct FS to the follow-on force as necessary.		
(2) Man contact and traffic control points and position guides as necessary.		
(3) Continue reconnaissance operations to maintain contact with enemy forces or surveillance of designated areas to provide information and answer the follow-on forces—		
(a) Information requirements (IR).		
(b) Priority intelligence requirements (PIR).		
(c) Locations of HPTs.		
(4) Establish restrictive FSCMs around reconnaissance elements and/or observation posts (OP) beyond the BHL, as required.		
(5) Establish voice and digital communications with the follow-on force, as necessary.		
(6) If applicable, collocate designated CPs.		
b. The XO/S-3 conducts reconnaissance handover with the accepting HQ when criteria are met. They take the following actions:		
(1) Provide guides and control movement and/or positioning of follow-on reconnaissance elements to accept reconnaissance and/or target handover, to include:		
(a) NAIs.		
(b) Preplanned targets.		
(c) HPTs and/or enemy/threat forces in contact.		
(2) Conduct reconnaissance handover when the follow-on force acknowledges it is observing designated locations and/or has gained contact with designated enemy forces.		
c. The XO/S-3 conducts BHO with accepting HQ when criteria are met. They take the following actions:		
(1) Coordinate movement of follow-on forces behind the BHL until BHO.		

TASK STEPS AND PERFORMANCE MEASURES	GO	NO-GO
(2) Report and receive acknowledgement of BHO within the BCT/BN using MCS, FBCB2, and voice communications.		
(3) Report BHO completion to common higher HQ using MCS and voice communications.		
6. The BCT/BN conducts BHO with a stationary force to its rear IAW order and/or SOP. They take the following actions:		
a. Prepare for the BHO. Take the following actions:		
(1) Confirm stationary force has occupied positions to provide overwatch and assist the rearward passage of lines.		
(2) Assure that air corridors are current and available for aviation elements.		
(3) Coordinate advance positioning of artillery units behind the BHL and movement of sustainment elements.		
(4) Employ indirect fires to suppress enemy in contact and screen friendly movement.		
(5) Control disengagement of subordinate units while maintaining contact using reconnaissance elements.		
b. The XO/S-3 conducts reconnaissance handover with accepting HQ when criteria are met. They take the following actions:		
(1) Guide and control movement and/or positioning of stationary reconnaissance elements forward of the BHOL to gain contact or initiate surveillance to include:		
(a) NAIs.		
(b) Preplanned targets.		
(c) HPTs and/or enemy forces in contact.		
(2) Ensure withdrawing elements establish contact with stationary force forward reconnaissance elements.		
(3) Maintain surveillance of enemy forces until stationary force elements confirm redundant surveillance is ongoing.		
(4) Conduct reconnaissance handover when the follow-on force acknowledges it is observing designated locations and/or has gained contact with designated enemy forces.		
c. The XO/S-3 conducts BHO with accepting HQ when criteria are met. They take the following actions:		
(1) Control movement of stationary forces forward of the BHL until BHO.		
(2) Report and receives acknowledgement of BHO within the BCT/BN using MCS, FBCB2, and voice communications.		
(3) Report BHO completion to common higher HQ using MCS and voice communications.		
7. During battle handover, the fires cell conducts FS handover with accepting HQ when criteria are met. They take the following actions:		
a. Coordinate movement and positioning of artillery assets prior to FS handover to ensure responsive fires from all supporting artillery assets.		

TASK STEPS AND PERFORMANCE MEASURES	GO	NO-GO
b. Control movement and guides positioning as necessary stationary force target acquisition assets to assume surveillance of designated targets IAW the FS plan and/or attack guidance.		
c. Establish or shifts FSCMs as required.		
d. Account for stationary force EFSTs and attack guidance in executing fires.		
e. Process calls for fire by the forward, follow-on, and/or stationary forces until FS handover.		
f. Conduct FS handover when criteria are met.		
8. During battle handover, the BCT/BN ENCOORD confirms that gaps or lanes through friendly force obstacles are open for the duration of the handover, closed at its duration, and status reported to moving units.		
Assess		
* 9. The BCT/BN leaders assess the operation. They take the following actions:		
a. Monitor the situation during all phases of the operation.		
b. Direct adjustments to ensure that operations remain aligned with the commander's intent.		
8. The BCT/BN consolidate as necessary. (Refer to Task 07-6-5037, Conduct Consolidation [Battalion-Brigade]).		
9. The BCT/BN reorganize as necessary. (Refer to Task 07-6-5082, Conduct Reorganization [Battalion-Brigade]).		
10. The BCT/BN continue operations as directed.		

* Indicates a leader task step.

Task Number	Task Title
07-6-5037	Conduct Consolidation (Battalion-Brigade)
07-6-5082	Conduct Reorganization (Battalion-Brigade)
07-6-1081	Conduct a Passage of Lines as Passing Unit (Battalion-Brigade)
07-6-1082	Conduct a Passage of Lines as a Stationary Unit (Battalion-Brigade)
17-6-1007	Control Intelligence, Surveillance, and Reconnaissance (ISR) Operations (Battalion-Brigade)
71-8-2210	Perform Intelligence Preparation of the Battlefield (Battalion–Corps)
71-8-5110	Plan Operations Using the Military Decision-making Process (Battalion-Corps)
71-8-5123	Task Organize for Operations (Battalion-Corps)
71-8-5145	Composite Risk Management (Battalion–Corps)

TASK: Conduct Mobility, Countermobility, and or Survivability (Battalion-Brigade) (07-6-6082)

(FM 3-90.6)   (FM 3-90.5)   (FM 3-34)

CONDITIONS: The brigade combat team (BCT) or battalion (BN) is conducting operations independently or as part of a higher headquarters (HQ) and receives an operation order (OPORD) or fragmentary order (FRAGO) to conduct a mission (offensive or defensive) at a specified time and location. All necessary personnel and equipment are available. The BCT/BN has communications with higher, adjacent, subordinate, and supporting elements. The unit is provided guidance by the rules of engagement (ROE) and may also have mission instructions such as a peace mandate, terms of reference, and status-of-forces agreement (SOFA). Military, civilian, joint and multinational partners, and news media may be present in the operational environment (OE). Some iterations of this task should be performed in mission-oriented protective posture (MOPP) 4.

TASK STANDARDS: The BCT/BN conducts mobility, countermobility, and/or survivability operations in accordance with (IAW) the standing operating procedures (SOPs), the order, and/or higher commander's guidance. The BCT/BN integrates and synchronizes warfighting functions based on the factors of mission, enemy, terrain and weather, troops and support available, time available, and civil considerations (METT-TC).The BCT/BN conducts extensive reconnaissance of enemy and friendly approaches, routes, and terrain. The BCT/BN executes engineer tasks IAW the commander's intent. The BCT/BN sites obstacles to provide force protection or breaches obstacles to provide freedom of maneuver. The BCT/BN complies with the ROE, mission instructions, higher HQs' orders, and other special orders. All communication and reporting is IAW the applicable SOP.

TASK STEPS AND PERFORMANCE MEASURES	GO	NO-GO
Plan		
* 1. The BCT/BN leaders gain and/or maintain situational understanding (SU) using available communications equipment, maps, intelligence summaries, situation reports (SITREPs), and other available information sources. Intelligence sources include human intelligence (HUMINT), signal intelligence (SIGINT), and imagery intelligence (IMINT) to include unmanned aircraft systems (UASs).		
* 2. The BCT/BN commander and staff receive an order or anticipate a new mission and begin the military decision-making process (MDMP). (Refer to Task 71-8-5110, Plan Operations using the Military Decision-Making Process [Battalion – Corps].) They take the following actions:		
a. Conduct a map reconnaissance.		
b. Update the joint common database and common operational picture (COP), and provide current SU to disseminate timely and accurate information for intelligence preparation of the battlefield (IPB) and the planning process.		
c. Conduct intelligence preparation of the battlefield (IPB). (Refer to Task 71-8-2210, Perform Intelligence Preparation of the Battlefield [Battalion – Corps].)		
d. Organize the unit to accomplish the mission. (Refer to Task 71-8-5123, Task Organize for Operations [Battalion – Corps].) Take the following actions:		
(1) Designate the main effort as required.		
(2) Augment engineer support.		
(3) Designate the shaping efforts.		
(4) Designate a breach element as required.		
(5) Designate an assault element as required.		

TASK STEPS AND PERFORMANCE MEASURES	GO	NO-GO
(6) Designate a reserve as necessary and or as directed.		
e. Integrate and synchronize warfighting functions based on the factors of METT-TC. Take the following actions:		
(1) Synchronize fires. Take the following actions:		
(a) Coordinate fires to suppress, neutralize, or destroy critical enemy forces that most affect the unit's mission.		
(b) Assign priority of fires (artillery and mortars) or nonlethal effects and priority of targets.		
(c) Plan obscuration fires as required.		
(d) Plan deception fires to deceive the enemy as necessary.		
(e) Plan fires to support the reconnaissance effort.		
(f) Plan fires to cover friendly obstacles.		
(g) Plan and coordinate indirect fires and/or close air support (CAS), for approaching enemy or to delay and neutralize repositioning enemy forces and reserves.		
(h) Plan locations of critical friendly zones (CFZ) to protect critical actions such as support forces, breaching efforts, and artillery assets to prevent fratricide.		
(2) Synchronize engineer support. Take the following actions:		
(a) Confirm terrain visualization products from higher HQs are available and distributed for planned breach sites, possible bypasses, defending enemy positions or key weapons, and or friendly support-by-fire (SBF) positions.		
(b) Integrate obstacle intelligence (OBSTINTEL) requirements into the priority intelligence requirements (PIR) and reconnaissance and surveillance (R&S) plan.		
(c) Confirm OBSTINTEL receive immediate unit-wide dissemination, including supporting maneuver and sustainment units.		
(d) Identify required mobility tasks throughout the depth of the unit zone or axis.		
(e) Plan adequate mission command to rapidly shift priority of effort and support to reinforce success or respond to a changing situation.		
(f) Plan scatterable mine (SCATMINE) systems for flank security and hasty defense as required.		
(g) Develop a scheme-of-obstacle overlay and obstacle-execution matrix IAW the mission.		
(3) Plan to support defensive operations. Take the following actions:		
(a) Develop a plan that focuses on maintaining the unit's freedom of maneuver.		
(b) Plan an obstacle system that not only attacks the enemy where desired but also assists counterattacks and facilitates future operations IAW the commander's intent.		

TASK STEPS AND PERFORMANCE MEASURES	GO	NO-GO
(c) Identify critical engineer tasks early.		
(d) Develop operations security (OPSEC) measures and a specific counter reconnaissance plan. (Both prevent premature disclosure of the defense and are essential.)		
(e) Task organize engineers to support a rapid transition to the offense.		
(f) Designate engineers to support the reserve.		
(g) Plan obstacles to support spoiling attacks and counterattacks.		
<u>1.</u> Position situational obstacles early and link them to natural and other manmade obstacles.		
<u>2.</u> Integrate triggers for the execution of situational and reserve obstacles in the decision support template (DST).		
(h) Designate engineers not held in reserve but who are committed and working on the commander's priority tasks.		
(i) Plan obstacles for forward deployed forces.		
(j) Clear counterattack routes of obstacles.		
(k) Prepare breaches through friendly obstacles.		
(l) Construct combat roads and trails for counterattacks and lateral movement between fighting positions.		
(m) Plan breaching and assault-bridging operations for reserves or the counterattack force.		
(n) Plan multiple obstacle locations to support depth and flexibility in the defense.		
(o) Ensure adequate security for obstacle emplacement systems.		
(p) Focus the countermobility effort to cause the enemy to maneuver into engagement areas (EAs) where the BCT intends to kill them.		
(q) Ensure adequate mobility support for withdrawing security forces, the reserve, the counterattack force, and the repositioning of MBA forces.		
(r) Ensure the integration of survivability priorities for critical systems and units through the development and implementation of an execution matrix and timeline.		
(4) Plan to support offensive operations. Take the following actions:		
(a) Develop plan that focuses on sustaining the offense's momentum.		
(b) Integrate a highly mobile engineer force well forward into maneuver formations.		
(c) Designate engineers or maneuver elements that are responsible for reporting and marking lanes or bypasses through or around obstacles.		
(d) Identify engineer equipment such as replacement bridges for armored launchers, follow-on tactical bridging, lift capability for mine-clearing line charge (MICLIC) reloading, and lane-marking materials to replenish marking systems.		
(e) Plan for combined-arms obstacle-breaching rehearsals to ensure that all elements involved were synchronized.		

TASK STEPS AND PERFORMANCE MEASURES	GO	NO-GO
(f) Identify general engineering requirements that will increase during offensive combat since lines of communications (LOCs) would lengthen.		
(g) Plan for an on-call rapid-mining and rapid-obstacle emplacement capability that is essential for flank security.		
(h) Designate engineers to emplace obstacles rapidly to protect attacking forces from enemy counterattacks once on the objective.		
(i) Plan for a transition to the defense.		
(5) Synchronize air defense (AD) support. Take the following actions:		
(a) Coordinate adequate AD of the unit during movement.		
(b) Shift assets as required by phase of the operation.		
(c) Plan for increased AD coverage of areas where the unit is most vulnerable to air attacks such as during breaching operations or movements through restrictive terrain.		
f. Conduct composite risk management. (Refer to Task 71-8-5145, Conduct Composite Risk Management [Battalion–Corps].)		
* 3. The BCT/BN commander and staff conduct a confirmation briefing with subordinates to ensure subordinates understand commander's intent and concept.		
Prepare		
4. The BCT/BN prepares for the mission. They take the following actions:		
a. Refine the plan based on continuously updated intelligence.		
b. Conduct extensive reconnaissance of enemy and friendly approaches, routes, and terrain. Locate obstacles to determine:		
(1) Size and boundaries.		
(2) Composition and breaching requirements.		
(3) Gaps and bypass routes.		
(4) Detection of enemy weapons covering each obstacle.		
(5) Available amount of cover and concealment on routes and approaches.		
(6) Best terrain for sighting friendly obstacles.		
c. Conduct precombat checks.		
d. Supervise staff MDMP/subordinate troop-leading procedures to ensure planning and preparations are on track and consistent with the unit commander's intent.		
e. Conduct rehearsals during day and limited visibility if possible.		
f. Position forces IAW the plan.		
Execute		
5. The BCT/BN executes area defense tasks IAW the commander's intent. They take the following actions:		
a. Retain centralized control over engineer elements and their resources.		
b. Withdraw engineers to work on subsequent defenses in depth once the battle is underway.		
c. Emplace tactical obstacles to:		

TASK STEPS AND PERFORMANCE MEASURES	GO	NO-GO
(1) Force the enemy into engagement areas (EAs).		
(2) Block the enemy from further advance.		
(3) Block the enemy from using avenues of approach that would allow him to avoid the main defense.		
(4) Fragment the enemy force and allow the defender to deal with only a small portion of the enemy at a time.		
6. The BCT/BN breaches obstacles. They take the following actions:		
a. Report all friendly obstacles and enemy obstacles that impact friendly maneuver and/or movement. Locations of breaches are reported to the higher headquarters.		
b. Breach quickly considering the size and coverage of the obstacle.		
c. Mark lanes and distribute information within unit.		
d. Guide follow-on elements through the breach.		
7. The BCT/BN conducts survivability actions whenever the unit stops. They take the following actions:		
a. Position all vehicles in full defilade positions and use available concealment and camouflage.		
b. Protect all dismounted Soldiers against indirect fire.		
c. Confirm all vehicles have alternate and supplementary positions and cover routes as time allows.		
8. The BCT/BN conducts deliberate survivability actions whenever the unit stops for longer than eight hours.		
Assess		
* 9. The BCT/BN leaders assess the operation. They take the following actions:		
a. Monitor continuously the situation and the progress of the operation.		
b. Direct adjustments to ensure that operations remain aligned with the commander's intent.		
10. The BCT/BN consolidates as necessary. (Refer to Task 07-6-5037, Conduct Consolidation [Battalion – Brigade].)		
11. The BCT/BN reorganizes as necessary. (Refer to Task 07-6-5082, Conduct Reorganization [Battalion – Brigade].)		
12. The BCT/BN continues operations as directed.		

* indicates a leader task step.

Task Number	Task Title
05-2-1025	Provide Support for Mobility Operations
05-2-1701	Conduct Route Clearing Operations
05-3-1016	Perform a Route Classification
05-6-0092	Plan Engineer Countermobility Operations
05-6-0125	Plan Engineer Mobility requirements in the Area of Operation (AO)

Task Number	Task Title
07-2-1396	Employ Obstacles (Platoon-Company)
07-2-1477	Breach an Obstacle (Platoon-Company)
07-6-1252	Conduct a Combined Arms Breach of an Obstacle (Battalion - Brigade)
07-6-5037	Conduct Consolidation (Battalion – Brigade)
07-6-5082	Conduct Reorganization (Battalion – Brigade)
71-8-5110	Plan Operations using the Military Decision-Making Process (Battalion – Corps)
71-8-5123	Task Organize for Operations (Battalion – Corps)
71-8-5145	Conduct Composite Risk Management (Battalion – Corps)

TASK: Conduct Area Security (Battalion - Brigade) (07-6-1272)

(FM 3-90.6)   (FM 3-07)   (FM 3-07.1)

CONDITIONS: The brigade combat team (BCT) or battalion (BN) is conducting operations independently or as part of a higher headquarters (HQ) and receives an operation order (OPORD) or fragmentary order (FRAGO) to conduct area security operations at a specified location and time. The order requires the BCT/BN to establish a reserve force. All necessary personnel and equipment are available. The BCT/BN has communications with higher, adjacent, subordinate, and supporting elements. Local populace and factions may or may not be cooperative. The BCT/BN is provided guidance by the rules of engagement (ROE) and may also have mission instructions, such as a peace mandate, terms of reference, and status of forces agreement (SOFA). Military, civilian, joint and multinational partners and news media may be present in the operational environment (OE). Some iterations of this task should be performed in mission-oriented protective posture (MOPP) 4.

TASK STANDARDS: The BCT/BN conducts area security operations in accordance with (IAW) the SOP, the order, and/or higher commander's guidance. The BCT/BN maintains stability and reacts to hostile actions. The commander and staff establish priorities for protection of civil and/or military personnel, facilities, installations, and key terrain within the area of operation (AO). The commander designates a reserve force. All required overlays and graphics are provided in digital format and all communication and reporting is IAW the applicable SOP. The unit complies with the ROE, mission instructions, higher HQ order, and other special orders.

TASK STEPS AND PERFORMANCE MEASURES	GO	NO-GO
Plan		
* 1. The BCT/BN leaders gain and/or maintain situational understanding (SU) using available communications equipment, maps, intelligence summaries, situation reports (SITREPs), and other available information sources. Intelligence sources include human intelligence (HUMINT), signal intelligence (SIGINT), and imagery intelligence (IMINT) to include unmanned aircraft systems (UASs).		
2. The BCT/BN commander and staff receive an order or anticipate a new mission and begin the military decision-making process (MDMP). (Refer to Task 71-8-5110, Plan Operations using the Military Decision-making Process [Battalion-Corps].) They take the following actions:		
a. Conduct a digital or conventional map reconnaissance.		
b. Update the joint common database and common operational picture (COP), and provide current SU to disseminate timely and accurate information for intelligence preparation of the battlefield (IPB) and the planning process.		
c. Identify the following mission focus factors:		
(1) The enemy.		
(2) The force being protected.		
(3) A protected asset.		
(4) Any combination of above.		
d. Conduct IPB, with emphasis on influencing factors. (Refer to Task 71-8-2210, Perform Intelligence Preparation of the Battlefield [Battalion–Corps] for further details.) The following factors are considered:		
(1) The natural defensive characteristics of the terrain.		
(2) Existing roads and waterways for military lines of communication and civilian commerce.	.	

TASK STEPS AND PERFORMANCE MEASURES	GO	NO-GO
(3) The control of land and water areas and avenues of approach surrounding the area to be secured, extending to a range beyond that of enemy artillery, rockets, and mortars,		
(4) The control of airspace.		
(5) The proximity to critical sites such as airfields, power generation plants, and civic buildings.		
(6) Sources external to the BCT AO causing instability in the local population.		
e. Determine what the enemy is capable of and what they prefer to do in like situations if unconstrained in the AO.		
f. Identify force requirements to execute the mission.		
g. Provide the following to subordinate elements that will accomplish security missions:		
(1) Purpose of mission.		
(2) Special constraints.		
(3) Unique tasks associated with the mission.		
(4) Updates to local situation.		
(5) Additional guidance as required.		
(6) Necessary attachments and special equipment.		
(7) Rules of engagement..		
h. Establish a reserve by taking the following actions:		
(1) Designate the reserve element.		
(2) Designate control measures.		
(3) Define linkup procedures.		
(4) Identify conditions for employment.		
i. Identify force protection requirements.		
j. Identify special equipment requirements.		
k. Establish performance criteria for continuous patrolling and reconnaissance.		
l. Establish route clearance and control measures.		
m. Plan checkpoints and or roadblocks.		
n. Determine documentation to be presented by persons passing through a checkpoint, roadblock, or other access controlled area.		
o. Establish priorities for protection of civil and or military personnel, facilities, installations, and key terrain within the AO.		
p. Integrate and synchronize warfighting functions based on the mission variables of mission, enemy, terrain and weather, troops and support available, time available and civil considerations (METT-TC). They take the following actions:		
(1) Synchronize fires. Take the following actions:		
(a) Plan for use of smoke and other nonlethal munitions.		
(b) Plan triggers for suppression and smoke.		

TASK STEPS AND PERFORMANCE MEASURES	GO	NO-GO
(c) Assign priority of fires (artillery and mortars) or nonlethal effects and priority of targets.		
(d) Plan fires to support the reconnaissance effort.		
(e) Plan locations of critical friendly zones (CFZ) to protect critical assets and to prevent fratricide.		
(2) Synchronize engineer support. Take the following actions:		
(a) Ensure terrain visualization products from higher HQ are available and distributed.		
(b) Identify survivability tasks.		
(c) Identify required mobility tasks throughout the depth of the unit zone or axis.		
(d) Integrate obstacle intelligence (OBSTINTEL) requirements into the priority intelligence requirements (PIR) and reconnaissance plan.		
(e) Confirm OBSTINTEL is immediately disseminated to all BCT/BN units and supporting elements.		
(f) Plan adequate mission command to rapidly shift priority of effort and support to reinforce success or respond to a changing situation.		
(3) Plan and coordinate air defense (AD) support, (if support has been provided by the BCT/BN).		
(4) Plan for increased AD coverage of areas where the unit was most vulnerable to air attacks such as movement through restrictive terrain.		
q. Plan Soldier and leader engagements with the local population and media.		
r. Conduct composite risk management. (Refer to Task 71-8-5145, Conduct Composite Risk Management [Battalion–Corps].)		
* 3. The BCT/BN commander and staff conduct confirmation briefings with subordinates immediately after OPORD is issued to ensure subordinates understand commander's intent and concept.		
Prepare		
4. The BCT/BN prepare for security operations. They take the following actions:		
a. Refine the plan based on continuously updated intelligence.		
b. Conduct extensive reconnaissance operations.		
c. Provide intelligence requirements to patrols, observation posts (OPs) and other U.S. elements operating in the AO.		
d. Coordinate for liaison officers, local guides, and interpreters as required.		
e. Coordinate fire support plans with adjacent or supported units.		
f. Coordinate for augmentations such as civil military detachments, military police teams, military working dogs, and tactical HUMINT teams.		
g. Conduct precombat checks as required.		
h. Supervise subordinate troop-leading procedures to ensure planning and preparations are on track and consistent with the unit commander's intent.		

TASK STEPS AND PERFORMANCE MEASURES	GO	NO-GO
i. Conduct rehearsals during day and limited visibility if possible.		
Execute		
5. The BCT/BN executes security operations. They take the following actions:		
a. Assign sub element AOs.		
b. Establish zones of separation if necessary.		
c. Conduct civil military operations (CMO) activities as required.		
d. Implement plans to protect civil and/or military personnel, facilities, installations, and key terrain.		
e. Supervise subordinate elements in support of and conduct of area security missions that may consist of:		
(1) Area, route, or zone reconnaissance.		
(2) Screen.		
(3) Attack.		
(4) Perimeter defense.		
(5) Battle positions.		
(6) Convoy and route security.		
(7) High value asset security (including fixed site security and personal security detachments).		
(8) Combat outposts.		
(9) Security patrols with host nation forces.		
(10) Stability tasks, such as:		
(a) Ensure liaison/negotiation and establish civil-military operations centers.		
(b) Secure activities/projects for civil-military operations.		
(c) Conduct compliance inspections.		
(d) Support presence operations (i.e., supporting company/platoon checkpoints, presence patrols).		
(11) Deliver supplies or render humanitarian aid.		
(12) React to civil disturbance.		
(13) React to media.		
(14) Ensure leader and Soldier engagements with the local population.		
Assess		
6. The BCT/BN leaders assess the operation. They take the following actions:		
a. Monitor continuously the situation and the progress of the operation.		
b. Direct adjustments to ensure that operations remained aligned with the commander's intent.		
7. The BCT/BN consolidates as necessary. (Refer to Task 07-6-5037, Conduct Consolidation [Battalion – Brigade].)		

TASK STEPS AND PERFORMANCE MEASURES	GO	NO-GO
8. The BCT/BN reorganizes as necessary. (Refer to Task 07-6-5082, Conduct Reorganization [Battalion – Brigade].)		
9. The BCT/BN continues operations as directed.		

* indicates a leader task step.

SUPPORTING COLLECTIVE TASKS

Task Number	Task Title
01-6-0436	Coordinate Air-Ground Integration and the Close Combat Attack
05-1-1006	Plan for Counter-IED (C-IED) Operations (UNCLASSIFIED/FOR OFFICIAL USE ONLY) (U//FOUO)
06-5-5082	Establish Fire Support Operations
06-6-5066	Employ Lethal Fires in Support of the BCT
07-6-1225	Employ a Reserve Force (Battalion - Brigade)
07-6-5037	Conduct Consolidation (Battalion – Brigade)
07-6-5082	Conduct Reorganization (Battalion – Brigade)
07-6-6073	Secure Civilians During Operations (Battalion - Brigade)
17-6-0308	Synchronize Close Air Support (Battalion - Brigade)
17-6-1007	Control Intelligence, Surveillance, and Reconnaissance (ISR) Operations (Battalion - Brigade)
71-8-2210	Perform Intelligence Preparation of the Battlefield (Battalion – Corps)
71-8-5110	Plan Operations using the Military Decision-Making Process (Battalion – Corps)
71-8-5145	Conduct Composite Risk Management (Battalion – Corps)

TASK: Secure Civilians During Operations (Battalion-Brigade) (07-6-6073)

(FM 3-19.4)   (FM 3-90.6)

CONDITIONS: The brigade combat team (BCT) or battalion (BN) is conducting operations independently or as part of a higher headquarters (HQ). The BCT or BN receives an operation order (OPORD) or fragmentary order (FRAGO) to secure civilians and protect them from injuries that could occur during BCT/BN full spectrum operations. The civilians may be refugees and some may be inhabitants of the area in which the BCT/BN is operating. Some civilians may be openly hostile toward friendly forces. The BCT/BN has communications with higher, adjacent, subordinate, and supporting elements. The BCT/BN receives guidance on the rules of engagement (ROE). Military, civilian, joint, and multinational partners and news media may be present in the operational environment (OE).

TASK STANDARDS: The BCT/BN secures civilians during operations in accordance with (IAW) standing operating procedures (SOP), the order, and/or higher commander's guidance. The BCT/BN identifies and segregates combatants and non-combatants, searches them, safeguards them, and moves them out of the immediate area of operations (AO). The BCT/BN complies with ROE.

TASK STEPS AND PERFORMANCE MEASURES	GO	NO-GO
Plan		
* 1. The BCT/BN leaders gain and/or maintain situational understanding (SU) using available communications equipment, maps, intelligence summaries, situation reports (SITREPs), and other available information sources. Intelligence sources include human intelligence (HUMINT), signal intelligence (SIGNINT), and imagery intelligence (IMINT) to include unmanned aircraft systems (UASs).		
* 2. The BCT/BN commander and staff receive an order or anticipate a new mission and begin the military decision-making process (MDMP) for securing the civilians. (Refer to Task 71-8-5110, Plan Operations using the Military Decision-making Process [Battalion–Corps].) They take the following actions:		
a. Conduct a map reconnaissance if not familiar with the AO.		
b. Organize the unit to accomplish the mission. (Refer to Task 71-8-5123, Task Organize for Operations [Battalion–Corps], for further details.) Take the following actions:		
(1) Identify security elements.		
(2) Identify search elements.		
(3) Identify guard elements.		
c. Conduct intelligence preparation of the battlefield (IPB). (Refer to Task 71-8-2210, Perform Intelligence Preparation of the Battlefield [Battalion–Corps].)		
d. Request interpreters to help interface with the local populace if necessary.		
e. Develop control measures for expected or unexpected situations.		
f. Designate an intermediate collection point to assist with large numbers of civilians.		
g. Coordinate for additional warfighting functions assets as required.		
h. Integrate and synchronize warfighting functions based on the mission variables of mission, enemy, terrain and weather, troops and support available, time available, and civil considerations (METT-TC).		
i. Select and designate methods of communications.		

TASK STEPS AND PERFORMANCE MEASURES	GO	NO-GO
j. Plan casualty evacuation.		
k. Develop a media plan.		
l. Conduct composite risk management. (Refer to Task 71-8-5145, Conduct Composite Risk Management [Battalion–Corps].)		
3. The BCT/BN commander and staff conducts confirmation briefings with subordinates immediately after OPORD is issued to ensure subordinates understand commander's intent and concept.		
Prepare		
4. The BCT/BN prepare for the mission. They take the following actions:		
a. Refine the plan based on continuously updated intelligence.		
b. Conduct extensive reconnaissance IAW the commander's intent.		
c. Conduct precombat checks IAW the commander's intent.		
d. Supervise staff MDMP/subordinate troop-leading procedures to ensure planning and preparations are on track and consistent with the unit commander's intent.		
e. Conduct rehearsals if possible.		
f. Position forces IAW the plan.		
Execute		
5. The BCT/BN executes the mission. They take the following actions:		
a. Establish and maintains 360 degree and three-dimensional security in the AO in which civilians have gathered.		
b. Segregate civilians identified as being combatants or suspected war criminals and treat them like enemy prisoners of war (EPWs).		
c. Search civilians and keeps identification papers with civilians under all circumstances, regardless of status.		
d. Restrain and detain noncombatants who do not follow instructions. Take the following actions:		
(1) Safeguard noncombatants and provides humane but firm treatment at all times.		
(2) Move noncombatants away from fire fights and the immediate combat area.		
e. Provide food, water, and medical attention based upon the medical ROE for civilian medical treatment.		
f. Assign guards to escort civilians out of the immediate AO to a processing and reception station or to an intermediate collection point.		
g. Report this situation and status in a timely manner to higher HQ..		
h. Give proper consideration to the situation of the press and local officials following ROE guidance as to whether the local civilians and officials are to be considered friendly, hostile, or uncertain.		
6. The BCT/BN intelligence section processes combatants and or suspected war criminals as EPWs, IAW the OPORD, FRAGO, SOP, or other guidance. They take the following actions:		

TASK STEPS AND PERFORMANCE MEASURES	GO	NO-GO
a. Process captured documents.		
b. Process captured material and equipment.		
c. Coordinate with the unit logistics officer to evacuate captured material, equipment, and EPWs.		
d. Identify and report time sensitive information to higher HQ immediately using a SPOTREP with at least an IMMEDIATE precedence.		
Assess		
* 7. The BCT/BN leaders assess the operation by taking the following actions:		
a. Continuously monitor the situation and the progress of the operation.		
b. Ensure civilians are treated with respect.		
c. Enforce ROE.		
d. Ensure elements understand procedures for dealing with news media.		
e. Use FRAGOs and graphic control measures as necessary to ensure that operations remain aligned with the commander's intent.		
8. The BCT/BN consolidates as necessary. (Refer to Task 07-6-5037, Conduct Consolidation [Battalion–Brigade].)		
9. The BCT/BN reorganizes as necessary. (Refer to Task 07-6-5082, Conduct Reorganization [Battalion–Brigade].)		
10. The BCT/BN continues operations as directed.		

* indicates a leader task step.

SUPPORTING COLLECTIVE TASKS

Task Number	Task Title
07-3-9022	Conduct a Security Patrol
07-6-5037	Conduct Consolidation (Battalion – Brigade)
07-6-5082	Conduct Reorganization (Battalion – Brigade)
19-3-3107	Process Detainee(s) at Point of Capture (POC)
71-8-2210	Perform Intelligence Preparation of the Battlefield (Battalion – Corps)
71-8-5110	Plan Operations using the Military Decision-Making Process (Battalion – Corps)
71-8-5123	Task Organize for Operations (Battalion – Corps)
71-8-5145	Conduct Composite Risk Management (Battalion – Corps)

TASK: Conduct Lines of Communication Security (Battalion - Brigade) (17-6-9406)

(FM 3-20.96)   (FM 3-90)   (FM 3-90.6)

CONDITIONS: The brigade combat team (BCT) or battalion (BN) is ordered to secure lines of communication (LOC) in a division, corps, or joint task force (JTF) rear area. The forward units may be occupying a noncontiguous area of operation (AO). All necessary personnel and equipment are available. The BCT/BN may be augmented with a rotary-wing aviation element. The BCT/BN has communications with higher, adjacent, subordinate, and supporting elements. All overlays and graphics are provided. Military, civilian, joint and multinational partners, and news media may be present in the operational environment (OE). Contact is possible. The BCT/BN received guidance on the rules of engagement (ROE). Some iterations of this task should be conducted during limited visibility. Some iterations of this task should be performed in mission-oriented protective posture (MOPP) 4.

TASK STANDARDS: The BCT/BN coordinates the LOC security mission with the higher headquarters (HQ). The BCT/BN conducts initial route reconnaissance and establishes a screen, patrols, and defensive positions along the route(s). Units establish combat outposts and/or patrols to overwatch critical points, bases/base clusters, choke points, and bridges along the route(s). The BCT/BN aviation assets perform reconnaissance, security, attack, and defensive operations in support of the BCT/BN. The BCT/BN establishes a reserve or quick reaction force (QRF) at BCT/BN and/or lower echelon level to respond to threat actions. The BCT/BN conducts convoy security missions along the route(s). All communication and reporting are in accordance with (IAW) applicable standing operating procedures (SOP). The BCT/BN complies with the ROE.

TASK STEPS AND PERFORMANCE MEASURES	GO	NO-GO
Plan		
* 1. The BCT/BN leaders gain and/or maintain situational understanding (SU) using available communications equipment, maps, intelligence summaries, situation reports (SITREPs), and other available information sources. Intelligence sources include human intelligence (HUMINT), signal intelligence (SIGINT), and imagery intelligence (IMINT) to include unmanned aircraft systems (UASs).		
* 2. The BCT/BN commander and staff receive an order of a new mission and begin the military decision-making process (MDMP). (Refer to Task 71-8-5110, Plan Operations using the Military Decision-Making Process [Battalion – Corps].) They take the following actions:		
a. Develop a reconnaissance plan and deploy reconnaissance assets. Develop a plan that focuses on:		
(1) The enemy.		
(2) The force being protected.		
(3) A protected asset.		
Or		
(4) Any combination of the following:		
b. Employ reconnaissance units and MI units early in the MDMP process. (Refer to Task 71-8-2300, Coordinate Intelligence, Surveillance, and Reconnaissance ISR Effort [Battalion – Corps].)		
c. Coordinate with higher HQ and adjacent units to obtain required intelligence products and other terrain products.		

TASK STEPS AND PERFORMANCE MEASURES	GO	NO-GO
d. Conduct a map reconnaissance of all assigned routes and the terrain that controls those routes.		
e. Update the joint common database and common operational picture (COP) providing current SU, to provide timely and accurate information for intelligence preparation of the battlefield (IPB) and the planning process.		
f. Integrate and synchronize warfighting functions based on the mission variables of mission, enemy, terrain and weather, troops and support available, time available and civil considerations (METT-TC).		
g. Conduct IPB. (Refer to Task, 71-8-2210, Perform Intelligence Preparation of the Battlefield [Battalion – Corps].)		
h. Develop and disseminate the situation template (SITEMP) that includes:		
(1) Location and orientation of enemy forces in the rear area, including irregular and special operations forces.		
(2) Weapons and tactics of the enemy.		
(3) Attitudes of civilians in the rear area and their willingness to support or cooperate with enemy forces		
(4) Locations of choke points, ambush sites, and possible obstacles along the route(s).		
(5) Enemy air avenues of approach (AA).		
i. Plan for convoy escort. Take the following actions:		
(1) Organize convoy security into advance guard, security, escort elements, and reaction force.		
(3) Coordinate the following with escorted elements:		
(a) Current threat situation to include paramilitary and criminal organizations.		
(b) Threat trends and recent activities.		
(c) Potential ambush sites.		
(d) Civilian traffic situation, to include refugees and potential congested areas.		
(e) Route conditions, choke points, and off-road trafficability.		
(4) Designate movement order, vehicle distances, and march rates.		
(5) Designate locations of leaders, communications, medical support, and critical weapons systems within the convoy.		
(6) Plan actions at danger and congested areas.		
(7) Plan the following actions on contact to include escorted vehicles and the security element, escort element, and QRF:		
(a) Indirect fire and air attack.		
(b) Obstacles clearance or bypass.		
(c) Sniper fire.		
(d) Near and far ambush.		
(e) Civilian demonstrations and disturbances.		

TASK STEPS AND PERFORMANCE MEASURES	GO	NO-GO
j. Establish a reserve by:		
(1) Designating the reserve element.		
(2) Designating control measures.		
(3) Defining linkup procedures.		
(4) Identifying conditions for employment.		
k. Coordinate with the higher HQ rear area command post (CP) for:		
(1) Routes and movement schedules.		
(1) Known or suspected friendly/enemy activity.		
(2) Existing obstacles or contamination that affects the LOCs.		
(3) Choke points that may canalize movement.		
(4) Location of bridges, over/underpasses, and past ambush sites.		
(5) Frequencies and call signs.		
(6) Status of host nation police or military forces in the rear area.		
l. Conduct composite risk management (CRM). (Refer to Task 71-8-5145, Conduct Composite Risk Management [Battalion – Corps].)		
Prepare		
3. The BCT/BN prepares to conduct LOC security. They take the following actions:		
a. Refine the plan based on continuously updated intelligence.		
b. Conduct extensive reconnaissance.		
c. Conduct rehearsal during daylight and periods of reduced visibility, if possible.		
e. Complete task organization.		
f. Position forces.		
Execute		
4. The BCT/BN conducts route security missions IAW area commander's guidance and METT-TC. (Refer to Task 07-2-1450 Secure Routes [Platoon – Company].)		
5. Units conduct convoy security missions IAW area commander's guidance and METT-TC. They take the following actions:		
a. Conduct route reconnaissance in advance of convoy.		
b. Accept and transfer control of security of the convoy to the designated organization at the specified location.		
c. Clear route by reducing obstacles, defeating threat ambushes and attacks, or controlling civilians.		
d. Units conduct convoy escort and defend convoy against ambushes and attacks. They take the following actions:		
(1) Reconnaissance element conducts route reconnaissance.		
(2) Security element organizes to conduct advance, rear guard, and flank screens.		
(3) Escort element disperses throughout the march order.		
(4) Reserve or QRF is positioned where it can best react to threat based on terrain and trafficability.		

TASK STEPS AND PERFORMANCE MEASURES	GO	NO-GO
(5) The BCT/BN aviation elements, if available, take the following actions:		
(a) Reconnoiter in advance or to the flanks of the reconnaissance element.		
(b) Establish a moving flank screen for the convoy's main body.		
(c) Employ indirect fire support and coordinate close air support (CAS), as needed.		
(d) Serve as a reserve or QRF and responds to ambushes or attacks on convoys, bases, or checkpoints on the LOC.		
Assess		
6. The commander and staff conduct assessment throughout the mission. They take the following actions:		
a. Continuously monitor and update the COP and the progress of the operation.		
b. Direct adjustments to ensure that operations remain aligned with the commander's intent.		
7. The BCT/BN consolidates as necessary. (Refer to Task 07-6-5037, Conduct Consolidation [Battalion – Brigade].)		
8. The BCT/BN reorganizes as necessary. (Refer to Task 07-6-5082, Conduct Reorganization [Battalion – Brigade].)		
9. The BCT/BN continues operations as directed.		

* indicates a leader task step.

SUPPORTING COLLECTIVE TASKS

Task Number	Task Title
07-2-1450	Secure Routes (Platoon-Company)
07-6-5082	Conduct Reorganization (Battalion-Brigade)
17-6-1272	Conduct Area Security (Battalion - Brigade)
19-2-2401	Supervise the Establishment of Roadblocks and Checkpoints
19-3-1102	Conduct Route Reconnaissance and Surveillance
19-3-2406	Conduct Roadblock and Checkpoint
19-6-2406	Plan Roadblocks and Checkpoints (BCT PM)
63-6-2036	Develop the Operational Areas Security Plan
71-8-2210	Perform Intelligence Preparation of the Battlefield (Battalion – Corps)
71-8-2300	Coordinate Intelligence, Surveillance, and Reconnaissance ISR Effort (Battalion – Corps)
71-8-5110	Plan Operations using the Military Decision-Making Process (Battalion – Corps)
71-8-5145	Conduct Composite Risk Management (Battalion – Corps)
07-2-1450	Secure Routes (Platoon – Company)

TASK: Conduct Fire Support Planning Using MDMP (06-6-1118)

(FM 3-09.32)   (FM 3-0)

CONDITIONS: The Fires brigade, brigade combat team (BCT) is conducting the military decision-making process (MDMP) while preparing for or engaged in operations. Additional fire support agencies such as the tactical air control party (TACP) or air and naval gunfire liaison company (ANGLICO) are integrated into the Fires Cell. The BCT has established communications and digital connectivity via the Army Battle Command System (ABCS), when equipped, with subordinate, adjacent, and higher headquarters, and is passing information in accordance with (IAW) higher headquarters' and the BCT's standing operating procedures (SOP). Some iterations of this task should be performed in MOPP4.

TASK STANDARDS: The Fires Cell assisted in the development of intelligence preparation of the battlefield (IPB) and ISR planning to develop the ISR order. The Fires Cell conducted mission analysis and developed the scheme of fire support for all courses of action (COA). The Fires Cell revised the scheme of support during COA analysis and comparison. The Fires Cell recommended COA and completed the fire support plan. The Fires Cell produced the high-payoff target list (HPTL), essential tasks for fire support, attack guidance matrix (AGM), target selection standard (TSS), and the fire support annex (with overlay) for the BCT order.

TASK STEPS AND PERFORMANCE MEASURES	GO	NO-GO
NOTE: The task steps below will be accomplished using ABCS when indicated in the performance measures. When preformatted messages do not exist, free text messages may be substituted for other Force XXI Battle Command brigade and Below (FBCB2) and Maneuver Control System (MCS) messages identified in task steps and performance measures below.		
1. FSCOORD/DFSCOORD assists in the development of the initial intelligence preparation of the battlefield (IPB).		
NOTE: IPB is initiated upon receipt of intelligence products and driven by additional products and intelligence, surveillance, and reconnaissance (ISR) feeds. The battle staff assists the S2 in preparing the initial IPB; and although the performance measures are presented separately, they may be performed simultaneously with some of the following task steps.		
a. Participates in the IPB huddle to-		
(1) Receive information.		
(2) Define operational environment.		
(3) Update timelines.		
(4) Identify area of operation (AO) and area of interest (AOI).		
(5) Identify initial intelligence requirements.		
b. Gathers the following overlays and reports, via Advanced Field Artillery Tactical Data System (AFATDS), using the web browser and Common Operating Environment Message Processor (CMP) to establish a start point for AOI and performs initial analysis of the battlefield environment to include terrain and weather.		
(1) Brigade AO overlay, if available.		
(2) Fires brigade AOI overlays.		
(3) Modified combined obstacle overlay (MCOO).		

TASK STEPS AND PERFORMANCE MEASURES	GO	NO-GO
(4) Reports which identify the significant characteristics of the environment.		
(a) Transportation network (road specifications).		
(b) Natural or manmade obstacles.		
(c) Weather effects on terrain.		
(5) Potential position areas for artillery (PAA).		
c. Performs initial analysis of the battlefield's effects on enemy and friendly capabilities.		
(1) Cross country mobility.		
(2) Visibility.		
d. FSCOORD/targeting officer assists the S2 in evaluating the threat by providing the current information on the enemy and his fire support capabilities through All Source Analysis System (ASAS), AFATDS, and FBCB2; evaluates the threat to identify its doctrinal fire support capabilities.		
(1) Addresses known enemy artillery units and their capabilities that may affect the operation.		
(2) Addresses other assets such as mortar, air support, and naval gunfire that the enemy may employ.		
(3) Addresses enemy nuclear and chemical fire support capabilities.		
(4) Identifies recent trends in the way enemy fire support has been used based on battle damage assessment (BDA), observed fires and reports.		
(5) Identifies enemy fire support target acquisition and delivery systems locations capable of ranging the brigade AO.		
(6) Using the order of battle, identifies unaccounted fire support assets and likely areas the enemy fire support target acquisition and delivery systems are capable of ranging the brigade AO.		
(7) Fires Cell creates the AOI overlay as directed by the targeting officer on the common operational picture (COP)/Joint Common Database (JCDB) updates.		
(8) Fires Cell exports the AOI overlay to the S2 section for consolidation.		
e. Assists the S2 in the integration of enemy fire support into the enemy courses of action (ECOA) and initiates target value analysis (TVA) to identify high-value targets (HVT).		
(1) Assists S2 in developing enemy fire support template.		
(2) Integrates execution of enemy lethal and nonlethal fires into the ECOAs.		
(3) Considers target characteristics (such as composition, disposition, degree of protection, size, location, shape, and mobility).		
(4) Considers impact of terrain and weather on enemy employment and positioning of fires.		
(5) Identifies HVTs considering the ECOAs by identifying assets and capabilities the enemy commander requires.		
(6) Nominates named area of interest (NAI), targeted area of interest (TAI), and detection assets for inclusion in the BCT and ISR plan.		
f. Fires Cell tracks the status of fire support systems.		

TASK STEPS AND PERFORMANCE MEASURES	GO	NO-GO
g. Analyzes effects of IPB on fire support.		
2. FSCOORD initiates the planning process based on the receipt of warning order (WO) 1 or anticipated mission.		
NOTE: The MDMP commences with the receipt of a higher headquarters order or by direction of the commander or deputy commanding officer (DCO) anticipating a mission.		
a. Updates staff estimates and COP in AFATDS.		
b. Understands higher maneuver and fire support plan.		
c. Identifies refined AO and AOI.		
d. Receives commander's guidance for fire support.		
(1) Authorizes movement only to support any immediate requirements.		
(2) Initial intelligence requirements of mission analysis.		
e. Coordinates with the brigade operational law team (BOLT) on current rules of engagement (ROE) for indirect fire, or for requesting modification to the ROE, if applicable.		
3. FSCOORD assists in the ISR planning.		
NOTE: Initial ISR planning is conducted concurrently with IPB and the decision-making process. Developing the ISR plan may be considered an independent, simultaneous decision-making process. Although these performance measures are presented separately here, for training purposes they may be performed concurrently with the following task steps.		
a. Identifies ISR fire support requirements and conduct ISR mission analysis.		
(1) Higher headquarters tasks.		
(2) Additional support requirements.		
(3) Pre-positioning of field artillery (FA) assets.		
(4) Recommended essential tasks for fire support.		
b. Participates in the ISR huddle to receive the commander's ISR guidance and engagement criteria.		
c. Develops the fire support scheme of support.		
(1) Target acquisition plan.		
(a) Conducts time analysis.		
(b) Organizes and analyzes facts.		
(c) Identifies specified and implied tasks.		
(d) Identifies NAIs and TAIs.		
(e) Translates status of assets into capabilities.		
(f) Allocates/organizes assets (Strikers) to ensure redundancy.		
(g) Details observer to shooter criteria.		
(h) Establishes quick-fire net for observer to shooter.		
(2) PAAs for batteries.		
(3) Priority of fires.		
(4) Priority targets.		

TASK STEPS AND PERFORMANCE MEASURES	GO	NO-GO
(5) Fire support coordination measures (FSCM).		
(6) Deception plan.		
d. Participates in wargaming to analyze the ISR COAs.		
e. The commander or DCO approves the ISR plan.		
f. FSCOORD completes the ISR fire support plan and prepares fire support paragraph, with graphics and FSCMs, for ISR order.		
g. Participates as necessary in the ISR rehearsal.		
h. Revises the plan after rehearsals.		
4. The Fires Cell conducts mission analysis.		
NOTE: The BCT may receive additional higher headquarters WOs, intelligence feeds and summaries, and the OPORD during this step.		
a. During mission analysis, the FSCOORD/targeting officer determines known facts about fire support operations.		
NOTE: FSCOORD oversees and integrates all members of the fire support cell (TACP, SBCT ANGLICO team).		
(1) Determines BCT fire support missions from higher echelon orders.		
(2) Determines unit locations and capabilities/limitations with the assistance of BFT and AFATDS.		
(3) Determines ammunition availability and identifies discrepancies/shortfalls in controlled supply rate (CSR).		
(a) Amount of ammunition required for operations (required supply rate [RSR]).		
(b) Recent usage and trends.		
(c) CSR.		
(4) Organizes FA assets to support future operations and plans for their relocation and resupply, if necessary.		
(5) Determines electronic warfare (EW) asset requirements.		
b. FSCOORD participates in the facts/assumptions huddle.		
(1) Presents facts on friendly order of battle, fire support capabilities, and limitations, to include but not limited to-		
(a) Current fire support unit's status.		
(b) Higher headquarters fire support requirements.		
(c) CSR and RSR.		
(d) Unit locations.		
(e) Weapons capabilities.		
(f) Other fire support assets (CAS, naval gunfire, and mortars, EW. PSYOP, CMO, SOI, PAO). Addresses specific FA, air support, naval gunfire, and target acquisition assets/requirements to include their capabilities and limitations.		
(g) Fire support missions.		

TASK STEPS AND PERFORMANCE MEASURES	GO	NO-GO
(2) Presents assumptions on the availability, capabilities, and employment of target acquisition assets.		
(a) Projected fire support unit's status.		
(b) Possible follow-on support requirements.		
(3) Presents constraints.		
(a) FSCMs.		
(b) Munitions employment.		
(c) Target restrictions (FSCM, ROE, Social, Moral, Political).		
c. Determines fire support specified and implied tasks.		
(1) Specified.		
(2) Implied.		
(3) Support for higher headquarters planned fires.		
d. Participates in task huddle to present specified and implied tasks.		
e. BCT DCO conducts the targeting huddle to focus the targeting effort.		
NOTE: BCT commander receives support from the FSCOORD on all aspects of fire support planning, coordination, and synchronization with maneuver and the maneuvering of FA assets.		
(1) FSCOORD briefs recommended high-payoff targets (HPT) and impact of environmental effects (terrain and weather) based on initial TVA.		
(2) FSCOORD provides the following input to the commander:		
(a) Recommends essential tasks for fire support for operation to include task and purpose.		
(b) Recommends targets for engagement (type, location, and time).		
(c) Determines if recommended targets can be acquired.		
(d) Recommends delivery/attack system best suited for attack and ensures system meets established guidance (effects) and targeting objective with the least expenditure of ammunition, and sufficient ammunition by type is available to support the fire plan.		
(e) Recommends clearance-of-fires guidance.		
(f) Recommends, in coordination with the BOLT, changes to indirect fire ROE, if not addressed in the clearance-of-fire guidance.		
(3) Commander issues the following guidance:		
(a) Approves HPTs.		
(b) Approves draft essential tasks for fire support that must be accomplished by fires. This includes the "when" and "why" it must be accomplished in relation to other events in the battle.		
(c) How he intends to shape the battlespace with fires in terms of time and space.		
(d) The critical enemy formation or function that, if successfully attacked by fires, will lead most directly to mission accomplishment.		
(e) Target attack criteria to include target effects.		

TASK STEPS AND PERFORMANCE MEASURES	GO	NO-GO
(f) Desired effects for each critical fire support task. This will include a desired targeting objective.		
(g) BDA/MOE requirements.		
f. FSCOORD completes conventional TVA to complete the draft AGM. Develops the HPTL, AGM, and TSS protected target list and assists with the collection plan, in concert with the targeting team (DCO, S2, S3, engineers, air defense artillery [ADA], intelligence, electronic warfare [EW], and BOLT) considering the following:		
(1) Commander's essential tasks for fire support and target engagement priorities.		
(2) Accuracy of target location.		
(3) Engagement criteria.		
(4) Fire support status.		
(5) Fire support capabilities and limitations, to include weapons and munitions available.		
(6) Observers available.		
g. Provides the BCT S4 with an initial projection of ammunition required for the operations based on available information on possible targets and target types.		
h. Participates in the mission analysis brief.		
NOTE: Information previously briefed to the commander is not repeated.		
i. After mission analysis, the FSCOORD participates in the commander's huddle and provides recommendations for fire support to include-		
(1) Essential tasks for fire support that support the commander's intent. Essential tasks for fire support are expressed in terms of task, purpose, method, and effects.		
(2) Attack and engagement criteria.		
(3) Priorities for target engagement.		
(4) Purpose of fires (overall, by asset, and for special munitions such as smoke, illum, Copperhead, area denial artillery munition [ADAM]/remote anti-armor mine [RAAM]).		
(5) Allocation of assets to accomplish fire support tasks.		
(6) Restrictions. Includes FSCMs, AGM, TSS guidance, and the protected target list.		
(7) Nomination of initial HPTs, by phase, to support the essential tasks for fire support.		
(8) AFATDS database development, to include commander's guidance, filtering guidance, and screening guidance.		
j. Develops the AGM with HPTL and TSS protected target list and assists with the collection plan, in concert with the targeting team.		
k. Coordinates timing for fire support rehearsals with DCO and Fires battalion.		
l. Provides input to the S3 for the second WO.		
m. Passes information to direct support (DS) FA battalion tactical operations center (TOC) to allow the Fires battalion to start their planning process.		

TASK STEPS AND PERFORMANCE MEASURES	GO	NO-GO
5. During COA development, the FSCOORD, in coordination with the S3, develops the scheme of support of essential tasks for fire support for the operation, to include-		
NOTE: The FSCOORD may have to develop separate schemes of support for multiple COAs.		
a. Participates in the COA development and provides advice for the employment of fire support.		
(1) Where to find and attack essential tasks for fire support formation, the decisive point (where to mass the effects of combat power), and TVA.		
(2) Shaping and decisive operations (sketch of the broad concept of the operation).		
(3) The purpose of the shaping and decisive operations.		
(4) Revises specified and implied tasks based on requirements for shaping and decisive operations.		
b. Develops scheme of fire support.		
(1) Analyzes relative combat power by-		
(a) Arranging specified and implied tasks for shaping and decisive operations on the battlefield in time and space.		
(b) Analyzing friendly capabilities pertaining to the operation (combat and combat support).		
(c) Using battle calculus to test feasibility analyzing relative force fire support ratios (friendly versus enemy) necessary to achieve the tasks.		
(2) Identifies HVTs, with methods of engagement (maneuver, lethal, nonlethal) and desired effects, for tentative HPTs.		
(3) Selects tentative positions and allocation of sensors (radars, critical friendly zones [CFZ], call-for-fire zones, striker platoon, fire support team [FIST], and combat observation lazing team [COLT]) for the detect function of the targeting process.		
(4) Nominates FA movement techniques and position areas. Selects tentative positions, movement plans, and allocation of firing systems for the deliver function of the targeting process.		
(5) Prioritizes targets that should be attacked during shaping and decisive operations.		
(6) Quantifies effects (criteria of success) (MOE).		
(7) Selects tentative triggers for initiating delivery of fires, positioning of assets, or cuing radars.		
(8) Identifies FSCMs that facilitate the attack of targets.		
(9) Completes a tentative observation plan that addresses the detection of targets and the combat assessment of essential tasks for fire support.		
(10) Prioritizes initial targets/scheduling of fires needed to support each COA.		
(11) Coordinates the effort with aviation, engineer, electronic warfare, G3 air, naval gunfire liaison officer (LNO), IOWG, and TACP elements.		
(12) Allocates all fire support assets to include CAS and naval gunfire to meet the commander's intent and accomplish the essential tasks for fire support.		

TASK STEPS AND PERFORMANCE MEASURES	GO	NO-GO
(13) Allocates target and radar zones.		
(14) Establishes a no later than (NLT) time for targets to be added or refined.		
(15) Assists the S2 in collection plan refinement.		
c. FSCOORD participates in hasty wargame to determine the scheme of support feasibility and suitability of COAs.		
NOTE: S3 identifies the critical event/phase to be wargamed. Follow these performance measures for each event/phase wargamed.		
(1) Briefs essential tasks for fire support and HPTs with shaping and decisive operations.		
(2) Briefs FA organization for battle and allocation of FS resources at the start of wargaming for each COA.		
(3) FS section provides input to the S3 section Battlefield Planning and Visualization (BPV) or moves and positions FA elements during the event.		
(4) Describes target acquisition and execution of fires for shaping and decisive operations.		
(5) Briefs FSCMs.		
(6) Records results and adjusts or modifies the fire support plan as necessary.		
(a) Essential tasks for fire support and HPTL.		
(b) Scheme of support.		
(c) Organization for combat.		
(d) PAAs.		
(e) FSCMs.		
(7) Upon completion of wargaming, reviews branch options for each COA.		
d. If necessary, briefs the scheme of support during the COA brief.		
NOTE: Each wargaming session is conducted in a similar manner.		
(1) Essential tasks for fire support.		
(2) Fire support assets available (FA, FIST, radar, COLT, Fires Cells, brigade reconnaissance troop [BRT]).		
(3) FSCMs.		
(4) Units to receive priority of fires.		
(5) AGM with HPTs.		
(6) Draft concept of fires.		
(7) FA positioning and movement plan.		
(8) Fire support execution matrix (FSEM), that answers who, what, when, and where for planned fires and how they accomplish the essential tasks for fire support.		
(9) Draft target list worksheet and overlay.		
(10) Draft or modified target synchronization matrix (TSM).		
(11) Fires planned by and/or availability of fire from higher headquarters.		

TASK STEPS AND PERFORMANCE MEASURES	GO	NO-GO

(12) Collection/reconnaissance and surveillance plan.
 	
6. During COA analysis the BCT FSCOORD/targeting officer references the AGM, and TSS.
 	
    a. Receives the DCO's evaluation criteria and description.
 	
    b. Participates in hasty wargame to expand the scheme of support and identify advantages and disadvantages with each COA.
 	
NOTE: S3 identifies the critical event/phase to be wargamed. Follow these performance measures for each event/phase wargamed.
 	
    (1) Lists fire support critical events, decision points, essential tasks for fire support, FS TAIs, and HPTs.
 	
    (2) Briefs FA organization for battle and allocation of fire support resources at the start of wargaming for each COA.
 	
    (3) Fires Cell provides input to the S3 section BPV or moves and positions FA elements during the event.
 	
    (4) Describes and records the following:
 	
        (a) Identifies movement and displacement requirements for fire support delivery systems, and ensures that they are accounted for in the scheme of maneuver.
 	
        (b) Describes target acquisition and execution of fires for shaping and decisive operations.
 	
        (c) Describes integration of psychological operations (PSYOP) assets, chemical fires, electronic warfare (EW), CAS, air interdiction (AI), and naval gunfire support.
 	
        (d) Simulates engagement of attack systems against HPTs to determine volume and volley of fires, desired target effects, and BDA collection requirements.
 	
States the enemy vulnerabilities created by loss of certain functions and capabilities.
 	
        (e) The FSCOORD in conjunction with the S2, determines what targets on the list can be acquired by BCT assets and what targets are translated into requests to higher headquarters.
 	
    (5) Briefs FSCMs.
 	
    (6) Records results and adjusts or modifies the fire support plan as necessary:
 	
        (a) Essential tasks for fire support and HPTL.
 	
        (b) Scheme of support.
 	
        (c) Organization for combat.
 	
        (d) PAAs.
 	
        (e) FSCMs.
 	
        (f) Combat service support (CSS) requirements to include RSR and casualty evacuation (CASEVAC).
 	
    (7) AGM and FSEM with shaping and decisive operations.
 	
    (8) Target acquisition and TSS targeting.		

TASK STEPS AND PERFORMANCE MEASURES	GO	NO-GO
(9) Upon completion of wargaming, reviews branch options for each COA.		
c. Targeting officer coordinates the exchange of information between the brigade and the Fires battalion S2 and the Fires Cell. Specific functions performed are-		
(1) Determines specific target aspects and vulnerabilities, aided by the S2 and FSCOORD, to include target location error requirements and dwell times for viable attack.		
(2) States the enemy vulnerabilities created by loss of certain functions and capabilities.		
(3) Determines requirements for unmanned aerial vehicle (UAV) support.		
d. Analyzes results of hasty wargaming to provides an overall assessment of the supportability for each COA, including the relationship of time versus space and the ability of the available FS assets to accomplish the essential tasks for fire support.		
(1) Evaluates each COA against the stated evaluation criteria focusing on how well each COA accomplishes the critical tasks and effects.		
(a) Refines COAs based on fire support insights gained during wargaming process.		
(b) Rejects COAs based on fire support insights gained during wargaming process.		
(2) Fires Cell and targeting team record battlefield functional area (BFA) specific advantages and disadvantages of COA with emphasis on supportability for use in COA comparison.		
(3) Develops initial AGM for each COA to portray critical events in time and space.		
(4) Develops the initial FSEM.		
(5) Identifies fire support CSS assets required for all COAs.		
(6) Records fire support strengths and weaknesses for each COA, to include risk assessment to subordinate, supporting, and supported elements. Determines specific target aspects and vulnerabilities, aided by the S2 and FSCOORD, to include target location error requirements and dwell times for viable attack.		
7. FSCOORD conducts COA comparison.		
a. FSCOORD provides following fire support information for each COA during the comparison huddle-		
(1) FSCOORD evaluates the advantages and disadvantages of each COA from a fire support perspective.		
(a) Ensures that the FA will be able to accomplish the essential tasks for fire support.		
(b) Identifies fire support assets available.		
(c) Develops initial HPTL.		
(d) TSS.		
(e) Presents findings to staff members for consideration.		
(2) Scores each COA using the evaluation criteria.		

TASK STEPS AND PERFORMANCE MEASURES	GO	NO-GO
(a) Highlights COA advantages and disadvantages.		
(b) Provides analysis to the S3 section.		
b. Presents results during the COA decision brief.		
(1) Assists the DCO in choosing a recommended COA for presentation to the commander for the decision brief.		
(2) Has available--		
(a) Updated fire support estimate.		
(b) Advantages, disadvantages and supporting rationale for each COA.		
8. BCT commander approves COA and issues additional guidance, if necessary, and directs formal wargaming.		
a. Approves COA and HPTL.		
NOTE: FSCOORD follows the previous wargaming performance measures in completing the scheme of support.		
b. Participates in formal wargame to finalize and synchronize the scheme of support with the scheme of maneuver.		
(1) Ensures scheme of fires is synchronized with and supports the scheme of maneuver. This includes--		
(a) A clear sequence of essential tasks for fire support.		
(b) Triggers for the essential tasks for fire support.		
(c) Allocation of and positions for target acquisition.		
(d) FSCMs.		
(e) Specific attack systems and volleys of fire.		
(f) Detailed battlefield calculus of time and volume of fires required to accomplish the essential tasks for fire support - movement, ready-to-fire times, time to build up smoke, fire ADAM/RAAM mission, fire a battalion 6, shift from one target to the next-and identification of critical periods for fire support.		
(g) If necessary, planned targets from higher and adjacent units into the BCT plan.		
(h) Assigned primary and backup observers for all targets on the target list worksheet.		
(2) At the end of wargaming, provides an overall assessment of supportability for each COA, including the relationship of time versus space, and the ammunition or assets required. During the accelerated tactical decision-making process (TDMP), this step is accomplished after COA development.		
(3) Approves the HPTL developed by the DFSCOORD, S3, S2, air defense officer, assistant brigade engineer (ABE), air liaison officer (ALO), targeting officer, and BOLT.		
c. Wargames results--		
(1) Fires paragraph with essential tasks for fire support.		
(2) Fire support annex to include-		

TASK STEPS AND PERFORMANCE MEASURES	GO	NO-GO
(a) AGM.		
(b) Target list.		
(c) Target overlay.		
(d) TSM or modified TSM.		
d. Once the HPTL is approved, the FSCOORD ensures that fire planning and fire support requests are processed according to the BCT commander's guidance.		
e. Provides input for the third WO.		
f. Fire support noncommissioned officer (FSNCO) ensures the fire support operator inputs target data into AFATDS.		
g. Targeting officer facilitates the exchange of information between the BCT and the Fires battalion S2s and the Fires Cell. Specific functions he performs are-		
(1) Helps the S2 and the FSCOORD determine specific target aspects and vulnerabilities. This includes target location error requirements and dwell times for a viable attack. He and the S2 are responsible for producing the target selection standard for the BCT.		
(2) Coordinates intelligence and electronic warfare (IEW) targeting taskings with the supporting military intelligence (MI) unit and the MI battalion.		
(3) States the enemy vulnerabilities created by loss of certain functions or capabilities.		
(4) In coordination with the FSCOORD, consolidates, and distributes the restricted target list.		
(5) During operations, monitors compliance with the restrictions and reports incidents where the restrictions have been violated.		
h. The DCO ensures targeting requirements, confirmed during wargaming, are met to produce the HPTL, AGM, and TSS.		
9. Fires Cell completes the fire support plan and assists with orders production.		
a. Ensures the plan-		
(1) Contains the commander's guidance received after the mission analysis, including:		
(a) Concept of fires (overall, by asset, and for special munitions such as smoke, illum, Copperhead, ADAM/RAAM).		
(b) AGM.		
(c) HPTL.		
(d) TSS.		
(e) Essential tasks for fire support (task, purpose, method, and effects) for each phase that would support the commander's intent.		
(f) The organization combat and employment of munitions to accomplish all tasks.		
(2) Supports forces in contact.		
(3) Synchronizes the fire support systems in time and space with maneuver.		

TASK STEPS AND PERFORMANCE MEASURES	GO	NO-GO
(4) Prioritizes the effects of all indirect-fire assets, to include CAS and naval gunfire, to meet the commander's intent.		
(5) Allocates targets and zones.		
(6) Establishes a NLT time for targets to be added or refined.		
(7) Includes guidance on the employment of Fire Support Teams.		
(8) Contains guidance on suppression of enemy air defense (SEAD) (if applicable).		
(9) Details FSCMs.		
b. The detailed scheme of fires; targets; triggers; task, purpose, method, and effects for each target; primary and backup observers; and allocation of resources to accomplish each Essential task for fire support.		
c. FSCOORD prepares the fires portion of the concept of the operation paragraph for inclusion in the SBCT OPORD/operations plan (OPLAN).		
(1) Prepares fire support paragraph/annex for OPORD.		
(a) Purpose.		
(b) Priority.		
(c) Allocation.		
(d) Restrictions.		
(2) Submits fire support paragraph/annex with all accompanying matrixes/lists/graphics to the S3 for inclusion in the OPORD. Ensures the plan includes: FSEM, target list worksheet, and target overlay; and that they provide a detailed scheme of fires.		
(a) Fire support estimate.		
(b) Fire support annex to OPORD/OPLAN (Annex D).		
(c) Fire support overlay.		
(d) Target list matrix.		
(e) Essential task for fire support list.		
(f) HPTL.		
(g) Fire support execution matrix (FSEM).		
(3) Ensures the essential tasks for fire support are clearly stated by task, purpose, method, and effects (lethal and nonlethal).		
(4) Recommends decision criteria to shift from one essential task for fire support to the next and/or to shift the focus of fires from deep to close and/or from one task force to another.		
10. FSCOORD assists in revising plan after rehearsals.		
a. Participates in the combined arms, fire support, and service support rehearsals as necessary.		
b. Provides input for FRAGO, as necessary.		

* indicates a leader task step.

SUPPORTING COLLECTIVE TASKS

Task Number	Task Title
06-6-5059	Coordinate Target Attack
71-8-3310	Conduct Fires (Brigade – Corps)

TASK: Coordinate Air-Ground Integration and the Close Combat Attack (01-6-0436)

(FM 3-04.126)   (FM 3-0)   (AR 385-10)

CONDITIONS: A mounted coalition brigade combat team (BCT) is conducting the Military Decision-Making Process (MDMP) for a close combat attack. Aviation brigade assets are establishing a command and support relationship with the BCT. The BCT has established communications and digital connectivity via the Army Battle Command System (ABCS), when equipped, with the aviation brigade, BCT subordinates, adjacent, and higher headquarters. The BCT is passing information IAW higher headquarters' and the BCT's standing operating procedures (SOP). Some iterations of this task should be performed in MOPP4.

TASK STANDARDS: The aviation brigade received a warning order (WARNORD) to support the BCT in the close combat attack. The aviation brigade staff was integrated into the BCT planning and the MDMP. Airspace utilization conflicts were resolved. The aviation brigade OPCON assets were integrated into the mounted BCT scheme of maneuver and employed IAW the BCT commander's intent. The air mission commander (AMC) performed the correct actions en route to the objective and during mission execution. The aviation team provided accurate aerial weapons delivery and there were no fratricide casualties or equipment damage to friendly units as a result of close combat fire support.

TASK STEPS AND PERFORMANCE MEASURES	GO	NO-GO
NOTE: If equipped, the task steps below may be accomplished using ABCS if applicable. Units without ABCS will follow unit SOPs. When pre-formatted messages do not exist, free text messages may be substituted for Force XXI Battle Command brigade and Below (FBCB2) and Maneuver Control System (MCS) messages identified in task steps and performance measures.		
* 1. The aviation brigade commander and staff directly coordinate with the mounted BCT commander and staff, to gain knowledge of the ground tactical plan.		
a. The commanders visualized how the battlefield will look at various stages and develop a scheme of maneuver.		
b. The staffs war-gamed enemy COAs at critical points and developed integrated aviation-ground COAs to maintain the initiative.		
c. The aviation brigade commander received and reviewed the BCT's air-ground integration SOP for close combat attack and made recommendations as appropriate.		
d. The aviation brigade commander recommended that fully qualified aviation liaison officers (LNOs) participate in the BCT MDMP and related staff planning.		
e. The aviation brigade commander requested a ground LNO join the aviation brigade staff.		
NOTE: The aviation brigade commander must implement an LNO certification program at home station to ensure that aviation LNOs are proficient in the full spectrum of air-ground integration. Fully qualified aviation LNOs should be captain career course graduates and have pilot-in-command (PC) experience. They should possess a strong knowledge of the aircraft and the units in the aviation brigade.		
* 2. The aviation brigade commander and staff obtain the minimum planning requirements required to better integrate aviation into the BCT ground scheme of maneuver and ensure accurate and timely support.		

TASK STEPS AND PERFORMANCE MEASURES	GO	NO-GO
NOTE: If equipped, digital transmission of information, such as coordinates, is faster and more accurate; however, voice communication is still necessary for clarification.		
a. Plotted the BCT friendly forces' locations, enemy air defense artillery (ADA) locations, tentative engagement area (EA) coordinates, and the BCT area of operations (AO).		
b. Received the BCT and battalion level graphics via MCS, or aviation mission planning system (AMPS), or radio communications to update critical items including limit of advance (LOA), fire-control measures, and maneuver graphics.		
c. Received fire support coordination information including location of direct support (DS) artillery, organic mortars, call signs, and frequencies.		
d. Identified routes into and out of the AO including air passage points into sector or zone, and air routes to the holding area (HA) or landing zone (LZ).		
e. Received BCT command frequencies and call signs of the BCT ground units in contact, to facilitate air-ground coordination down to company level, and provide situational awareness (SA) to all elements.		
f. Coordinated the correct time for the global positioning system (GPS) and the single channel ground and airborne radio system (SINCGARS).		
* 3. The aviation brigade operations officer (S3) briefs and dispatches aviation LNOs to the BCT S3.		
* 4. The senior aviation LNO works with the BCT S3-Air to advise and assist the BCT commander and staff.		
a. Received the missions of aviation forces OPCON to the BCT and coordinated same with the aviation brigade commander and aviation brigade S3.		
b. Understood the BCT commander's intent, scheme of maneuver, and how the aviation assets are integrated into it.		
c. Alerted the appropriate aviation units of their mission.		
d. Informed the aviation brigade commander and aviation brigade S3 of the status of aviation assets OPCON to the BCT.		
e. Advised the BCT commander and the BCT S3 on the proper employment and missions for Army aviation.		
f. Coordinated with the BCT S2 and extracted information pertinent to Army aviation planning, such as-		
(1) Target location(s), objective, and EA.		
(2) Summary or synopsis of the intelligence preparation of the battlefield (IPB).		
(3) Commander's Critical Information Requirements (CCIR).		
(4) Weather and terrain.		
g. Advised the BCT S3 on requesting additional aviation assets, with supporting elements, as required.		
h. Assisted the BCT S3 in the development of the OPORD, to include-		
(1) Air corridors to and from the forward line of own troops (FLOT), to include penetration corridor.		
(2) Movement to the objective.		

TASK STEPS AND PERFORMANCE MEASURES	GO	NO-GO
(3) Suppression of enemy air defense (SEAD) operations.		
(4) Actions on the objective.		
(5) Movement from the objective.		
(6) Deception plan.		
(7) Special instructions for Army aviation integration into the BCT air defense effort.		
(8) Coordination instructions.		
i. Acted as liaison between air defense units and air traffic control units.		
5. The aviation LNO and the BCT S3-Air coordinate Army aviation employment with the air defense (AD) officer.		
a. Received, processed, and disseminated AD information to the aviation brigade staff and aviation units OPCON to the BCT		
(1) Provided early warning intelligence information.		
(2) Friendly ADA unit locations.		
(3) Identification, friend or foe (IFF)/selective identification feature (SIF) procedures for Army aircraft, to include location of IFF/SIF line.		
(4) Known enemy ADA locations.		
(5) Minimum risk routes.		
(6) Army Airspace Command and Control (A2C2) rules and procedures.		
(7) Coordinating flight altitudes.		
(8) All known positive and procedural controls.		
b. Established coordination with friendly high-to-medium-altitude air defense (HIMAD) units and advised the aviation brigade staff and aviation units OPCON to the BCT, of HIMAD locations and frequencies.		
c. Advised friendly ADA commander on types of aircraft and unmanned aerial vehicles (UAVs) in use.		
d. Coordinated aviation information with the fire support element (FSE).		
e. Coordinated Army aviation communications and logistical requirements.		
f. Coordinated the following information with the aviation brigade A2C2 element located at division-		
(1) BCT AO.		
(2) Air defense warnings.		
(3) Rules of Engagement (ROE) (weapons control status and hostile criteria).		
(4) Coordinating altitudes.		
(5) Weather.		
(6) Positive and procedural control measures.		
(7) Types of aircraft and UAVs in use.		
6. The aviation LNO and BCT S3-Air monitor aviation operations.		

TASK STEPS AND PERFORMANCE MEASURES	GO	NO-GO
a. Ensured aviation forces are properly employed and in compliance with the BCT commander's intent and overall scheme of maneuver.		
b. Ensured aviation-related reports to higher headquarters are accurate and submitted in a timely manner.		
c. Maintained a current status of aviation assets.		
d. Coordinated all current and future logistical requirements with the combat service support (CSS) staff.		
7. During operations, the aviation LNO and BCT S3-Air assist in the identification and resolution of airspace conflicts.		
a. Monitored current operations of airspace users.		
b. Monitored intelligence reports.		
c. Disseminated unscheduled high-volume use of airspace.		
d. Informed airspace users at each echelon of any loss of communication affecting any airspace user.		
e. Identified and correlated situations affecting airspace use for unscheduled events.		
f. Analyzed airspace use on the situation map (SITMAP) to determine and resolve conflicts.		
g. Recommended shifting or ending fires when affecting high priority aviation missions.		
h. Disseminated changes of control or restriction measures affecting airspace users.		
i. Analyzed future OPORDs/OPLANs for possible conflicts of flight control measures, friendly field artillery (FA)/ADA locations, and flight obstructions.		
(1) Determined impact on aviation and BCT operations.		
(2) Developed and recommended alternatives.		
8. The aviation LNO, BCT S3-Air, and AMC coordinate aviation mission execution actions with the BCT units in close combat with the enemy.		
a. The aviation LNO coordinated/confirmed the locations for the HA (or orbiting area) within FM communications range of the ground unit, LZ, forward arming and refueling point (FARP), initial point (IP), battle position (BP), attack by fire (ABF), and/or support by fire (SBF) position.		
NOTE: The BP and ABF/SBF positions are normally offset from the flank of the friendly ground position, but close enough to facilitate efficient target handoffs.		
b. The BCT S3-Air called for SEAD and informed the ground unit leader that supporting attack aircraft are inbound to their location.		
c. The aviation LNO coordinated/confirmed the use of the joint standard nine-line format for the close combat attack briefing with the BCT units in close combat with the enemy.		
d. While en route to the HA, the attack AMC contacted the supported ground unit leader on the unit's FM command network for a SITREP on the enemy and friendly situation.		

TASK STEPS AND PERFORMANCE MEASURES	GO	NO-GO
(1) The close combat SITREP consisted of the front line trace, enemy ADA threat, location of enemy vehicles/equipment and their direction of movement.		
(2) The SITREP included the ground unit's mission, location of friendly ground elements in contact, location of friendly flank units, how they are marking their position, and how they will mark the enemy target.		
(3) The SITREP included the call sign/frequency verification and method of contact.		
NOTE: Locations may be expressed by grid coordinates, distance/direction from a known point, or common graphics.		
9. The attack AMC conducts the aviation team check-in and close combat brief with the ground unit leader on the unit's FM command network.		
a. The attack AMC provided the ground unit leader his concept of the operation, to include his attack route and the time required to move from the HA/orbiting area to the IP/BP.		
b. Upon arrival at the HA/orbiting area, the attack AMC conducted the aviation team check-in with the ground unit leader.		
(1) Made initial contact and informed the ground unit leader of his arrival.		
(2) Gave the aviation team composition, altitude, and location.		
(3) Stated what weapons and munitions were available for the attack.		
(4) Estimated how long the aviation team could remain on station.		
(5) Stated night vision capabilities/type: image intensification, thermal, or both.		
c. After the aviation team check-in, the ground unit leader presented the close combat attack briefing to the AMC, using the joint standard nine-line format (without the line numbers), as follows:		
(1) Target location by grid coordinates, from a known reference point (IP, BP, ABF, or friendly location), or terrain feature.		
(2) Magnetic heading to target from a known point (IP, BP, ABF, or friendly location).		
(3) Distance to target in meters from a known point (IP, BP, ABF, or friendly location).		
(4) Target elevation in feet mean sea level.		
(5) Target description.		
(6) Target location in grid coordinates, or location from a known point/terrain feature.		
(7) Target marking (white phosphorous, laser, infrared, beacon), day/night code, and laser to target line in degrees, if appropriate.		
(8) Location of friendly troops by grid coordinates, or distance from a known point/terrain feature, to include type of marking (If smoke is used, AMC verifies color).		
NOTE: The marking of friendly positions is done with great caution due to force protection.		
(9) Egress direction to avoid the enemy.		

TASK STEPS AND PERFORMANCE MEASURES	GO	NO-GO
NOTE: A remarks line may be added to include special instructions, laser to target line (degrees), time on target (TOT), time-to-target (TTT), etc.		
NOTE: When identifying a position by grid coordinates, during joint operations, include the map datum data. Combat lessons learned have shown that simple conversion to latitude/longitude is not sufficient. The location may be referenced on several different databases; for example, land-based versus sea-based data.		
10. The attack AMC and the ground unit leader consider the risk to friendly forces and select the weapons/munitions to engage the target.		
11. The attack AMC moves the aviation team from the HA/orbiting area to the BP and engages the target.		
12. The attack AMC and the ground unit leader maintain open communication and coordination to ensure desired effect.		
13. The attack AMC provides battle damage assessment (BDA) to the ground unit leader who determines if a reattack is required.		

* indicates a leader task step.

SUPPORTING COLLECTIVE TASKS

Task Number	Task Title
01-1-0344	Direct the Aviation Brigade/Battalion Staff
71-8-5110	Plan Operations Using the Military Decision-Making Process (Battalion – Corps)

TASK: Coordinate Target Attack (06-6-5059)

    (FM 3-09.32)   (FM 3-0)

CONDITIONS: The fires brigade is operating in support of an associated maneuver force in a joint and/or combined environment. The force is engaged in combat or in a condition where combat is imminent. The brigade command posts are deployed and operational. Some iterations of this task should be performed in MOPP4.

TASK STANDARDS: All available fire support assets were used to support maneuver force operations. The operation was successful and the maneuver force accomplished their stated mission. The FSC continually updated attack guidance and made recommendations to revise the commander's criteria as needed to best support operations. The purpose of all essential tasks for fire support was met.

TASK STEPS AND PERFORMANCE MEASURES	GO	NO-GO
1. The Fires Cell performs target analysis. Automated systems may be used to perform some analysis of a target. The operator must still perform certain aspects of this analysis not performed by the automated system.		
a. They analyze designated targets.		
b. They analyze targets on the basis of time available.		
c. They consider the following:		
(1) Target characteristics; composition, degree of protection, size, shape, and mobility.		
(2) Target location, proximity to friendly troops, and accuracy of target location.		
(3) Terrain and weather.		
(4) Weapons and munitions available.		
(5) Commander's attack guidance and desired effects.		
2. Provides target information to attack assets.		
3. Expedites processing planned fire support requests.		
a. Monitors all requests for planned fires including: On-Call targets, scheduled targets, counterfire programs, SEAD, and FS programs.		
b. Ensures planned fires are continually updated on the basis of the tactical situation and FSCMs.		
c. Determines the priority of missions and assigns an alternative means of FS if available.		
4. Expedites immediate fire support requests.		
a. Reviews and process requests for immediate fires to ensure the following:		
(1) Request is consistent with the commander's guidance. NOTE: In automated Fires Element sections this will be done automatically with the commander's criteria.		
(2) Most effective means of FS is requested. NOTE: This will be accomplished automatically when automated means are used.		
(3) Ensures airspace corridors are in effect and entered in the automated system. NOTE: this is very important when processing CAS missions.		

TASK STEPS AND PERFORMANCE MEASURES	GO	NO-GO
b. Coordinates with responsible agency to cancel original requests if needed.		
c. Passes target to appropriate FS asset for attack.		
d. Notifies the requester of any cancellation and tells him the reason for cancellations and what FS asset to use. NOTE: The cancellation is automatically sent in those units equipped with automated systems. the coordination for other assets needs to be made via voice.		
5. Coordinates the attack of HPTs and orders the execution of joint air attack operations (JAAT). ⸱		
6. Orders the execution of localized joint suppression of enemy air defenses (J-SEAD), as needed.		
7. Orders counterfire for the attack of identified enemy indirect fire support.		
8. Continuously coordinates target intelligence information and target production for timely and accurate engagement.		
a. Maintain appropriate standing request for information with intelligence and TOC agencies as appropriate.		
b. Request specific information form intelligence and TOC agencies.		
c. Maintain appropriate MOI files.		
9. Coordinates with other target attack supporting agencies.		
a. Coordinates with air liaison officer (ALO), aviation, and other attack assets, as appropriate to avoid duplication.		
b. Coordinates times and sequences of attack with other FS assets.		
c. Requests additional attack assets as needed from reinforcing units, USAF, USN, and other supporting agencies as needed.		
d. Coordinates counterbattery fires for the desired effects on identified enemy artillery, rocket, missile, and mortar fires.		
10. Requests BDA from S2.		
a. Obtains enemy casualty figures.		
b. requests vehicle and facility damage assessment.		
c. Requests any additional effects needed to accurately assess damage to the target.		
d. Requests evaluation of overall effects and recommendations for restrike.		
11. The fire support cell recommends changes to current attack guidance as needed.		
12. Establishes a continuous, direct, and responsive interface between the analysis and control element (ACE), FCE, targeting team, and subordinate FS elements as defined by unit TSOPs.		
a. Facilitates liaison concerning the threat and enemy COAs.		
b. Provides intelligence estimate/IPB products to the targeting element, and subordinate FA HQ as soon as possible to support the COA development, wargaming, and selection processes.		
c. Advises the targeting team on targeting priorities during the planning process, to include the definition of the TSS and attack guidance.		

TASK STEPS AND PERFORMANCE MEASURES	GO	NO-GO
d. Selects targeting information from all-source intelligence assets and nominates target to the targeting team for target value analysis (TVA) consideration and inclusion into the HPTL.		
e. Provides collection managers TSS criteria addressing FA weapon and TA system accuracy and time standard requirements.		
f. Integrates targeting considerations (HPTs, TSS, BDA, etc.) into the force intelligence collection plan.		
13. Continuously monitors the enemy situation and keeps the targeting team informed.		
a. Assists the ACE in target development, advising attack managers of requirements for timely target identification.		
b. Assists the S2/collection managers in determining the eligibility of targets for attack by matching FS system accuracy and time standard requirements to collection systems target location errors.		
c. Passes HPTs identified by intelligence analysts and validated against TSS and the HPTL immediately to the FCE for attack as provided for in the FS annex.		
d. Passes suspected targets to the FCE for correlation and may recommend use of additional collection assets.		
14. The FAIO recommends to the targeting team changes to targeting priorities, HPTs, TSS, attack means, etc. during mission preparation and execution.		
15. Coordinates the retrieval of BDA data with collection managers, monitoring feedback from near real-time collectors and observers during target engagement.		
16. Helps determine if fires produced desired effects and advises the FSCOORD/targeting team accordingly.		

* indicates a leader task step.

SUPPORTING COLLECTIVE TASKS

Task Number	Task Title
06-6-5431	Execute Targeting Process
06-6-5074	Analyze Targets
06-6-1079	Conduct Battle Tracking

TASK: Employ Lethal Fires in Support of the BCT (06-6-5066)

(FM 3-90.6)   (FM 5-0)   (FM 6-0)

CONDITIONS: The Fires Brigade/ brigade combat team (BCT) is engaged in combat operations. The S3 is developing or has issued an order. Fire support planning and establishment of fire support coordination measures (FSCM) are ongoing to support maneuver elements. The FiB/BCT has established communications and digital connectivity via the Army Battle Command System (ABCS), when equipped, with subordinate, adjacent, and higher headquarters, and is passing information in accordance with (IAW) higher headquarters' and the FiB/BCT's standing operating procedures (SOP). Some iterations of this task should be performed in MOPP4.

TASK STANDARDS: The Fires Cell employed all available lethal fires assets to support the commander's intent and execute the essential fire support tasks.

TASK STEPS AND PERFORMANCE MEASURES	GO	NO-GO
1. FSCOORD, in conjunction with other members of the Fires Cell, processes planned fire support requests (FBCB2/Advanced Field Artillery Tactical Data System [AFATDS] or FM).		
NOTE: The task steps below will be accomplished using ABCS when indicated in the performance measures. When preformatted messages do not exist, free text messages may be substituted for other Force XXI Battle Command brigade and Below (FBCB2) and Maneuver Control System (MCS) messages identified in task steps and performance measures below. BCTs without ABCS will substitute appropriate SOP procedures for task steps that require ABCS.		
a. Receives subordinate unit requests for planned fires to include, but not limited to-		
(1) Preparatory fires (planned or on call).		
(2) Counterfire.		
(3) Suppression of enemy air defense (SEAD).		
(4) Priority targets.		
(5) Counterpreparation fires.		
(6) On-call targets.		
(7) Targets of opportunity.		
b. Reacts to changing situations; for example-		
(1) Planned fire support assets are not available because of a change in commander's guidance or additional requirements.		
(a) Determines priority of mission.		
(b) If other fires are available, assigns an alternate means of fire support, such as close air support (CAS) or naval gunfire, to attack the target.		
(2) CAS has been scheduled against a target but has not yet arrived on station. Fires Cell determines the desirability and feasibility of engaging the target with less effective means of fire support until air assets arrive.		
2. FSCOORD processes combat assessment.		

TASK STEPS AND PERFORMANCE MEASURES	GO	NO-GO
a. Fire support noncommissioned officer (FSNCO) requests assessment from observing unit FSO.		
b. FSCOORD requests, through the S2, the appropriate intelligence collection agency to determine damage on selected targets identified during the decide phase of the targeting process.		
c. FSCOORD determines if another attack is necessary based on results of the combat assessment and makes a recommendation to the commander and S3 based on his assessment.		
3. FSNCO monitors the current situation.		
a. Maintains the status of all available fire support agencies, to include-		
(1) Locations.		
(2) Missions.		
(3) Capabilities.		
(4) Ammunition status.		
(5) Equipment status.		
b. Collects and maintains friendly and known enemy situation, to include-		
(1) Maneuver graphics.		
(2) Locations of maneuver and indirect fire elements (battalion mortars, and fires battalion firing and trains elements).		
(3) Observer locations as reported by maneuver observers via FBCB2 and by artillery observers using the Forward Observer System (FOS).		
(4) FSCMs via AFATDS graphic depiction and MCS common operational picture (COP)/Joint Common Database (JCDB) update.		
(5) Host nation (HN) restrictive fire measures via AFATDS update.		
(6)) Friendly and enemy obstacles via MCS COP/JCDB updates.		
c. Anticipates when and where the FSCOORD will need to make decisions, recommendations, or take actions. Identifies what information requirements the FSCOORD will need for those actions, recommendations, and decisions.		
(1) Uses troop-leading procedures (TLP) to prepare the Fires Cell. Briefs the plan, scheme of fires, and critical events (friendly and enemy). Assigns specific tasks based on mission, enemy, terrain, troops and time available, and civil considerations (METT-TC). Rehearses key battle drills (such as simultaneous attacks on the same target with both CAS and artillery).		
(2) Remains abreast of changes to the scheme of maneuver and scheme of fires during the battle and adjusts/informs the Fires Cell of changing information requirements.		
d. Establishes and maintains the AFATDS current operations screen, other situation maps (SITMAP) and target planning maps.		
e. Records FA-delivered mines (coordinated with the engineer), if applicable, on operations map and overlays, and ensures they are posted to the MCS COP/JCDB and are disseminated across the brigade via FBCB2 entity data messages.		
f. Passes and receives intelligence data to/from the S2.		

TASK STEPS AND PERFORMANCE MEASURES	GO	NO-GO
4. FSNCO coordinates with higher, subordinate, and adjacent units.		
a. Informs or confirms with higher headquarters the location of maneuver elements, scheme of maneuver, and proposed locations.		
b. . Provides and receives FSCMs and ensures they are posted to the MCS COP/JCDB update.		
c. Exchanges targeting information with higher headquarters intelligence agencies, and subordinate fire support agencies.		
d. Assists battle captain in clearance of fires.		
5. FSCOORD coordinates fire support for the FiB/BCT.		
a. Key targeting team member at the BCT battle map (with executive officer [XO], S2, and battle captain):		
(1) Anticipates fire support events 30 to 60 minutes out.		
(2) Makes decisions, recommendations, and takes action as required by the scheme of fires.		
(3) Tasks the FSNCO and targeting officer to execute his decisions while he remains focused 30 to 60 minutes out.		
b. Monitors nets of subordinate Fires Cells to ensure that established procedures are being followed.		
c. If coordination of fires across boundaries is required, coordinates for clearance of fires.		
d. Fires Cell analyzes targets and calls-for-fire to ensure they meet the commander's intent. For targets of opportunity, coordinates with appropriate asset for attack. In addition:		
(1) Requests adjacent/higher unit engages target if possible.		
(2) Advises the fires battalion if the target will not be engaged by fires battalion elements.		
(3) Advises the requesting agency of the asset engaging the target.		
e. If adjacent/higher element allows engagement, the Fires Cell does the following:		
(1) Notifies the fire support resource that they are cleared to fire.		
(2) Notifies the requester that the mission is cleared to fire.		
f. Ensures all current targeting information is maintained in the AFATDS database.		

* indicates a leader task step.

SUPPORTING COLLECTIVE TASKS

Task Number	Task Title
06-6-1079	Conduct Battle Tracking
06-6-1118	Conduct Fire Support Planning Using MDMP
06-6-5059	Coordinate Target Attack

TASK: Synchronize Close Air Support (Battalion-Brigade) (17-6-0308)

<u>(FM 3-09.32)</u>   (FM 3-90.6)   (FM 6-20-50)

CONDITIONS: The brigade combat team (BCT) or battalion (BN) is conducting operations independently or as part of a higher headquarters (HQ) and must synchronize close air support (CAS). Combat intelligence and unit reports are being received. Friendly forces have air superiority or can achieve air superiority temporarily over key areas. The BCT/BN has CAS available. The BCT/BN has communications with higher, adjacent, supported, and subordinate elements. The BCT/BN received guidance on the rules of engagement (ROE). Military, civilian, joint, and multinational partners and news media may be present in the operational environment (OE). Some iterations of this task should be performed in mission-oriented protective posture (MOPP) 4.

TASK STANDARDS: Close air support is planned and coordinated in conjunction with the air liaison officer (ALO). Any CAS requests from units are consolidated and forwarded to higher HQ. Subordinate units were notified of any CAS requests that were denied. All communications and reporting are in accordance with (IAW) applicable standing operating procedures (SOP).

TASK STEPS AND PERFORMANCE MEASURES	GO	NO-GO
Plan/Prepare		
* 1. The BCT/BN commander and staff receive an order or anticipate a new mission and begin the military decision-making process (MDMP). (Refer to Task 71-8-5110, Plan Operations using the Military Decision-Making Process [Battalion–Corps] for further details.)		
* 2. The BCT/BN leaders gain and/or maintain situational understanding (SU) using available communications equipment, maps, intelligence summaries, situation reports (SITREPs), and other available information sources. Intelligence sources include human intelligence (HUMINT), signal intelligence (SIGINT), and imagery intelligence (IMINT) to include unmanned aircraft systems (UASs). They take the following actions:		
a. Update the joint common database and common operational picture (COP), providing current SU to provide timely and accurate information for intelligence preparation of the battlefield (IPB) and the planning process.		
b. Fires cell and ALO initiate CAS planning. They take the following actions:		
(1) Notify subordinate units of the no later than (NLT) time to submit requests to fires cell.		
(2) Prepare preplanned requests for tactical air (TACAIR) sorties based on commander's concept of the operation.		
(3) Evaluate the surface-to-air threat and plan/coordinate suppression of enemy air defenses (SEAD) to counter the threat.		
(4) Obtain number of CAS sorties distributed to the BCT/BN for planning.		
(5) Advise subordinate units of number of CAS sorties available for planning purposes.		
(6) Confirm the NLT time for submitting preplanned requests to Fires cell.		
(7) Consider other planning considerations:		
(a) Weather.		

TASK STEPS AND PERFORMANCE MEASURES	GO	NO-GO
(b) Target acquisition.		
(c) Suppression of SEAD.		
(d) Target identification.		
(e) Identification of friendly forces.		
(f) General ordnance characteristics.		
(g) Final attack heading.		
(h) Troop safety.		
(i) Integration of CAS and artillery.		
* 3. S-3 supervises CAS support planning. They take the following actions:		
a. Ensure CAS support, SEAD, and friendly air defense artillery (ADA) controls are integrated into the fires plan based on commander's concept of the operation and guidance.		
b. Ensure preplanned requests comply with commander's concept and priorities.		
c. Assign priority and precedence to each CAS request.		
d. Consider the impact of successful battle damage assessment (BDA) on the concept of the operation.		
e. With the commander's approval, make revisions to the fires and maneuver plans, as necessary.		
f. Synchronize the Army airspace command and control (AC2) plan.		
Execute		
* 4. Fires cell and tactical air control party (TACP) process preplanned CAS requests. They take the following actions:		
a. Ensure all subordinate preplanned requests are received at BCT/BN by the NLT time stated in the operation order (OPORD).		
b. Ensure preplanned requests are complete and properly prepared.		
c. Approve or disapprove preplanned requests.		
d. Consolidate all approved requests in priority and precedence order.		
e. Submit the consolidated requests by the NLT time specified in the OPORD.		
f. Notify subordinate units of requests that are disapproved.		
g. Complete combat assessment, approve reattack recommendation, and modify scheme of maneuver, as appropriate.		
h. Adjust preplanned missions through higher HQ, as appropriate.		
i. Plan for alternate means of engagement for preplanned targets if CAS aircraft are diverted to higher priority targets.		
j. Inform subordinate units of revisions to fires and maneuver plans.		
5. S-3 or Fires cell process immediate CAS support requests. They take the following actions:		
a. Commander, S3, ALO, and fires cell evaluate requests.		
b. A2C element, fires cell, air support operations center (ASOC), and ALO deconflict airspace.		

TASK STEPS AND PERFORMANCE MEASURES	GO	NO-GO
c. The TACP transmits approved request directly to the ASOC via Air Force request net(s).		
Assess		
* 6. The BCT/BN leaders assess the operation. They take the following actions;		
a. Monitor the situation during all phases of the operation.		
b. Direct adjustments to ensure that operations remain aligned with the commander's intent.		
7. The BCT/BN leaders continue operations as directed.		

* indicates a leader task step.

Task Number	Task Title
71-8-3000	Provide Fire Support (Battalion-Corps)
71-8-5110	Plan Operations using the Military Decision-Making Process (Battalion–Corps)
71-8-5700	Develop Airspace Usage Priorities (Brigade-Corps)
71-8-5702	Determine Integrated Airspace User Requirements (Brigade-Corps)
71-8-5703	Develop Airspace Coordinating Measures to Support Planned Operations (Brigade-Corps)
71-8-5712	Monitor Assigned Airspace and Airspace Users within Assigned AO (Brigade-Corps)

TASK: Execute the Operations Process (Battalion - Corps) (71-8-5100)

(FM 5-0) (FM 3-0) (FM 6-0)

CONDITIONS: The unit has received an Operations Plan, Warning, Operations, or Fragmentary Order from higher headquarters and is exercising mission command. The commander has issued planning guidance for executing the operations process. Communications are established with subordinate and adjacent units, and higher headquarters. Mission Command Information Systems are operational and passing information in accordance with Tactical Standing Operating Procedures. The unit has received guidance on the rules of engagement. Some iterations of this task should be performed in MOPP4.

TASK STANDARDS: The unit executes the operations process in accordance with the operations or fragmentary order, and the higher commander's guidance and intent. The unit plans, prepares, executes, and assesses operations. The unit complies with the rules of engagement.

Note: Task steps and performance measures may not apply to every unit or echelon. Prior to evaluation, coordination should be made between evaluator and the evaluated units' higher headquarters to determine the task steps and performance measures that may be omitted.

TASK STEPS AND PERFORMANCE MEASURES	GO	NO-GO
* 1. The commander and staff maintain a shared situational understanding during operations through knowledge and information management to include an accurate common operational picture provided by the staff.		
2. The unit plans operations.		
a. Conducts the military decision-making process.		
b. Integrates requirements and capabilities.		
c. Develops commander's critical information requirements.		
d. Establishes target priorities.		
e. Integrates space capabilities.		
3. The unit prepares for tactical operations.		
a. Establishes coordination and liaison.		
b. Performs rehearsals.		
c. Task organizes for operations.		
d. Revises the plan.		
e. Conducts pre-operations checks and inspections.		
f. Integrates new units and Soldiers into the force.		
4. The unit executes tactical operations.		
a. Performs ongoing functions.		
b. Performs planned actions, sequels, and branches.		
c. Adjusts resources, concept of operations, or mission.		
d. Synchronizes actions to produce maximum effective application of military power.		
e. Conducts transitions.		
f. Reconstitutes tactical forces.		

TASK STEPS AND PERFORMANCE MEASURES	GO	NO-GO
5. The unit assesses tactical situations and operations.		
a. Monitors situation or progress of operations.		
b. Evaluates situation or operation.		
6. The unit continuously performs composite risk management.		
7. The unit assesses the operation and recommends adjustments to the plan ensuring operations meet the higher commander's guidance and intent.		
8. The unit complies with the rules of engagement.		
9. The unit consolidates and reorganizes to meet operations, or as directed by higher headquarters.		
10. The unit conducts primary stability tasks in accordance with the mission or operational variables.		

* indicates a leader task step.

SUPPORTING COLLECTIVE TASKS

Task Number	Task Title
71-8-2210	Perform Intelligence Preparation of the Battlefield (Battalion - Corps)
71-8-2321	Develop the Intelligence, Surveillance, and Reconnaissance Plan (Brigade - Corps)
71-8-3300	Implement the Targeting Process (Brigade - Corps)

TASK: Conduct the Military Decision-Making Process (Battalion - Corps) (71-8-5111)

(FM 5-0)   (FM 3-0)   (FM 2-0)   (FM6-0)

CONDITIONS: The staff is conducting or preparing to conduct operations. Communications are established with subordinate, adjacent units, and Higher Headquarters (HQ). Command and Control (C2) Information Systems (INFOSYS) are operational and are passing information in accordance with Tactical Standing Operating Procedures (TACSOP). The command has received a Warning Order (WARNO) from higher headquarters and is exercising mission command. Some iterations of this task should be performed in MOPP 4.

TASK STANDARDS: The staff analyzes a mission received from Higher Headquarters (HQ), develops, analyze and compare Courses Of Action (COA) against criteria of success and each other, selected the optimum COA to accomplish the mission, and produce and disseminate an Operations Plan/Operations Order (OPLAN/OPORD) to subordinates.

Note: Task steps and performance measures may not apply to every unit or echelon. Prior to evaluation, coordination should be made between evaluator and the evaluated units' higher headquarters to determine the task steps and performance measures that may be omitted.

TASK STEPS AND PERFORMANCE MEASURES	GO	NO-GO
* 1. Upon receipt of mission, or anticipation of a new mission, the staff begins the planning process by:		
a. Alerting the staff of the pending planning requirements.		
b. Gathering the necessary tools, to include, but not limited to:		
(1) Higher headquarter order or plan and operational graphics.		
(2) Maps of the Area of Operations (AO).		
(3) Unit and higher headquarters Tactical Standing Operating Procedures (TACSOP).		
(4) Appropriate doctrinal references and regulations.		
(5) Current running estimates.		
(6) Other items dictated by necessity or TACSOP.		
c. Updating running estimates.		
d. Performing an initial assessment, which includes determining:		
(1) Time available from mission receipt to mission execution.		
(2) Time needed to plan and prepare for mission, for Higher Headquarters(HQ) and subordinate units.		
(3) Currentness of Intelligence Preparation of the Battlefield (IPB) and other available intelligence products.		
(4) Currentness of running estimates and determining those needing updating.		
(5) Time required to position critical elements, to include Command and Control (C2) nodes.		
(6) The staff's experience, cohesiveness and level of rest or stress.		
e. Based upon the initial assessment, the Plans section prepares initial operational timeline, which includes staff planning timeline.		

TASK STEPS AND PERFORMANCE MEASURES	GO	NO-GO
f. The commander issues initial guidance, which includes:		
(1) Initial operational timeline.		
(2) How to abbreviate the Military Decision-Making Process (MDMP), if required.		
(3) Necessary coordination to perform, to include Liaison Officer (LNO)s required.		
(4) Authorized movements, to include positioning of C2 nodes.		
(5) Additional staff tasks, to include Specific Information Requirements (SIR).		
(6) Collaborative planning times and locations, if desired.		
(7) Initial Information Requirements (IR) or Commander's Critical Information Requirements (CCIR), as required.		
g. Issuing of initial Warning Order (WARNO) (#1) by the staff, which at a minimum, includes:		
(1) Type of operation.		
(2) General location of operation.		
(3) Initial operational timeline.		
(4) Movements to initiate.		
(5) Collaborative planning sessions directed by the commander.		
(6) Initial IR and CCIR.		
(7) Intelligence, Surveillance and Reconnaissance (ISR) tasks.		
2. Upon receipt of commander's initial guidance, the staff conducts mission analysis by:		
a. Analyzing the higher HQs order to understand the:		
(1) Commander's intent.		
(2) Mission.		
(3) Available assets.		
(4) Higher HQs AO.		
(5) Concept of operations.		
(6) Operational timeline.		
(7) Missions of adjacent, supporting and supported units.		
(8) AO.		
(9) Unit's mission in the context of and in relation to the higher headquarters mission and commander's intent (two levels up).		
b. Conducting initial IPB by:		
(1) Defining the operational environment.		
(2) Describing the operations effects.		
(3) Evaluating the threat.		
(4) Determining threat Courses Of Action (COA).		
c. Identifying specified, implied and essential tasks.		

TASK STEPS AND PERFORMANCE MEASURES	GO	NO-GO
d. Reviewing available assets.		
e. Identifying higher headquarters mission constraints.		
f. Identifying critical facts and assumptions.		
g. Performing risk assessment, to include:		
(1) Identification of hazards.		
(2) Assessment of hazards.		
(3) Development of controls and decisions on risks.		
(4) Implementation plan of controls.		
(5) Supervision and evaluation plan.		
h. Determining initial CCIR.		
i. Determining the initial Intelligence, Surveillance and Reconnaissance (ISR) plan. At a minimum, the ISR plan should contain:		
(1) The AOs for surveillance and reconnaissance assets.		
(2) ISR tasks.		
(3) Provisions for communications, logistics, and fire support.		
(4) Task organization.		
(5) The reconnaissance objective.		
(6) CCIR and IR.		
(7) Line of Departure (LD) or Line of Contact (LC) time.		
(8) Initial Named Areas of Interest (NAIs).		
(9) Routes to the AO, and passage of lines instructions.		
(10) Fire Support Coordination Measures (FSCMs) and Airspace Control Measures (ACMs).		
(11) Provisions for Medical Evacuation (MEDEVAC).		
j. Updating the operational timeline and the staff planning timeline.		
k. Writing the proposed restated mission, which contains the following five elements (who, what, when, where, why):		
(1) Who will execute the operation (unit/organization).		
(2) What is the unit/organization's essential task (tactical mission task).		
(3) When the operation will begin (by time or event) or the duration of the operation.		
(4) Where the operation will occur (AO, objective, grid coordinate).		
(5) Why the unit will conduct the operation (purpose).		
l. Delivering a mission analysis brief to the commander consisting, at a minimum, of the following:		
(1) Mission and commander's intent of headquarters two levels up.		
(2) Mission, commander's intent, concept of operation, and military deception plan or deception objectives of the headquarters one level up.		
(3) Review of the commander's initial guidance.		

TASK STEPS AND PERFORMANCE MEASURES	GO	NO-GO
(4) Initial IPB products, including Modified Combined Obstacle Overlay (MCOO) and Situation Template (SITTEMP)s.		
(5) Pertinent facts and assumptions.		
(6) Specified, implied, and essential tasks.		
(7) Constraints.		
(8) Forces available.		
(9) Initial risk assessment.		
(10) Recommended initial CCIR, which include the Essential Elements of Friendly Information (EEFI) and Priority Information Requirements (PIR).		
(11) Recommended timelines.		
(12) Recommended collaborative planning sessions.		
(13) Recommended restated mission.		
m. Gaining the commander's approval of the restated mission.		
n. Developing the initial commander's intent. The commander's intent includes the following components:		
(1) Expanded purpose (if desired).		
(2) Key tasks.		
(3) End state.		
o. Receiving the commander's planning guidance, which at a minimum, addresses:		
(1) The decisive operation.		
(2) Identification of a decisive point or points.		
(3) Potential key decisions.		
(4) Specific COAs to consider or not, both friendly and enemy, and the priority for addressing them.		
(5) Initial CCIR.		
(6) Surveillance and reconnaissance guidance.		
(7) Risk.		
(8) Military deception.		
(9) Fires.		
(10) Mobility and countermobility.		
(11) Security operations.		
(12) Priorities for the warfighting functions.		
(13) The operational timeline.		
(14) The type of order to issue.		
(15) Collaborative planning sessions to be conducted.		
(16) Movements to initiate (including C2 nodes).		
(17) The type of rehearsal to conduct.		
p. Issuing a WARNO (#2), which at a minimum, contains:		

TASK STEPS AND PERFORMANCE MEASURES	GO	NO-GO
(1) The approved unit mission statement.		
(2) The commander's intent.		
(3) Task organization changes.		
(4) Attachments and detachments.		
(5) The CCIR and EEFI.		
(6) Risk guidance.		
(7) Surveillance and reconnaissance instructions.		
(8) Initial movement instructions.		
(9) Security measures.		
(10) Military deception guidance.		
(11) Mobility and countermobility guidance.		
(12) Specific priorities.		
(13) The updated operational timeline.		
(14) Guidance on collaborative events and rehearsals.		
q. Reviewing facts and assumptions to assess the impact of changes on the plan and making adjustments as needed.		
3. Upon receipt of the restated mission, the commander's intent and the commander's planning guidance, the staff develops COAs by:		
a. Ensuring each proposed COA meets the following criteria:		
(1) Feasible. A COA must enable the unit to accomplish the mission within the available time, space, and resources.		
(2) Acceptable. The advantage gained by executing a COA must justify the cost in resources, especially casualties.		
(3) Suitable. A COA must accomplish the mission and comply with commander's guidance.		
(4) Distinguishable. Each COA must differ significantly from one another.		
(5) Complete. A COA must show how: decisive operation accomplishes mission; shaping operations create and preserve conditions for success of decisive operations; sustaining operations enable shaping and decisive operations.		
b. Analyzing relative combat/operational power to determine feasibility of proposed COAs by:		
(1) Computing force ratios.		
(2) Analyzing intangible aspects of combat/operational power, which include:		
(a) Environmental factors.		
(b) Human factors.		
(c) Friction.		
(d) Enemy will.		
(e) Enemy intentions.		

TASK STEPS AND PERFORMANCE MEASURES	GO	NO-GO
(3) Comparing friendly strengths against enemy weaknesses and vice verse, for the elements of combat/operational power listed below:		
(a) Movement and maneuver.		
(b) Intelligence		
(c) Fires.		
(d) Sustainment		
(e) Command and control		
(f) Protection.		
(g) Leadership.		
(h) Information.		
(4) Comparing force ratio with historic minimum planning ratios and estimating the extent which intangible factors affect relative combat/operational power.		
c. Generating options for proposed COAs by:		
(1) Determining doctrinal requirements for each type of operation being considered.		
(2) Considering possibilities created by attachments.		
(3) Ensuring the decisive operation issued in commander's planning guidance is nested within higher headquarters concept of operations.		
(4) Determining the decisive operation's purpose (if not stated by the commander).		
(5) Determining the best way to mass the effects of overwhelming power to achieve the purpose.		
(6) Considering shaping operations.		
(7) Establishing a purpose for each shaping operation that is tied to creating or preserving a condition for the decisive operation.		
(8) Determining sustaining operations necessary to create and maintain the combat power required for the decisive operation and shaping operations.		
(9) Developing the operational organization for each COA.		
(10) Determining the essential tasks for the decisive operation and each shaping and sustaining operation.		
(11) Examining each COA to determine if it satisfies the COA screening criteria.		
(12) Changing or eliminating COAs as appropriate.		
d. Arraying initial forces for each proposed COA by:		
(1) Considering:		
(a) The higher commander's intent and concept of operation.		
(b) The unit mission statement and commander's intent and planning guidance.		
(c) The air and ground avenues of approach.		
(d) As many possible enemy COAs as time permits, starting with the most likely and including the most dangerous.		

TASK STEPS AND PERFORMANCE MEASURES	GO	NO-GO
(2) Determining relative power required to accomplish each task, starting with the decisive operation and continuing through all shaping operations.		
(3) Determining the combination of tangible and intangible assets required to accomplish each task.		
(4) Determining a proposed Forward Edge of the Battle Area (FEBA) (in the defense) or an LD (in the offense).		
(5) Considering military deception operations.		
(6) Making an initial array of friendly forces, starting with the decisive operation and continuing with all shaping and sustaining operations, arraying ground forces two levels down.		
(7) Identifying the total number of units needed and possible methods of dealing with the enemy.		
(8) Determining whether to request additional resources, accept risk, or execute tasks required for COA sequentially (phased) rather than simultaneously, if a force shortfall is identified.		
e. Developing the concept of operations, by including the following:		
(1) The purpose of the operation.		
(2) Identifying where the commander will accept tactical risk.		
(3) Identification of critical friendly events and transitions between phases (if operation is phased).		
(4) Designation of the decisive operation, with its task and purpose, linked to how it supports the higher HQ concept.		
(5) Designation of shaping operations, with their tasks and purposes, linked to how they support the decisive operation.		
(6) Designation of sustaining operations, along with their tasks and purposes, linked to how they support the decisive and shaping operations.		
(7) Designation of reserve, including its location and composition.		
(8) ISR operations.		
(9) Security operations.		
(10) Identification of maneuver options that may develop during an operation.		
(11) Location of Engagement Areas (EAs), or attack objectives and counterattack objectives.		
(12) Assignment of subordinate AOs and identify unit unassigned operational environment.		
(13) Concept of fires.		
(14) Information Operations (IO) concept of support including military deception, and nonlethal fires.		
(15) Stability operations concept of support.		
(16) Prescribed formations or dispositions, when necessary.		
(17) Priorities for each warfighting function.		
(18) Integration of obstacle effects with maneuver and fires.		

TASK STEPS AND PERFORMANCE MEASURES	GO	NO-GO
(19) Considerations of the effects of enemy Weapons of Mass Destruction (WMD) on the force.		
(20) Graphic control measures.		
f. Assigning headquarters to create a task organization, as necessary.		
g. Preparing COA statements and sketches by:		
(1) Developing the COA statement which:		
(a) Portrays how the unit will accomplish the mission.		
(b) Explains the concept of operations, to include main and supporting efforts and decisive, shaping and sustaining operations.		
(c) Is written in terms of the battlefield organization.		
(d) Includes mission and end state.		
(2) Developing the COA sketch which, at a minimum, includes:		
(a) Unit and subordinate boundaries.		
(b) Subordinate locations or movement formations (but not subordinate unit formations).		
(c) The FEBA, LD, or LC, and phase lines if used.		
(d) Reconnaissance and security graphics.		
(e) Ground and air axes of advance.		
(f) Assembly Areas (AAs), Battle Positions (BPs), strong points, Engagement Areas (EAs) and objectives.		
(g) Obstacle control measures and tactical mission graphics.		
(h) FSCMs.		
(i) Designation of the decisive operation and shaping operations.		
(j) Location of Command Posts (CP)s and critical INFOSYS nodes.		
(k) Enemy known or templated locations.		
h. Conducting a COA brief to the commander, which includes:		
(1) An IPB update.		
(2) Possible enemy COAs (event templates).		
(3) The unit mission statement.		
(4) The commander's and higher commanders' intent.		
(5) COA statements and sketches.		
(6) The rationale for each COA, including:		
(a) Considerations that might affect enemy COAs.		
(b) Critical events for each COA.		
(c) Deductions resulting from the relative combat/operational power/troop to task analysis.		
(d) The reason units are arrayed as shown on the sketch.		
(e) The reason the staff used the selected control measures.		

TASK STEPS AND PERFORMANCE MEASURES	GO	NO-GO
(f) Updated facts and assumptions.		
(7) Recommended evaluation criteria.		
i. Upon completion of the COA briefing, the commander provides additional guidance, which includes:		
(1) Acceptance of COAs.		
(2) Rejection of COAs.		
(3) Creation of new COAs.		
(4) Directions on which COAs to analyze.		
4. Upon approval of COAs and receipt of commander's guidance, the staff conducts COA analysis (wargaming) to identify the best COA by:		
a. Gathering the required tools, to include, but not limited to:		
(1) Current running estimates.		
(2) Event templates.		
(3) A recording method.		
(4) Completed COAs, including maneuver, reconnaissance and surveillance, and security graphics.		
(5) A means to post or display enemy and friendly unit symbols.		
(6) A map of the AO.		
b. Listing the friendly forces.		
c. Listing assumptions.		
d. Listing known critical events and decision points, to include:		
(1) Events that trigger actions or decisions.		
(2) Complicated actions requiring detailed study.		
(3) Essential tasks.		
e. Determining evaluation criteria.		
f. Selecting the wargaming method from one of the following methods or by developing a different technique:		
(1) Belt method. Dividing AO into belts (areas) running the width of AO.		
(2) Avenue-in-depth method. Focusing on one avenue of approach at a time, beginning with the decisive operation.		
(3) Box Method. Detailed analysis of critical areas (i.e. EAs or Landing Zones [LZs]).		
(4) Any combination of the three methods.		
g. Selecting a method to record and display results, from one of two methods:		
(1) Synchronization Matrix.		
(2) Sketch note technique.		
h. Wargaming the operation and assessing the results by:		
(1) Executing action/reaction/counteraction analysis through each selected event of COAs.		

TASK STEPS AND PERFORMANCE MEASURES	GO	NO-GO
(2) Considering all possible forces, including templated enemy outside the AO that can influence the operation.		
(3) Evaluating each friendly move to determine assets and actions required to defeat the enemy at that point.		
(4) Considering branches to the plan that promote success against likely enemy counteractions.		
(5) Listing assets used in appropriate columns of worksheets and lists totals.		
(6) Examining the following areas in detail:		
(a) All enemy capabilities.		
(b) Movement considerations.		
(c) Closure rates.		
(d) Lengths of columns.		
(e) Formation depths.		
(f) Ranges and capabilities of weapons systems.		
(g) Desired effects of fires.		
(7) Assessing risk to friendly forces and ways to reduce vulnerability.		
(8) Identifying warfighting function assets required to support the concept of the operations.		
(9) Recommending priorities if requirements exceed available assets.		
(10) Validating the composition and location of the decisive operation, shaping operation, and reserve forces.		
(11) Identifying situations, opportunities or additional critical events that require further analysis by staff.		
(12) Performing any additional analysis quickly and incorporating the results into wargame record.		
i. Identifying the following wargame results:		
(1) Refined COAs with branches and sequels to become on-order or be-prepared missions.		
(2) Locations and times of decisive points and critical events.		
(3) Identification of key and decisive terrain.		
(4) Enemy event template and matrix.		
(5) Refined task organization.		
(6) Tasks unit retains and tasks assigned to subordinate elements.		
(7) Assets allocated to subordinate commanders to accomplish mission.		
(8) Synchronization matrix.		
(9) Decision Support Template (DST).		
(10) Estimation of the duration of entire operation and each critical event.		
(11) Projection of percentage of enemy force defeated overall and at each critical event.		

TASK STEPS AND PERFORMANCE MEASURES	GO	NO-GO
(12) Likely times and areas for enemy use of WMD.		
(13) Potential times and locations for committing the reserve.		
(14) Most dangerous enemy COA.		
(15) Location of commander, CPs, and INFOSYS nodes.		
(16) Warfighting function support requirements.		
(17) Military deception requirements.		
(18) Graphic control measures and updated operational graphics.		
(19) Refined CCIR and IR - including Latest Time Information Of Value (LTIOV) - and their incorporation into the ISR and Information Management (IM) plan.		
(20) ISR plan and graphics.		
(21) IO objectives and tasks.		
(22) Fire support, engineer, air and missile defense, IO, and sustainment plans and graphic control measures.		
(23) Effects of friendly and enemy actions on civilian population and infrastructure, and how these will affect military operations.		
(24) Location of NAIs, TAIs, DPs, and IR needed to support them.		
(25) Timing for concentration of forces and starting attack or counterattack (if applicable).		
(26) Movement times and tables for critical assets, including INFOSYS nodes.		
(27) Strengths and weaknesses of each COA.		
(28) Targeting data: High-Payoff Targets (HPTs) and attack guidance.		
(29) Risk assessment, hazards and controls.		
j. Conducting a wargame brief to the commander (OPTIONAL), which includes the following:		
(1) Higher headquarters mission, commander's intent, and military deception plan.		
(2) Updated IPB.		
(3) Friendly and enemy COAs that were wargamed, to include:		
(a) Critical events.		
(b) Possible enemy actions and reactions.		
(c) Modifications to the COAs.		
(d) Strengths and weaknesses.		
(e) Results of the wargame.		
(4) Assumptions.		
(5) Wargaming technique used.		
5. Upon completion of Analysis, the staff conducts COA comparison by:		
a. Determine the comparison technique that facilitates reaching the best recommendation and decision.		

TASK STEPS AND PERFORMANCE MEASURES	GO	NO-GO
b. Determine the weight of each criterion, developed before the wargame, based on its relative importance and the commander's guidance.		
c. Comparing COAs individually, by warfighting function.		
d. Staff responsible for warfighting function, score each COA using the established criteria.		
e. Multiplying their score by weights to determine the criterion value.		
f. Totaling all values, by category, to determine best COA.		
g. Comparing feasible COAs to identify the one with the highest probability of success against most likely enemy COA and most dangerous enemy COA.		
h. Developing a recommendation for the COA that best accomplishes the mission by:		
(1) Posing the minimum risk to the unit and mission accomplishment.		
(2) Placing the unit in the best posture for future operations.		
(3) Providing the maximum latitude for initiative by subordinates.		
(4) Providing the most flexibility to meet unexpected threats and opportunities.		
* 6. Upon conclusion of analysis and comparison, the staff seeks COA approval from the commander by:		
a. Conducting a COA decision briefing, which includes:		
(1) The intent of the higher and next higher commander.		
(2) The status of the unit and its components.		
(3) Current IPB.		
(4) The COAs considered, which include:		
(a) Assumptions used.		
(b) Results of staff running estimates.		
(c) Summary of wargame for each COA to include critical events, modifications to any COA, and wargame results.		
(d) Advantages and disadvantages (including risk) of each COA. (Discussed in terms of numerical or subjective analysis through a decision matrix).		
(5) The recommended COA.		
b. Obtaining the commander's decision on a COA.		
c. Receiving the commander's final planning guidance, which includes:		
(1) Refined commander's intent (if necessary).		
(2) New CCIR to support execution.		
(3) Additional guidance on priorities for warfighting function activities, orders preparation, rehearsals, and preparation.		
(4) Priorities for resources needed to preserve freedom of action and assure continuous sustainment.		
(5) The risk that the commander is willing to accept.		
d. Issuing WARNO (#3) to subordinate headquarters, which includes:		

TASK STEPS AND PERFORMANCE MEASURES	GO	NO-GO
(1) Mission.		
(2) Commander's intent.		
(3) Updated CCIR and EEFI.		
(4) Concept of operations.		
(5) AO.		
(6) Principal tasks assigned to subordinate units.		
(7) Preparation and rehearsal instructions not included in TACSOP.		
(8) Final timeline for the operations.		
7. Upon receiving the commander's approval for a COA, the staff produces the plan or order by:		
a. Converting the selected COA into a clear, concise concept of operations and supporting information by writing a complete five-paragraph field order with supporting annex's and operational graphics.		
b. Submitting the plan or order to the commander for review and approval, prior to reproduction and dissemination.		
c. Briefing the plan or order to subordinate commanders.		
d. Conducting confirmation briefings with subordinates immediately after orders brief.		
e. Reviewing subordinate commander's plans or orders, upon their completion.		

* indicates a leader task step.

Task Number	Task Title
71-8-5114	Establish Target Priorities (Battalion - Corps)
71-8-5113	Develop Commander's Critical Information Requirements (Battalion - Corps)
71-8-5121	Establish Coordination and Liaison (Battalion - Corps)

TASK: Prepare for Tactical Operations (Battalion - Corps) (71-8-5120)

(FM 3-0)   (FM 5-0)   (FM 6-0)

CONDITIONS: The staff is conducting or preparing to conduct operations. Communications are established with subordinate, adjacent units, and Higher Headquarters (HQ). Command and Control (C2) Information Systems (INFOSYS) are operational and are passing information in accordance with Tactical Standing Operating Procedures (TACSOP). The command has received a Warning Order/Operations Plan/Operations Order/Fragmentary Order (WARNO/OPLAN/ OPORD/FRAGO) from higher headquarters and is exercising mission command. The commander has issued guidance. Some iterations of this task should be performed in MOPP4.

TASK STANDARDS: The staff prepares to conduct tactical operations by initiating reconnaissance operations early. New information collection is used to revise and refine the Operations Plan/Operations Order (OPLAN/OPORD). The staff conducts extensive coordination to synchronize activities and ensure mutual understanding of the situation and commander's concept of the operation; conduct rehearsals; inspect key Command and Control (C2) operating systems; and coordinate the movement of forces and C2 elements to initial positions in preparation for the start of operations.

Note: Task steps and performance measures may not apply to every unit or echelon. Prior to evaluation, coordination should be made between evaluator and the evaluated units' higher headquarters to determine the task steps and performance measures that may be omitted.

TASK STEPS AND PERFORMANCE MEASURES	GO	NO-GO
1. The staff conducts an assessment of the units preparations by:		
a. Monitoring readiness procedures and activities for compliance with the unit Tactical Standing Operating Procedures (TACSOP)/Readiness Standing Operating Procedures (RSOP).		
b. Evaluating preparations against criteria of success established in the TACSOP/RSOP and developed during planning to identify variances.		
c. Updating running estimates to maintain current situational awareness.		
2. The staff incorporates commander critical information requirements into the Operations Plan/Operations Order (OPLAN/OPORD) and disseminates them to subordinate units.		
3. The Current Operations section directs reconnaissance operations in order to update and improve situational understanding by:		
a. Initiating reconnaissance early, before completing the OPLAN/OPORD.		
b. Requesting Intelligence, Surveillance and Reconnaissance (ISR) collection assistance, as required, from higher headquarters.		
c. Continuously reviewing and assessing intelligence products for new information.		
d. Ensuring all reconnaissance efforts are synchronized with the ISR plan.		
e. Modifying the collection plan to redirect ISR assets based on new information.		
4. The Current Operations section initiates security operations to prevent surprise and reduce uncertainty by:		
a. Identifying the commander's essential elements of friendly information.		
b. Coordinating security operations with subordinates.		

TASK STEPS AND PERFORMANCE MEASURES	GO	NO-GO
c. Synchronizing security operations with local security.		
5. The staff conducts Force Protection (FP) integration to prevent or mitigate hostile actions against Department of Defense (DoD) personnel (to include family members), resources, facilities and critical information by:		
a. Developing active and passive FP measures/actions.		
b. Initiating FP measures/actions upon receipt of mission/warning order.		
c. Monitoring FP measures.		
d. Evaluating FP measures for effectiveness.		
e. Modifying and/or directing new measures/actions, if applicable.		
6. The staff revises the plan In Accordance With (IAW) the commander's guidance based on new information to include:		
a. Information that validates assumptions.		
b. Reconnaissance information specifically addressing:		
(1) Changes in enemy situation, dispositions and actions.		
(2) Changes in friendly situation, dispositions and actions.		
7. The Current Operations section prepares and disseminates execution information through plans and orders.		
8. The Current Operations section, conducts coordination with higher, lower, adjacent, supporting and supported units to synchronize actions by:		
a. Sending and receiving liaisons teams.		
b. Establishing communications links.		
c. Exchanging Standing Operating Procedures (SOP), as needed.		
d. Synchronizing security and reconnaissance plans.		
e. Coordinating and exchanging graphic control measures.		
f. Keeping units informed by passing relevant information quickly.		
9. The staff assists subordinate units by:		
a. Providing resources the commander allocates to them.		
b. Representing subordinates' concerns to the commander.		
c. Clarifying orders and directives.		
10. The staff conducts rehearsals to ensure the staff and subordinates understand the commander's intent and concept of operation by:		
a. Revealing unidentified external coordination requirements.		
b. Synchronizing key points in the upcoming operation by identifying times and locations requiring coordination, and solutions for coordinating actions.		
c. Identifying internal coordination tasks.		
d. Updating internal coordination techniques such as the synchronization matrix and decision support template.		
11. The staff task organizes forces to establish command and support relationships.		

TASK STEPS AND PERFORMANCE MEASURES	GO	NO-GO
12. The staff conducts training to build teamwork, trust and mutual understanding necessary among the staff, subordinates, and supporting units to exercise mission command.		
13. The staff coordinates troop movements by positioning or re-positioning units for execution.		
14. The staff conducts pre operations checks and inspections to ensure all Command and Control (C2) information systems are fully operational and ready to execute.		
15. The Sustainment section conducts logistic preparations to ensure that sustainment support requirements are fully integrated in accordance with the commander's concept of the operation.		
a. Issuing, resupply, and maintenance of special supplies or equipment.		
b. Positioning of logistics assets.		
c. Enforcing Operation Security (OPSEC) measures to conceal preparations and friendly intentions.		
16. The Current Operations section integrates new units/Soldiers into the force to ensure they are assimilated into their units and/or the staff by:		
a. Proving new Soldiers and units with SOPs.		
b. Orienting new Soldiers and units on their places and roles in the unit and operation.		
c. Conducting orientation briefings and rehearsals.		
d. Establishing C2.		
e. Establishing communications links.		
f. Training them on unit TACSOP/RSOP and mission essential tasks for the tactical operation.		
17. The SJA section reviews Rules of Engagement (ROE) to ensure they are enforceable, understood, tactically sound, and legally sufficient.		
REMARKS:		
RELATED AUTL (ART) TASKS:		
ART 7.5.1 Establish and Conduct Coordination and Liaison ART 7.5.2 Conduct Rehearsals ART 7.5.3 Task Organize/Organize for Operations ART 7.5.4 Revise and Refine the Plan ART 7.5.5 Conduct Preoperations Checks and Inspections ART 7.5.6 Integrate New Units/Soldiers into the Force		
ASSOCIATED JOINT (OP) TASKS:		
OP 5.1.1 Monitor Strategic Situation OP 5.2 Assess Operational Situation		
(NOTE: Associated Joint (OP) Tasks are derived from JFCOM which lists 67 OP tasks as "Baseline Functional" and "Warfighting" tasks that a JTF should train for IAW JTF HQ Master Training Guide (MTG), CJCSM 3500.05A).		

* indicates a leader task step.

Task Number	Task Title
71-8-5111	Conduct the Military Decision-Making Process (Battalion - Corps)
71-8-5113	Develop Commander's Critical Information Requirements (Battalion - Corps)
71-8-5200	Conduct Command Post Operations (Battalion - Corps)

TASK: Assess Tactical Situation and Operations (Battalion - Corps) (71-8-5130)

(FM 3-0)   (FM 5-0)   (FM 6-0)

CONDITIONS: The staff is conducting or preparing to conduct operations. Communications are established with subordinate, adjacent units, and Higher Headquarters (HQ). Command and Control (C2) Information Systems (INFOSYS) are operational and are passing information in accordance with Tactical Standing Operating Procedures (TACSOP). The command has received a Warning Order/Operations Plan/Operations Order/Fragmentary Order (WARNO/OPLAN/ OPORD/FRAGO) from higher headquarters and is exercising mission command. The commander has issued guidance. Some iterations of this task should be performed in MOPP4. Some iterations of this task should be performed in MOPP4.

TASK STANDARDS: The staff continuously monitors the current situation and progress of the operation and assesses the situation or operation against criteria of success allowing the commander and staff timely decisions and necessary adjustments to the plan, prepare and execute process (planning, preparation, execution and assessment).

Note: Task steps and performance measures may not apply to every unit or echelon. Prior to evaluation, coordination should be made between evaluator and the evaluated units' higher headquarters to determine the task steps and performance measures that may be omitted.

TASK STEPS AND PERFORMANCE MEASURES	GO	NO-GO
1. Upon receipt of a mission the commander and staff, during planning, assesses the tactical situation and operations by:		
NOTE: Assessment is the continuous monitoring - throughout planning, preparation, and execution - of the current situation and progress of an operation and the evaluation of it against criteria of success (identified by the staff IAW commander's) to make decisions and adjustment to the plan. Assessing consists of two tasks: monitoring the current situation and progress of the operation and evaluating the operation against criteria. Together, they allow the commander to assess the situation in terms of expectations and the progress of the plan.		
a. Maintaining situational understanding based on the Common Operational Picture (COP).		
b. Developing and evaluating Course of Action (COA)s.		
c. Identifying gaps in information.		
d. Establishing the initial criteria of success for the operation during COA analysis in order to:		
(1) Compare COA.		
(2) Evaluate operations during preparation and execution.		
e. Assessing the enemy situation and environment.		
f. Using running estimates to update conclusions and recommendations.		
g. Identifying criteria for success.		
2. The staff assesses how well the unit is prepared for operations during preparation by:		
a. Determining the progress of readiness to execute operations.		
b. Refining plans and running estimates.		
c. Evaluating criteria of success established during planning to determine variances.		

TASK STEPS AND PERFORMANCE MEASURES	GO	NO-GO

3. The commander and staff, lead by the Intelligence section assesses reconnaissance operations by:
 	
  a. Integrating reconnaissance missions and surveillance means to form an integrated Intelligence, Surveillance and Reconnaissance (ISR) plan.
 	
  b. Synchronizing reconnaissance missions with other ISR components to continuously update and improve the situational understanding.
 	
  c. Modifying the collection plan to account for new information and redirect the ISR effort through Fragmentary Orders (FRAGO).
 	
  d. Continuously reviewing intelligence products and synchronizing the reconnaissance efforts within the ISR plan by focusing on:
 	
    (1) Important intelligence gaps.
 	
    (2) Emphasizing the established or revised Commander's Critical Information Requirements (CCIR).
 	
4. The commander and staff continuously assess security operations by:
 	
  a. Coordinating security operations among all subordinates.
 	
  b. Synchronizing local unit security.
 	
5. The commander and the staff continuously assesses force protection by monitoring and evaluating the effectiveness of force protection measures identified during planning.
 	
6. The commander and staff continuously revises and refines the plans based on:
 	
  a. Confirmation of enemy actions and disposition.
 	
  b. Assumptions made during planning that are proven true or false.
 	
  c. Changes to friendly situations.
 	
7. The commander or Executive Officer/Chief of Staff conduct rehearsals as part of preparation to:
 	
  a. Ensure the staff understands the intent and concept of the operation.
 	
  b. Ensure operations are synchronized at times and places critical to successful mission accomplishment.
 	
  c. Reveal unidentified external coordination requirements.
 	
  d. Support internal coordination by identifying tasks needed to accomplish external coordination.
 	
  e. Update internal coordination techniques, such as synchronization matrixes and decision support templates.
 	
8. The staff continuously assesses the operation during execution by:
 	
  a. Recommending when to execute planned action such as:
 	
    (1) Phases.
 	
    (2) Branches.
 	
    (3) Sequels.
 	
  b. Updating staff running estimates by:
 	
    (1) Comparing forecasted outcomes to actual events using the criteria for success to judge operational progress toward success.		

TASK STEPS AND PERFORMANCE MEASURES	GO	NO-GO
(2) Identifying the magnitude and significance of variances to determine the need for adjustments to the plan.		
9. The commander continuously assesses the execution of the operation/tasks in order to determine:		
a. Whether the current plan is still valid.		
b. Impacts on potential future operations.		
REMARKS:		
RELATED AUTL (ART) TASKS:		
ART 7.3 Assess Tactical Situation and Operation ART 7.3.2.1 Develop Staff Estimates ART 7.3.2.2 Evaluate Progress ART 7.3.1 Monitor Situation or Progress of Operations ART 7.3.2 Evaluate Situation or Operation ART 7.3.3 Provide Combat Assessment		
ASSOCIATED JOINT (OP) TASKS:		
OP 5.1.5 Monitor Strategic Situation OP 5.2 Assess Operational Situation		
NOTE: Associated Joint (OP) Tasks are derived from JFCOM which lists 67 OP tasks as "Baseline Functional" and "Warfighting" tasks that a JTF should train for IAW JTF HQ Master Training Guide (MTG), CJCSM 3500.05A.		

* indicates a leader task step.

Task Number	Task Title
71-8-5111	Conduct the Military Decision-Making Process (Battalion - Corps)
71-8-5316	Display a Common Operational Picture Tailored to User Needs (Battalion - Corps)
71-8-5144	Develop Running Estimates (Battalion - Corps)

TASK: Execute Tactical Operations (Battalion - Corps) (71-8-5131)

(FM 3-0)   (FM 6-0)   (FM 3-13)

CONDITIONS: The staff is conducting or preparing to conduct operations. Communications are established with subordinate, adjacent units, and Higher Headquarters (HQ). Command and Control (C2) Information Systems (INFOSYS) are operational and are passing information in accordance with Tactical Standing Operating Procedures (TACSOP). The command has received a Warning Order/Operations Plan/Operations Order/Fragmentary Order (WARNO/OPLAN/ OPORD/FRAGO) from higher headquarters and is exercising mission command. The commander has issued guidance. Some iterations of this task should be performed in MOPP4.

TASK STANDARDS: The staff combines and coordinates forces and warfighting functions in the most effective combinations to meet the requirements for mission accomplishment established by planning to support the commander in controlling tactical operations by providing him and subordinate commanders with a Common Operational Picture (COP) and execution information required to facilitate situational understanding. Prior to execution, forces are issued the OPORD and execution matrix with sequence and timing of each subordinate task throughout the operation and issues appropriate orders or requests to Higher Headquarters (HQ) as necessary to synchronize decisive, shaping and sustaining operations.

Note: Task steps and performance measures may not apply to every unit or echelon. Prior to evaluation, coordination should be made between evaluator and the evaluated units' higher headquarters to determine the task steps and performance measures that may be omitted.

TASK STEPS AND PERFORMANCE MEASURES	GO	NO-GO
1. The staff integrates Information Operations (IO) and Information Management (IM) activities to enhance situational understanding rapidly and accurately achieve information superiority and yield decisions that initiate or govern actions to accomplish tactical missions:		
a. Advising the commander and staff on capabilities, limitations, requirements, resources and employment, and all matters that deal with the units AOI (AOI).		
b. Providing Relevant Information (RI) to help the commander read the operational environment and keep abreast of the situation.		
c. Informing the commander of directives and policy guidance from higher headquarters dealing with the units AOI.		
d. Directing the staff to continuously monitor and update running estimates.		
2. The staff manages information:		
a. Receiving, processing and disseminating RI via digital Information System (INFOSYS).		
b. Analyzing RI to determine whether it is critical, exceptional, or routine.		
c. Deciding how to best display the information on digital INFOSYS for use by integrators and decision makers and incorporation into Tactical Standing Operating Procedures (TACSOP).		
d. Assess tactical situation and operations to determine if it is progressing satisfactorily In Accordance With (IAW) the current plan.		

TASK STEPS AND PERFORMANCE MEASURES	GO	NO-GO
e. Maintain the COP of decisive, shaping and sustaining operations by managing tactical information to ensure situational understanding.		
3. The staff conducts coordination through maintaining close contact and information exchange with the command and with corresponding commanders, staff officers, and sections at higher, subordinate, adjacent and supporting echelons of command.		
4. The Staff assists the commander in controlling tactical operations:		
a. Direct actions IAW Warning Order/Operations Plan/Operations Order/Fragmentary Order (WARNO/OPLAN/ OPORD/FRAGO) and execution and adjustment decisions (positive control).		
b. Regulate actions IAW, Standing Operating Procedures (SOP) (procedural control).		
c. Perform critical ongoing functions of execution.		
d. Synchronize the operation:		
(1) Assist the commander in synchronizing the operation to produce maximum effects on the threat.		
(2) Synchronize the operation in space and time across the warfighting functions with respect to decisive, shaping, and sustaining operations to gain or retain the initiative through the use of information dominance.		
(3) Verify staff officer's understanding in the operation and how it relates to everyone else's while supporting the commander's intent.		
5. The staff displays the COP and provides functional inputs IAW TACSOP:		
a. Provide sustainment input to the COP, consisting of support annex overlays and any logistics input required by the commanders Essential Elements of Friendly Information (EEFI) IAW TACSOP.		
b. Provide intelligence input to the COP, consisting of threat locations and type, CCIR, Priority Information Requirements (PIR) IAW TACSOP.		
6. The Human Resource Section and Inspector General (IG) section monitor trends:		
a. Analyze data from all sources to detect trends and identify solutions as they affect the mission:		
(1) Maintain updated IG technical information.		
(2) Review as necessary, other source data.		
b. Inquire into and report on matters about performance of the mission state of discipline, efficiency and economy.		
c. Consult staff elements, as appropriate, to obtain items for the special attention of inspectors and to arrange for technical assistance.		
d. Identify and monitor trends, both positive and negative, in all activities.		
e. Advise the commander and staff concerning matters noted.		
7. The staff leverages information management to support more precise and timely decisions.		
a. Conduct of operations security reviews of classified and unclassified documentation to ensure compliance with distribution statement requirements and command policy covering release of information into the public domain.		
b. Develop, publish, and maintain the EEFI list.		

TASK STEPS AND PERFORMANCE MEASURES	GO	NO-GO
c. Develop Operations Security (OPSEC) measures to recommend for implementation by the commander.		
d. Developing and publishing the unit OPSEC plan.		
8. The staff, develops EEFI in order to enhance friendly Decision-Making.		
9. The Operations Section integrates Information Operations (IO) that will cause the threat to make inappropriate, untimely, and irrelevant decisions that will give the commander a Decision-Making advantage:		
a. Obtain incoming tactical information and intelligence IAW the TACSOP.		
b. Monitor the digital INFOSYS, communications nets, and standard messages and reports IAW the TACSOP.		
c. Pass information requiring immediate action to the appropriate action officer, (battle captain, XO/COS, commander) IAW the TACSOP; which includes:		
(1) Support data for CCIR such as PIR, Friendly Force Information Requirements (FFIR), or when directed, EEFI.		
(2) Identify data that supports a decision the commander has to make.		
(3) Receive unexpected reports affecting the current operation.		
(4) Analyze and disseminating orders from higher headquarters requiring immediate action.		
d. Process tactical information and intelligence:		
(1) Focus efforts on threat not in contact (those able to influence the decisive battle) IAW CCIR.		
(2) Extract and collating essential intelligence information from messages and reports.		
(3) Determine the reliability of the source or agency.		
(4) Determine the credibility of incoming information.		
(5) Determine the validity of incoming data.		
(6) Determine the relevancy of the information to other staff elements and cells or headquarters.		
e. Evaluating the threat:		
(1) Identify the threat and information gaps.		
(2) Maintain threat models by creating or updating doctrinal template and patterns of operation.		
(3) Identify threat capabilities and vulnerabilities.		
(4) Prepare a consolidated staff assessment of threat capabilities and vulnerabilities, for the XO/COS.		
(5) Develop a full set of threat COAs available by establishing threat overlays.		
(6) Develop situation template overlays, COA descriptions and options, and High Value Targets (HVTs).		
(7) Evaluate and prioritizing each threat COA, particularly identifying the threat most likely and most dangerous.		

TASK STEPS AND PERFORMANCE MEASURES	GO	NO-GO
(8) Identify initial collection requirements to include an event template overlay and event matrix.		
f. Continuously assists the commander in conducting the ongoing functions of execution necessary to control operations:		
(1) Focus all assets on the decisive operation to include:		
(a) Confirm they are tasked to support the decisive operation or the main effort for a phase of an operation.		
(b) Confirm they are in the best position to support the decisive operation or main effort for a phase of an operation, or are moving to a location from where they can best support the decisive operation.		
(2) Conduct continuous Intelligence, Surveillance and Reconnaissance (ISR) to include:		
(a) Phase or sequencing ISR operations, IAW the commander's guidance, to ensure that assets are tasked to support the CCIR, available when needed, and maintain required coverage.		
(b) Synchronize the efforts of all ISR assets through dynamic re tasking and changes to the integrated ISR/collection plan based on changes to the situation and/or the commander's adjustment decisions.		
(3) Continue security operations to include:		
(a) Assess the command's security posture.		
(b) Update the EEFI to fit the situation.		
(c) Task subordinates to secure open flanks and gaps between units.		
(4) Adjust CCIR, based on the situation to include:		
(a) Analyze Information Requirements (IR) against changing operational circumstances.		
(b) Designate new IR that effect Decision-Making, success of the operation, and Decisive operations.		
(c) Disseminate CCIR as they are answered.		
(d) Update CCIR and EEFI as the situation changes.		
(5) Conduct battle tracking to:		
(a) Monitor the progress of air and ground troops.		
(b) Recommend changes in movement, as required.		
(6) Develop or adjust airspace and Fire Support Control Measures (FSCM) to include:		
(a) Maintain awareness of Airspace Control Measures (ACMs), their effects on ground operations and ground operations effects on ACMs.		
(b) Adjust ACMs as required.		
(c) Integrate new ACMs with ground operations.		

TASK STEPS AND PERFORMANCE MEASURES	GO	NO-GO
(7) Conduct targeting meetings to focus and synchronize the combat power and resources toward finding, tracking, attacking, and assessing High-Payoff Targets (HPTs).		
(8) Manage movement and position of sustainment units to include:		
(a) Determine where to mass effect.		
(b) Directing movements early enough to position all forces, including sustainment units, to accomplish that task.		
(9) Manage terrain to include:		
(a) Deconflict land use.		
(b) Track location and land use by all units.		
(c) Reverse-planning to determine which units require what space at what time.		
(d) Prioritizing land use to those units executing and supporting the decisive operation.		
10. The Operations section ICW the Plans section determine if an Order, FRAGO or a request to higher HQ is required to synchronize decisive, shaping and sustaining operations due to:		
a. Information received or analysis meets CCIR criteria or supports commander's decision.		
b. Information indicates unplanned or unforeseen situation that affects the current operation that requires an adjustment to the plan or request to higher HQ.		
11. The staff develops plans to sufficiently suppress or defeat the threat intelligence effort to allow the unit to conduct its mission with the element of surprise and with minimal losses:		
a. Prepare the Counterintelligence (CI) running estimate.		
b. Provide CI products.		
c. Provide input to the OPLAN/OPORD, to counter threat intelligence collection units and elements, and the structure or organization of paramilitary and/or terrorist groups in the AO.		
d. Provide CI support to battlefield deception.		
e. Provide CI support to OPSEC.		
12. The Staff, develops recommendations to the commander as a result of unplanned or extraordinary events (referred to as variances) critical to the current operation and requiring major adjustments to the plan:		
a. Determine if information received constitutes an unplanned or extraordinary event.		
b. Inform the Operations section.		
c. Inform the commander.		
d. Assemble action team or directing the Plans section, to develop a plan.		
e. Provide recommendations to the commander.		
f. Issue appropriate orders or requests to higher HQ.		

TASK STEPS AND PERFORMANCE MEASURES	GO	NO-GO
g. Identify variances from the initial plan.		
13. The Operations Section issues Orders, FRAGOs, or requests to higher HQ for information, as necessary, to implement the commander's decision based on CCIR, and to execute pre-planned decisions, respond to triggers, or conduct staff-to-staff coordination.		
a. Verify that CCIR has been answered.		
b. Inform Staff sections that CCIR has been answered.		
c. Inform the commander that CCIR has been answered.		
d. Review Decision Support Template (DST), synchronization matrix, and current situation.		
e. Present staff recommendation, if required, to the commander.		
f. Issue appropriate orders or submits requests to higher HQ.		
g. Receive information that requires execution of a pre-planned decision.		
h. Take appropriate actions to synchronize combat operations.		

* indicates a leader task step.

Task Number   **Task Title**
71-8-5113   Develop Commander's Critical Information Requirements (Battalion – Corps)
71-8-1121   Conduct Predeployment Activities (Battalion - Corps)
71-8-5200   Conduct Command Post Operations (Battalion - Corps)

This page intentionally left blank.

Appendix A

Reconnaissance and Surveillance Brigade Unit Task List

A-1. The UTL shown in Table A-1 is an example of a consolidated listing of all active collective tasks identified within CATS that the R&S brigade is organized, manned, and equipped to conduct IAW their TOE. The commander uses this list to develop his FSO METL. Commanders may accept risk and not train the entire UTL. The task numbers and task titles are listed under each of the six warfighting functions.

A-2. For current listing of all collective tasks that support the R&S brigade, refer to CATS.

Table A-1. Example R&S brigade unit task list

Task Number	Task Title
Command and Control	
01-6-0028	Coordinate Airspace Command and Control for Higher Commander
01-6-0436	Coordinate Air-Ground Integration when Providing Close Combat Attack (CCA) Support
01-6-0029	Maintain the BCT Current Situation for Aviation
01-6-0444	Employ Automated Mission Planning Equipment/TAIS
06-1-6008	Prepare the Logistic Plan
03-6-0404	Direct CBRN Defense Operations
06-1-1095	Transfer Fire Support Operations to an Alternate BN/CAB Fires Cell
06-1-1097	Conduct Rehearsals (BN Fires Cell)
06-1-5002	Execute Fires
06-1-5076	Synchronize Fires
06-5-5046	Conduct FIST/COLT Fire Missions
06-6-1079	Conduct Battle Tracking
06-6-1118	Conduct Fire Support Planning Using MDMP
06-6-5433	Plan Counterstrike Operations
11-4-8140	Establish the Warfighter Information Network (WIN) (S6)
11-5-0014	Operate the Enhanced Position Location Reporting System (EPLRS)
11-5-0201	Operate/Maintain/Troubleshoot Platform with Applique, Precision Lightweight GPS Receiver (PLGR) and SINCGARS System Improvement Program (SIP)
11-5-1102	Operate a Single Channel Ground and Airborne Radio System (SINCGARS) Frequency Hopping (FH) Net
11-6-7000	Conduct BCT/Support Brigade S6 Staff Functions (BDE S6)
11-6-7001	Provide S6 Support at the Brigade Main CP (BDE S6)
11-6-7002	Provide S6 Support at the Brigade TAC CP (BCT S6)
11-6-7004	Establish the Brigade S6 Element (BDE Main and Alternate CPs)

Table A-1. Example R&S brigade unit task list (continued)

Task Number	Task Title
11-6-7005	Conduct Brigade Network Activities (BDE S6)
11-6-7006	Operate the Brigade Network Operations & Security Center (BNOSC) (BDE S6)
11-6-7007	Exercise Technical Control (TECHCON) of the Brigade's LandWarNet (BDE S6)
11-6-7008	Operate the Brigade Help Desk (BDE S6 & NSC/NSD)
11-6-7009	Transfer BNOSC Network C2 During Relocation (BDE S6/NSC/NSD)
11-6-7010	Conduct Brigade TI/LAN Management (BDE S6/NSC/NSD)
11-6-7011	Conduct the Network Orders Planning Process (BDE S6/NSC/NSD)
11-6-7012	Develop Brigade Network Courses of Action (BDE S6/NSC/NSD)
11-6-7013	Conduct Brigade Information Protect (BDE S6/NSC/NSD)
11-6-7014	Conduct Brigade Information Assurance (IA) (BDE S6/NSC/NSD)
11-6-7015	Defend the Brigade's LandWarNet (BDE S6/NSC/NSD)
11-6-7016	Operate the Brigade Tactical Internet (TI) (BDE S6/NSC/NSD)
11-6-7017	Employ a Relay/Retransmission System (BDE S6/NSC/NSD)
11-6-7035	Conduct Information Systems & Network Engineering (BDE & BN S6s/NSC/NSD)
11-6-7036	Operate a Local Area Network (LAN) (BDE & BN S6s/NSC/NSD)
11-6-7037	Operate the GBS Transportable Ground Receive Suite (TGRS) (BDE & BN S6s/NSC/NSD)
11-6-7038	Operate Cable/Wire/Local Area Network (LAN) Systems (BDE & BN S6s/NSC/NSD)
11-6-7039	Recover Cable/Wire/Local Area Network (LAN) Systems (BDE & BN S6s/NSC/NSD)
11-6-8006	Maintain a Combat Network Radio Voice / Data Network
11-6-8050	Maintain Enhanced Position Location Reporting System (EPLRS) Network
34-2-9035	Manage Headquarters and Headquarters Company (HHC) Operations (BDE)
34-4-0823	Plan Multifunctional Team Missions
34-4-1203	Establish Connectivity with National Networks
34-4-1204	Access External Databases
34-5-0221	Synchronize the HUMINT Collection Effort (S2X)
34-5-0222	Coordinate HUMINT Operations (OMT)
34-5-0050	Establish the Common Ground Station (CGS) Site
34-5-0051	Conduct Common Ground Station (CGS) Pre-Mission Activities
34-5-0052	Conduct Common Ground Station (CGS) Mission Activities
34-5-0053	Conduct Common Ground Station (CGS) Post-Mission Activities
34-5-0054	Prepare the Common Ground Station (CGS) for Redeployment
34-5-0820	Manage Prophet Sensor Missions
34-5-0331	Coordinate HUMINT Operations (OMT) (BfSB)
34-6-0506	Implement Information Assurance Procedures
34-6-2036	Provide Meteorological Support to the Planning Process
34-6-2037	Prepare the Intelligence Estimate (BDE/BN)
34-6-2038	Process Captured Enemy Documents and Material

Table A-1. Example R&S brigade unit task list (continued)

Task Number	Task Title
34-6-2039	Conduct Intelligence Preparation of the Battlefield (IPB) in Support of Urban Operations (BDE/BN)
34-6-2040	Conduct Intelligence Preparation of the Battlefield (IPB)
34-6-2041	Produce Intelligence Products
34-6-2042	Process Specific Information Requirements (SIR)
34-6-2043	Maintain Situational Awareness (BDE/BN)
34-6-2044	Disseminate Combat Information and Intelligence
34-6-2045	Maintain the Current Threat Situation
34-6-2047	Provide Intelligence Support to Targeting
34-6-2048	Develop an Intelligence, Surveillance, and Reconnaissance (ISR) Plan
34-6-2049	Provide Intelligence Support to Deployment
34-6-2050	Conduct Long Range Surveillance (LRS) Staff Planning (BDE)
63-6-4854	Update Movement Plan
63-6-4866	Prepare Redeployment Movement Plan/Order
63-6-4871	Direct Integration Activities
63-6-4878	Direct Redeployment Activities
71-8-1420	Integrate Command and Control Warfare (Battalion – Corps)
71-8-2321	Develop the Intelligence, Surveillance, and Reconnaissance Plan (Battalion - Corps)
71-8-5100	Execute the Operations Process (Battalion - Corps)
71-8-5110	Plan Operations Using the Military Decision-Making Process (Battalion - Corps)
71-8-5111	Conduct the Military Decision-Making Process (Battalion – Corps)
71-8-5120	Prepare for Tactical Operations (Battalion – Corps)
71-8-5121	Establish Coordination and Liaison (Battalion - Corps)
71-8-5122	Perform Rehearsals (Battalion - Corps)
71-8-5130	Assess Tactical Situation and Operations (Battalion - Corps)
71-8-5131	Execute Tactical Operations (Battalion - Corps)
71-8-5137	Manage Sustainment Force Positioning (Battalion – Corps)
71-8-5139	Maintain Synchronization (Battalion – Corps)
71-8-5141	Monitor Situation or Progress of Operations (Battalion – Corps)
71-8-5142	Evaluate Situation or Operation (Battalion – Corps)
71-8-5143	Evaluate Combat Assessment (Battalion – Corps)
71-8-5144	Develop Running Estimates (Battalion – Corps)
71-8-5146	Perform Battle Damage Assessment (Battalion - Corps)
71-8-5200	Conduct Command Post Operations (Battalion - Corps)
71-8-5210	Monitor Continuous Operations (Battalion – Corps)
71-8-5250	Maintain Continuity of Command and Control (Battalion – Corps)

Table A-1. Example R&S brigade unit task list (continued)

Task Number	Task Title
71-8-5310	Manage Information and Knowledge (Battalion - Corps)
71-8-5315	Process Relevant Information to Create a Common Operational Picture (Battalion – Corps)
71-8-5316	Display a Common Operational Picture Tailored to User Needs (Battalion - Corps)
71-8-5715	Control Tactical Airspace (Division and Above)
Movement and Maneuver	
01-4-7927	Conduct Unmanned Aircraft System (UAS) Surveillance Missions
03-2-9208	Cross a Radiological Contaminated Area
03-2-9225	Conduct a Chemical Reconnaissance
03-2-9226	Cross a Chemically Contaminated Area
07-2-1342	Conduct Tactical Movement (Platoon-Company)
07-2-9003	Conduct a Defense (Platoon-Company)
07-2-9011	Conduct Tactical Movement in an Urban Area (Platoon-Company)
07-3-9013	Conduct Action on Contact
07-3-9017	Conduct Actions at Danger Areas
07-6-1234	Establish a Base of Operations (Battalion - Brigade)
07-6-1272	Conduct Area Security (Battalion - Brigade)
07-6-6073	Secure Civilians During Operations (Battalion - Brigade)
07-6-6082	Conduct Mobility, Countermobility, and or Survivability (Battalion - Brigade)
08-2-0220	Establish Operational Areas
11-3-0007	Secure and Defend Unit Position
17-1-4025	Conduct a Reconnaissance Handover
17-6-9225	Conduct a Screen (Battalion - Brigade)
17-6-9314	Conduct Zone Reconnaissance (Battalion - Brigade)
17-6-9315	Conduct Area Reconnaissance (Battalion - Brigade)
17-6-9406	Conduct Lines of Communication Security (Battalion - Brigade)
55-2-4003	Conduct Tactical Convoy
Intelligence	
05-3-6000	Collect Geospatial Information
05-3-6003	Provide Geospatial Information
05-3-6004	Produce Geospatial Products
05-3-6005	Provide Geospatial Analysis and Intelligence
06-6-5074	Analyze Targets
11-1-6723	Evaluate the Threat (IPB)
34-4-1205	Collaborate Analysis With Supporting Theater and National Intelligence Agencies Through JWICS and SIPRNET

Table A-1. Example R&S brigade unit task list (continued)

Task Number	Task Title
34-4-1723	Perform Intelligence Synchronization
34-5-0220	Conduct Human Intelligence (HUMINT) Screening
34-5-0702	Process Incoming Signals Intelligence (SIGINT) Information
34-5-1201	Establish the Operational Site (Trojan Spirit)
34-5-1202	Prepare the AN/TSQ-190 (V) for Operation (Trojan Spirit)
34-6-2034	Perform Analysis (BDE/BN)
34-6-2039	Conduct Intelligence Preparation of the Battlefield (IPB) in Support of Urban Operations (BDE/BN)
34-6-2040	Conduct Intelligence Preparation of the Battlefield (IPB)
34-6-2048	Develop an Intelligence, Surveillance, and Reconnaissance (ISR) Plan
71-8-2210	Perform Intelligence Preparation of the Battlefield (Battalion – Corps)
71-8-2300	Perform Intelligence, Surveillance, and Reconnaissance (Battalion - Corps)
71-8-2311	Develop Information Requirements (Battalion - Corps)
71-8-2410	Provide Intelligence Support to Targeting (Battalion - Corps)
Fires	
06-6-5059	Coordinate Target Attack
06-6-5062	Prepare the Fire Support Plan
06-6-5066	Employ Lethal Fires in Support of the BCT
17-6-0308	Synchronize Close Air Support (Battalion - Brigade)
34-6-0501	Implement Information Security Procedures
34-6-0502	Implement Personnel Security Program
71-8-3000	Plan Fire Support (Battalion - Corps)
71-8-5114	Establish Target Priorities (Battalion – Corps)
Sustainment	
07-2-5063	Conduct Composite Risk Management (Platoon-Company)
08-2-0001	Conduct Battlefield Stress Reduction and Prevention Procedures
08-2-0002	Perform Field Sanitation Functions
08-2-0003	Treat Casualties
08-2-0004	Evacuate Casualties
08-2-0123	Provide Preventive Medicine Services and Support
08-2-0232	Treat Chemical, Biological, Radiological, and Nuclear (CBRN) Contaminated Casualties
08-3-0311	Establish A Patient Decontamination Station
08-2-0313	Provide Emergency Medical Treatment -- Medical Units
08-2-0315	Provide Diagnostic Services
08-2-0316	Provide Sick Call Services

Table A-1. Example R&S brigade unit task list (continued)

Task Number	Task Title
08-2-0318	Provide Patient Holding
08-2-0319	Provide Ground Ambulance Evacuation Support
08-2-0352	Provide Area Ground Evacuation Support
08-2-4515	Provide Medical Supply Support (Note: Only if medical logistics personnel are organic to the unit)
08-2-0700	Conduct Preventive Medicine Operations
08-6-9001	Develop Health Service Support (HSS) Estimate - Surgeon
08-6-9002	Develop Courses of Action – Surgeon
08-6-9003	Analyze Courses of Action – Surgeon
08-6-9004	Produce Orders and Plans – Surgeon
08-6-9005	Evaluate Situation and Operations – Surgeon
08-6-9006	Monitor the Health of the Command - Surgeon
08-6-9007	Provide Health Service Support (HSS) Input During the Military Decision-Making Process (MDMP) – Surgeon
08-6-9008	Conduct Surgeon Section Activities - Surgeon
12-6-0003	Provide Morale, Welfare, and Recreation (MWR) Support
12-6-0004	Prepare Personnel for Deployment
12-6-0005	Conduct Casualty Operations
12-6-0006	Conduct Personnel Accounting and Strength Reporting (PASR)
12-6-0007	Perform Essential Personnel Services
12-6-0008	Conduct Unit Mail Services
12-6-0009	Process Replacements
12-6-0010	Prepare Personnel for Redeployment
16-5-1001	Conduct Religious Services
34-3-0003	Maintain Operations Security
34-3-0009	React to Indirect Fire (Platoon/Squad)
43-2-4522	Destroy Supplies and Equipment
44-3-3220	Perform Passive Air Defense Measures
44-3-3221	Perform Active Air Defense Measures
55-2-4803	Perform Predeployment Training Activities
55-2-4806	Prepare Equipment for Deployment
55-2-4809	Perform Sea Port of Embarkation Activities for Deployment
55-2-4810	Perform Aerial Port of Embarkation Activities for Deployment
55-2-4811	Perform Aerial Port of Debarkation Activities for Deployment
55-2-4812	Perform Sea Port of Debarkation Activities for Deployment
55-2-4818	Prepare Equipment for Redeployment
55-2-4819	Perform Sea Port of Embarkation Activities for Redeployment

Table A-1. Example R&S brigade unit task list (continued)

Task Number	Task Title
55-2-4820	Perform Aerial Port of Embarkation Activities for Redeployment
55-2-4821	Perform Aerial Port of Debarkation Activities for Redeployment
55-2-4822	Perform Home Station Activities Upon Redeployment
55-2-4823	Perform Sea Port of Debarkation Activities for Redeployment
55-2-4828	Plan Unit Deployment Activities Upon Receipt of a Warning Order
55-2-4829	Conduct Unit Redeployment
63-1-4015	Perform Advance/Quartering Party Activities
63-1-4028	Coordinate Sustainment and Field Maintenance Support
63-2-4113	Coordinate Sustainment Automation Support
63-2-4816	Perform Redeployment Supply Activities
63-2-4817	Perform Redeployment Maintenance Activities
63-6-4021	Provide Internal Sustainment
63-6-4853	Direct Deployment Activities
63-6-4854	Update Movement Plan
63-6-4860	Provide Deployment Logistics Support
63-6-4861	Perform Deployment Advance Party Activities
63-6-4862	Coordinate Onward Movement
63-6-4864	Perform Home Station Rear Detachment Activities
63-6-4865	Direct Reconstitution for Redeployment
63-6-4867	Provide Redeployment Support
63-6-4868	Perform Redeployment Advance Party Activities
63-7-2429	Provide Logistics Automation/STAMIS Support
71-8-4100	Provide Logistics Support (Battalion – Corps)
71-8-5115	Provide Operational Law Support (Battalion – Corps)
Protection	
03-2-9201	Implement CBRN Protective Measures
03-2-9203	React to Chemical or Biological (CB) Attack
03-2-9209	React to Obscuration
03-2-9222	React to the Residual Effects of a Nuclear Attack
03-2-9223	React to the Initial Effects of a Nuclear Attack
03-2-9224	Conduct Operational Decontamination
05-2-3091	React to a Possible Improvised Explosive Device (IED), Vehicle Borne IED, Suicide VBIED or Person Borne IED (UNCLASSIFIED / FOR OFFICIAL USE ONLY) (U//FOUO)
05-2-3092	Prepare for a Suspected Vehicle-Borne Improvised Explosive Device (VBIED)/Person-Borne IED (PBIED) Attack Against A Static Position
05-3-2019	Construct a Wire Obstacle
05-3-2022	Construct a Protective Obstacle
05-5-3009	Prepare Crew-Served Weapons Fighting Positions

This page intentionally left blank.

Appendix B

Corps/Division FSO METL

Table B-1 shows the R&S brigade's next higher HQ FSO METL, that of the corps/division. This METL, like that of brigade and higher units, is standardized by the Army.

Table B-1. R&S brigade higher HQ (corps/division) FSO METL

Corps/Division FSO METL
Core Mission: The corps/division deploys, conducts FSO as part of a joint task force (JTF) and on order redeploys. In order of priority, it operates as an intermediate/tactical HQ, ARFOR, JTF, JFLC.
Doctrinal Mission: The corps/division deploys, conducts FSO as part of a JTF and on order redeploys. In order of priority, it operates as an intermediate/tactical HQ, ARFOR, JTF, JFLC.
Conduct Command and Control (ART 5.0)
TG: Execute the Operations Process (Battalion - Corps) (71-8-5100)
TG: Integrate information Engagement Capabilities (Brigade - Corps) (71-8-5300)
TG: Provide Fire Support (Battalion - Corps) (71-8-3000)
Conduct Offensive Operations (ART 7.1)
TG: Conduct a Movement To Contact (Division - Corps) (71-8-7110)
TG: Conduct an Attack (Division - Corps) (71-8-7120)
TG: Conduct a Pursuit (Division - Corps) (71-8-7140)
TG: Conduct Entry Operations (Division - Corps) (71-8-1340)
Conduct Defensive Operations (ART 7.2)
TG: Conduct an Area Defense (Division - Corps) (71-8-7220)
Conduct Stability Operations (ART 7.3)
TG: Plan Restoration of Public Safety (Brigade - Corps) (71-8-7321)
TG: Coordinate Essential Services (Brigade - Corps) (71-8-7331)

This page intentionally left blank.

Appendix C

CATS Task Selection to FSO METL Matrix

The CATS task selection to FSO METL matrix table (Table C-1) is an example that displays a list of CATS task selections supporting the task groups of the unit's FSO METLs. For more information regarding a specific task selection found in this table, refer to the R&S brigade CATS at ATN and/or DTMS.

Table C-1. Example R&S brigade CATS task selection to FSO METL matrix

HHC, R&S Brigade		METs and Task Groups								
		C2	Perform ISR			Conduct Reconnaissance				Decide Surface Targets
Task Number	Task Title	Execute the Operations Process	Develop the ISR Plan	Perform ISR	Conduct LRS Staff Planning	Conduct Zone Reconnaissance	Conduct Area Reconnaissance	Conduct a Screen	Conduct Area Security	Conduct Fire Support Planning Using MDMP
06-TS-4360	Establish Fires Cell Operations	X								
06-TS-4361	Plan for Combat Operations - FEC	X								X
06-TS-4362	Prepare for Combat Operations - FEC	X								X
06-TS-4363	Execute Combat Operations - FEC	X								X
06-TS-4364	Conduct FEC Operations	X								X
06-TS-4365	Execute Targeting	X								X
06-TS-4366	Plan and Conduct Nonlethal Operations	X								X
06-TS-4412	Conduct Digital Sustainment Training	X								
11-TS-S601	Conduct Brigade S6 Operations	X								

Table C-1. Example R&S brigade CATS task selection to FSO METL matrix (continued)

HHC, R&S Brigade		METs and Task Groups									
		C2	Perform ISR			Conduct Reconnaissance				Decide Surface Targets	
Task Number	Task Title	Execute the Operations Process	Develop the ISR Plan	Perform ISR	Conduct LRS Staff Planning	Conduct Zone Reconnaissance	Conduct Area Reconnaissance	Conduct a Screen	Conduct Area Security	Conduct Fire Support Planning Using MDMP	
11-TS-S602	EIOMD a Brigade Network Operations & Security Center (BNOSC)	X									
11-TS-S603	EIOMD a Global Broadcast System (GBS)	X									
34-TS-6100	Conduct R&S Brigade Operations	X									
34-TS-6101	Deploy/Redeploy the Battlefield Surveillance Brigade	X									
34-TS-6102	Use Digital C4I Systems	X									
34-TS-6103	Plan and Prepare Intelligence, Reconnaissance, & Surveillance (MDMP)	X	X								
34-TS-6104	Conduct CP Operations	X									
34-TS-6105	Sustain the Battlefield Surveillance Brigade	X									
34-TS-6120	Protect the Force - CBRN	X									
34-TS-6121	Protect the Force - Defend, Movement, Casualties	X									

Table C-1. Example R&S brigade CATS task selection to FSO METL matrix (continued)

HHC, R&S Brigade		METs and Task Groups								
		C2	Perform ISR			Conduct Reconnaissance				Decide Surface Targets
Task Number	Task Title	Execute the Operations Process	Develop the ISR Plan	Perform ISR	Conduct LRS Staff Planning	Conduct Zone Reconnaissance	Conduct Area Reconnaissance	Conduct a Screen	Conduct Area Security	Conduct Fire Support Planning Using MDMP
34-TS-6130	Conduct Medical Treatment Team Operations	X								
34-TS-6131	Conduct Evacuation Squad Operations	X								
34-TS-6141	Perform S1/Surgeon/JAG/UMT Staff Section Functions	X								
34-TS-6142	Perform S-2/ISR Fusion Staff Section Functions	X	X		X					X
34-TS-6143	Perform S-3/S-5 Staff Section Functions	X	X		X					X
34-TS-6144	Perform S-4 Staff Section Functions	X								
34-TS-6145	Perform Common Ground Station Operations	X								
34-TS-6146	Perform ADAM/BAE Section Functions	X								X
34-TS-6147	Perform Geospatial Information & Services Functions	X								
34-TS-6148	Perform HUMINT Coordination Element Functions	X								

This page intentionally left blank.

Glossary

A

AA	assembly area
ABCS	Army Battle Command System
ABE	assistant brigade engineer
AC2	airspace command and control
ACE	analysis control element
ACP	air control point
AD	air defense
ADA	air defense artillery
ADAM	air defense and airspace management
AFATDS	Advanced Field Artillery Target Data System
AGM	attack guidance matrix
AI	air interdiction
ALO	air liaison officer
AMC	air mission commander
AMD	air and missile defense
ANGLICO	air and naval gunfire liaison company
AO	area of operation
AOI	area of interest
APS	Army pre-positioned stocks
ARFORGEN	Army force generation
ASAS	All-Source Analysis System
ASCOPE	areas, structures, capabilities, organizations, people and events
ASOC	air support operations center
ATN	Army Training Network
ATS	Army Training Strategy
AVN	aviation
AXP	Ambulance exchange point

B

BDA	battle damage assessment
BAE	brigade aviation element
BCT	brigade combat team
BDA	battle damage assessment
BDE	brigade
BDF	base defense force
BFA	battlefield functional area
BHL	battle handover line
BHO	battle handover
BN	battalion
BOLT	brigade operational law team
BP	battle position
BRT	brigade reconnaissance troop

C

C2	command and control
CA	civil affairs
CAS	close air support
CASEVAC	casualty evacuation
CATS	combined arms training strategy

CBRN	chemical, biological, radiological, and nuclear
CBRNE	chemical, biological, radiological, nuclear, and high-yield explosives
CCIR	commander's critical information requirement
CDS	Container Deliver System
CEF	contingency expeditionary force
CFZ	critical friendly zone
CFL	coordinate fire lines
CI	counter intelligence
CICA	counterintelligence coordination authority
CMO	civil military operations
CNR	combat net radio
COA	course of action
COLT	combat observation lazing team
COMSEC	communications security
CONPLAN	contingency plan
COO	combined obstacles overlay
COP	common operational picture
CP	command post
CPX	command post exercises
CRM	composite risk management
CSR	controlled supply rate
CTC	combat training center
D	
DA	Department of the Army
DC	displaced civilian
DCO	deputy commanding officer
DEF	deployment expeditionary force
DFSCOORD	deputy fire support coordinator
DIA	Defense Intelligence Agency
DOCEX	document exploitation
DoD	Department of Defense
DP	decision point
DS	direct support
DST	decision support template
DTMS	Digital Training Management System
DZ	drop zone
E	
EA	engagement area
ECOA	enemy course of action
EEFI	essential element friendly information
EFET	essential fires and effects task
EFST	essential fire support task
EMM	event menu matrix
ENCOORD	engineer coordinator
EP	electronic protection
EPLRS	Enhanced Position Location and Reporting System
EPW	enemy prisoner of war
ES	electronic surveillance
EW	electronic warfare
EWO	electronic warfare officer
F	
FA	field artillery

FAARP	forward area arming and refueling point
FAIO	field artillery intelligence officer
FASCAM	family of scatterable mines
FBCB2	Force XXI battle command brigade and below
FCE	forward command element
FEBA	forward edge of the battle area
FEMA	Federal Emergency Management Agency
FFIR	friendly forces information requirement
FIST	fire support team
FLOT	forward line of own troops
FM	field manual, frequency modulation
FOS	Forward Observer System
FORSCOM	Forces Command
FPF	final protective fires
FRAGO	fragmentary order
FS	fire support
FSCM	fire support control measure
FSCOORD	fire support coordinator
FSEM	fire support execution matrix
FSNCO	fire support noncommissioned officer
FSO	full spectrum operations
FSO METL	full spectrum operations mission-essential task list
FTX	field training exercise

G

GS	general support

H

HBCT	Heavy brigade combat team
HCT	HUMINT collection team
HD	high drag
HHQ	higher headquarters
HIMAD	high-to-medium altitude air defense
HN	host nation
HOC	HUMINT operations cell
HQ	headquarters
HQDA	headquarters, Department of the Army
HPT	high-payoff target
HPTL	high-payoff target list
HUMINT	human intelligence
HVT	high-value target

I

IAW	in accordance with
ICW	in conjunction with
IED	improvised explosive device
IEW	intelligence and electronic warfare
IGO	intergovernmental organization
IM	information management
IMINT	imagery intelligence
INFOSYS	information system
IO	information operations
IOWG	information operations working group
IPB	intelligence preparation of the battlefield
ISM	intelligence synchronization matrix
ISR	intelligence, surveillance, and reconnaissance

IR	information requirement
J	
JAAT	joint air attack operations
JCATS	Joint Conflict and Tactical Simulation
JCDB	joint common database
JFLC	joint force land component
JTF	joint task force
K	
KIA	killed in action
L	
LAPES	Low-Altitude Parachute Extraction System
LC	line of contact
LD	line of departure
LDS	leader development strategy
LNO	liaison officer
LOA	limit of advance
LOB	line of bearing
LOC	line of communication
LOGPAC	logistics package
LOS	line of sight
LRP	logistics release point
LTIOV	latest time information of value
LVCG	live, virtual, constructive, and gaming
LZ	landing zone
M	
MBA	main battle area
MCoE	Maneuver Center of Excellence
MCOO	modified combined obstacle overlay
MCS	Maneuver Control System
MDMP	military decision-making process
MEDCAP	medical civil action program
MEDEVAC	medical evacuation
METT-TC	mission, enemy, terrain, troops and time available, and civil considerations
MIE	military information environment
MET	mission essential task
METL	mission-essential task list
MFT	multifunctional team
MI	military intelligence
MILDEC	military deception
MLRS	Multiple Launch Rocket System
MOE	measure of effectiveness
MOI	message of interest
MOPP	mission-oriented protective posture
MP	military police
MPF	maritime pre-positioning force
MSEL	master scenario events list
MSR	main supply route
MTG	master training guide

N

NAI	named area of interest
NCO	noncommissioned officer
NFA	no fire area
NGF	naval gunfire
NGO	nongovernmental organization
NLT	not later than
NSFS	naval surface fire support

O

OAKOC	observation and fields of fire, avenues of approach, key and decisive terrain, obstacles, and cover and concealment
OBSTINTEL	obstacle intelligence
OE	operational environment
OMT	operational management team
OODA	observe, orient, decide, and act
OP	observation post
OPLAN	operations plan
OPORD	operations order
OPSEC	operations security
OT	observer trainer

P

PA	public affairs
PAA	position areas for artillery
PAG	public affairs guidance
PAO	public affairs officer
PASS	publish and subscribe service
PIR	primary intelligence requirement
PL	phase lines
PLD	probable line of deployment
PME	professional military education
PMESII-PT	political, military, economic, social, information, infrastructure, physical environment, and time
POL	petroleum, oils, and lubricants
PSG	platoon sergeant
PP	passage point
PSYOP	psychological operations
PVO	private voluntary organization
PZ	pickup zone

Q

QRF	quick reaction force

R

RATELO	radio telephone operator
RAAM	remote antiarmor mine
RC	Reserve Component
RFA	restrict fire area
RFI	request for information
RFL	restrict fire line
RI	relevant information
RLOS	radio line of sight
ROE	rules of engagement
R&S	reconnaissance and surveillance

RSOP	readiness standing operation procedure
RSR	required supply rate
RSTA	reconnaissance, surveillance, and target acquisition

S

SBF	support by fire
SCATMINE	scatterable mine
SBCT	Stryker brigade combat team
SBF	support by fire
SEAD	suppression of enemy air defenses
SEMA	state emergency management agency
SHORAD	short-range air defense
SIGINT	signal intelligence
SIP	source incentive program
SIR	specific information requirement
SITEMP	situation template
SITMAP	situation map
SITREP	situation report
SJA	staff judge advocate
SNR	signal-to-noise ratio
SOEO	scheme of engineer operations
SOFA	status-of-forces agreement
SOI	signal operations instruction
SOP	standing operating procedures
SOR	specific order or request
SP	start point
SPOTREP	spot report
STX	situational training exercise
SU	situational understanding

T

TA	target acquisition
TACAIR	tactical air
TACP	tactical air control party
TACREP	tactical report
TACSOP	tactical standing operation procedure
TAI	target areas of interest
TC	training circular
TCF	tactical combat force
T&EO	training and evaluation outline
FTLP	troop-leading procedures
TO	task organization
TOE	table of organization and equipment
TOT	time on target
TPME	task, purpose, method, and endstate
TRADOC	Training and Doctrine Command
TSM	target synchronization matrix
TSP	training support package
TSS	target selection standard
TTT	time to target
TVA	target value analysis

U

UAS	unmanned aircraft system
UAV	unmanned aerial vehicle
UMCP	unit maintenance collection point

UTL	unit task list
USAF	United States Air Force
USN	United States Navy

V

VBS2	virtual battlespace

W

WARNO, WO	warning order
WIA	wounded in action
WMD	weapons of mass destruction
WTSP	warfighter training support package

X

XO	executive officer

This page intentionally left blank.

References

SOURCES USED
These are the sources quoted or paraphrased in this publication.

JOINT AND DEPARTMENT OF DEFENSE PUBLICATIONS
JP 1-02, *Department of Defense Dictionary of Military and Associated Term,* 8 November 2010.

JP 3-0, *Joint Operations,* 17 September 2006.

JP 3-13, *Joint Doctrine for Information Operations,* 13 February 2006.

ARMY PUBLICATIONS
AR 220-1, *Army Unit Status Reporting and Force Registration-Consolidated Policies,* 15 April 2010.

AR 350-1, *Army Training and Leader Development,* 18 December 2009.

AR 350-28, *Army Exercises,* 9 December 1997.

ATTP 3-20.97, *Dismounted Reconnaissance Troop,* 16 November 2010.

DA Pam 350-38, *Standards in Training Commission,* 13 May 2009.

FM 1-01, *Generating Force Support for Operations,* 2 April 2008.

FM 1-02, *Operational Terms and Graphics,* 21 September 2004.

FM 2-22.3, *Human Intelligence Collector Operations,* 6 September 2006.

FM 3-0, *Operations,* 27 February 2008.

FM 3-20.96, *Reconnaissance and Cavalry Squadron,* 12 March 2010.

FM 3-20.971, *Reconnaissance and Cavalry Troop,* 4 August 2009.

FM 3-55.1, *Battlefield Surveillance Brigade,* 14 June 2010.

FM 3-55.93, *Long-Range Surveillance Unit Operations,* 23 June 2009.

FM 3-90.5, *The Combined Arms Battalion,* 7 April 2008.

FM 3-90.6, *Brigade Combat Team,* 14 September 2010.

FM 5-0, *The Operations Process,* 26 March 2010.

FM 5-19, *Composite Risk Management,* 21 August 2006.

FM 6-0, *Mission Command: Command and Control of Army Forces,* 11 August 2003.

FM 6-22, *Army Leadership,* 12 October 2006.

FM 7-0, *Training Units and Developing Leaders for Full Spectrum Operations,* 23 February 2011.

FM 7-15, *The Army Universal Task List,* 27 February 2009.

FORSCOM Circular 350-1, *Army Force Generation Training Support for an Operational Reserve,* 2 June 2010.

TRADOC Pam 525-3-0, *The Army Capstone Concept,* 21 December 2009.

TRADOC Pam 350-70-1, *Guide for Developing Collective Training Products,* 17 May 2004.

TRADOC Regulation 350-70, *Systems Approach to Training Management, Processes, and Products,* 9 March 1999.

OTHER PUBLICATIONS/DOCUMENTS
The Capstone Concept for Joint Operations, CCJO v3.0, 15 January 2009:
https://acc.dau mil/CommunityBrowser.aspx?id=341276.

Army, G-3/5/7 memorandum *Army Training and Leader Development Guidance,* FY 10-11, 31 July 2009:
https://atn.army mil/Media/docs/CSA%20ATLD%20GUIDANCE%202009.pdf.

Deputy Chief of Staff, G-3/5/7 memorandum, Army Training Strategy, 12 November 2009: https://atn.army.mil/Media/docs/Army%20Training%20Strategy%20%20Appendix%20A%2017%20Dec%2009.pdf.

The Army Leader Development Strategy for a 21st Century Army, 25 November 200: https://atn.army.mil/Media/docs/CSA%20ATLD%20GUIDANCE%202009df.

Forces Command Training Guidance Training Under Army Force Generation, 5 February 2010: https://fcportal.forscom.army.mil/sites/CmdGrp/KM_Admin/CGZone/FC_CG_Training_Guidance (Change1) 5 Feb 10.pdf.

REFERENCED FORMS

DA Form 2028, *Recommended Changes to Publications and Blank Forms.*

WEB SITES

Army Knowledge Online (accessed 24 February 2011): https://www.us.army.mil.

2009 Army Posture Statement (accessed 24 February 2011): http://www.army_mil/aps/09/information_papers/structured_self_development.html.

Army Training Network (accessed 24 February 2011): https://atn.army_mil/index.aspx.

Combined Arms Training Strategy (accessed 24 February 2011): ATN - CATS.

Digital Training Management System (accessed 24 February 2011): https://dtms.army.mil/DTMS/myWorkspace.aspx.

MCoE Collective Training Branch Home Page (accessed 24 February 2011): https://www.us.army_mil/suite/grouppage/130823

Joint publications (accessed 24 February 2011): http://www.dtic_mil/doctrine/doctrine/doctrine.htm.

Army doctrinal publications and regulations (accessed 24 February 2011): http://www.apd.army.mil.

Index

This page intentionally left blank.

By order of the Secretary of the Army:

MARTIN E. DEMPSEY
General, United States Army
Chief of Staff

Official:

JOYCE E. MORROW
Administrative Assistant to the
Secretary of the Army
1113808

DISTRIBUTION:
Active Army, Army National Guard, and U.S. Army Reserve: Not to be distributed; electronic media only.

www.ingramcontent.com/pod-product-compliance
Lightning Source LLC
Chambersburg PA
CBHW081358270326
41930CB00015B/3343